Prophecy Proof Insights on the End Times

Prophecy Proof Insights on the End Times

Biblical End Time Insights You Won't Hear in Church

Wayne Croley

Prophecy Proof Insights Publications

Antelope

eBook ISBN 13: 978-1-7322111-6-2

Paperback ISBN 13: 978-1-7322111-5-5

LCCN: 2022903779

Prophecy Proof Insights Publications

Antelope, CA

CONTENTS

ACKNOWLEDGMENTS

I want to thank parents because this book would not be possible without them. My late dad introduced Bible prophecy to me and was the main person I shared my Bible prophecy theories with. My mom has little interest in Bible prophecy, but she has strongly supported me in my endeavors nonetheless. I also want to acknowledge the following individuals:

- **Tiffany:** The Lord used Tiffany to push me towards studying Bible prophecy around my sixteenth birthday.

- **Julie:** Julie was a close friend while I wrote much of the text found in this book. I would not have come close to completing this book without her.

- **Gina:** Gina changed my life. She boosted my confidence immensely and allowed me to discover God-given abilities that I never realized I possessed. Gina encouraged me and motivated me to finish my work. She is someone who I will never forget and will always be grateful for.

- **John & Pat:** They helped me tremendously by providing me feedback during the writing process. They did not agree with all my conclusions, but they helped me to identify various areas that I could improve on, and they provided me with many suggested improvements.

You have all made a difference to me and have a part in helping people avoid being led astray in the future.

ABBREVIATIONS

Genesis: Gen	**Isaiah:** Isa	**Romans:** Rom
Exodus: Exod	**Jeremiah:** Jer	**1 Corinthians:** 1Cor
Leviticus: Lev	**Lamentations:** Lam	**2 Corinthians:** 2Cor
Numbers: Num	**Ezekiel:** Ezek	**Galatians:** Gal
Deuteronomy: Deut	**Daniel:** Dan	**Ephesians:** Eph
Joshua: Josh	**Hosea:** Hos	**Philippians** Phil
Judges: Judg	**Joel:** Joel	**Colossians:** Col
Ruth: Ruth	**Amos:** Amos	**1 Thessalonians:** 1Thess
1 Samuel: 1Sam	**Obadiah:** Obad	**2 Thessalonians:** 2Thess
2 Samuel: 2Sam	**Jonah:** Jonah	**1 Timothy:** 1Tim
1 Kings: 1Kgs	**Micah:** Mic	**2 Timothy:** 2Tim
2 Kings: 2Kgs	**Nahum:** Nah	**Titus:** Titus
1 Chronicles: 1Chr	**Habakkuk:** Hab	**Philemon:** Phlm
2 Chronicles: 2Chr	**Zephaniah:** Zep	**Hebrew:** Heb
Ezra: Ezra	**Haggai:** Hag	**James:** Jas
Nehemiah: Neh	**Zechariah:** Zech	**1 Peter:** 1Pet
Esther: Esth	**Malachi:** Mal	**2 Peter:** 2Pet
Job: Job	**Matthew:** Matt	**1 John:** 1John
Psalms: Ps	**Mark:** Mark	**2 John:** 2John
Proverbs: Prov	**Luke:** Luke	**3 John:** 3John
Ecclesiastes: Eccl	**John:** John	**Jude:** Jude
Song of Solomon: Song	**Acts:** Acts	**Revelation:** Rev

PREFACE

Today we can find information on just about any topic with ease. We can uncover a lot of information about Bible prophecy online, including on websites, blogs, forums, eBooks, podcasts, and videos. We can also find information on TV, radio, books, and at church.

Sadly, much of this information fails to give an accurate depiction of future events. As a result, many Christians live with a false sense of security and have little idea about how trying the future will truly be for them. This problem is the main reason this book exists.

MY BACKGROUND

My dad studied Bible prophecy after a supernatural event in his life sparked his interest in religion. He devoted all his free time to studying the subject with the hope that I would someday study it.

I was very reluctant to learn about Bible prophecy. I was scared and did not think I could learn it. But the Lord used events in my life to push me to study it when I turned sixteen.

The Lord seemed to turn on a switch in my mind to help me learn once I agreed to study the subject. I became a quick learner and my mind absorbed information like a sponge. My fear also went away. I was a changed person.

I quickly developed a strong desire to teach Bible prophecy and with that came the desire to write a comprehensive book about the end times. I considered writing a book about the end times to be the most important thing I could do in my life. However, I was unsure when I would complete this task as I had a lot of schooling ahead of me, including college and possibly graduate school. Nonetheless,

I preferred to not postpone writing a book until the latter stages of my life, since many key events may take place in my lifetime.

I have spent countless hours studying Bible prophecy since I began. As a teen, I devoted all my free time, including my lunch breaks at school and my summer vacations, to studying the topic. Also, I have spent thousands of hours from college until now comparing Scripture with Scripture in search of Bible prophecy truth.

As I studied, I saw a growing, pressing need for me to complete a comprehensive book about the end times. I found that many of today's popular Bible prophecy teachings are unscriptural.

Realizing the pressing need and desiring to finish a book at a young age, I devoted several years of my life to writing and further study. I made many personal and financial sacrifices during this time. As a result, I could not do many of the things my peers have done, including purchasing a home, getting married, and starting a family. I missed a lot in life during this time and often the thought of how I compared to my peers was depressing. However, I resisted the urge to quit by reminding myself that I could help many to not be caught off guard by the dangers of the future through my work.

Prophecy Proof Insights on the End Times is my effort to present many years of research on end time events. The book is designed to educate people of all levels of Bible prophecy understanding:

- Longtime students will learn new things about the end times and have long-held assumptions about end time events challenged.

- Beginners will find it easy to learn a lot about the end times. I wrote this book with the assumption that the average reader knows nothing about Bible prophecy.

- Both groups will benefit greatly from the unique way I present information in this book.

THE STRUCTURE OF THIS BOOK

The Concept of "Prophecy Proof"

My struggles with learning Math as a teen had a big effect on how I teach Bible prophecy. I struggled to grasp Math concepts and equations my peers found easy to understand. I could not just rely on memorizing things to get by. I needed to know the steps mathematicians took to derive a concept or equation. I often wrote down mathematical proofs and studied the various steps of the proofs.

As I stated, I developed a strong desire to help people understand Bible prophecy soon after I started to study the subject as a teen. I assumed that everyone I would help knew nothing about Bible prophecy and that learning about it was not a simple task.

With my struggles with Math fresh in my mind, I sought to devise a way to help anyone learn about Bible prophecy. I settled on helping people learn about Bible prophecy the same way I learned Math. I would try to present the key steps I took to derive a Bible prophecy teaching and the verses used to support those steps; a proof to support a Bible prophecy teaching: a "prophecy proof".

I will use the prophecy proof teaching method in this book.

The Formatted Text

The formatted text found in much of this book will help you grasp how different Bible verses and passages relate to each other more clearly. Many verses and passages overlap by discussing the same things but from different perspectives.

I believe you can learn quicker when you can easily see how various Bible verses and passages relate to each other.[1]

End of Chapter Timelines

I also want to help you see how end time events relate to each other chronologically. As a result, most chapters in this book will end with a timeline. Each timeline displays the order of events discussed and the relationship between these events.

The Appendix Studies

I tried to limit the length of the chapters in this book to help the flow and pacing of this book. Some topics like the identity of Babylon the Great require special attention, but not at the cost of interrupting the flow of this book, nor at the cost of confusing you with new information that you may not be ready to handle.

As a result, the appendix of this book has several studies of Bible prophecy significance.

A NOTE ABOUT THIS BOOK

Prophecy Proof Insights on the End Times is the title of an updated edition of *Prophecy Proof Insights of the End Times*. Much has changed since I published the first edition of *Prophecy Proof Insights of the End Times* in 2018. Since that time, I've learned more and received helpful feedback from readers.

My writing style has also evolved. I really strive to make my writing as easy to understand as possible.

As a result, I wanted to update this book to add new information, incorporate reader feedback, and to make it easier to understand.

The length of this book is much shorter than the first edition, but I believe the quality has not been affected.

A FINAL NOTE

I want you to know that I am under no pressure to conform to mainstream thought on Bible prophecy topics. I care far more about providing you with biblical truth than I care about being popular.

With all that said, I hope you read this book with an open mind, and I hope this book helps you in your study of Bible prophecy.

Notes

1. If you're reading on an eBook device or app, I suggest you turn on "continuous scrolling". This will make it easier to read the formatted text.

CHAPTER 1.

AN INTRODUCTION TO BIBLE PROPHECY

I want to repeat a key sentence in case you skipped the preface:

Many Christians live with a false sense of security and have little idea about how trying the future will truly be for them.

How trying? Let me be blunt. Christians, one way or another, will be spared from God's wrath, but they will face Satan's wrath.

Many Christians will be denied the essentials of life. Many will even be martyred for their beliefs. That is why Christians need to study Bible prophecy, why you need to study Bible prophecy, and why people need to be warned about what is coming.

BIBLE PROPHECY: THE ULTIMATE PUZZLE

A ton of Bible prophecy information is readily available. Unfortunately, much of that information is wrong. Sadly, many put too much faith in "experts" when they search for information. Few take the time to study the Bible to see if the teachings they hear are true.

Studying Bible prophecy is like putting a jigsaw puzzle together. The Bible contains many prophecies. The goal is to put all the pieces together to get a clear picture of the future:

- Pieces like the Book of Revelation and Matthew 24 can help us form the outer edge of the puzzle if they are understood correctly.

- The challenge is to use verses found in books like Isaiah, Malachi, Zechariah, and Jeremiah to fill in the detail of the prophecy puzzle.

Bible prophecy is the ultimate puzzle. There are so many ways you can put verses together without it being obvious whether all the pieces you work with fit. No picture of the solved puzzle exists and almost a countless number of ways to assemble verses exist. As a result, people have different views about the future. For instance, some believe in the Pre-Tribulation (Pre-Trib) Rapture, the belief that the gathering of the righteous to meet Christ can come at any moment, while others reject it.

Bible has over 31,000 verses and nearly 800,000 words. If you count each Bible verse as a piece of the puzzle, the Bible would be one of the world's largest jigsaw puzzles.

However, we cannot fully equate a Bible verse with a jigsaw puzzle piece because many verses contain words or phrases that apply to multiple places. For instance, Daniel 9:27 covers:

- The start of the seventieth week of Daniel (see chapter five).

- The midpoint of the seventieth week of Daniel.

- The end of the "desolate" (the Antichrist).

> And he shall confirm the covenant with many for one week: and in the midst of the week he shall cause the sacrifice and the oblation to cease, and for the overspreading of abominations he shall make it desolate, even until the consummation, and that determined shall be poured upon the desolate. (Dan 9:27)

This means that Daniel 9:27 has three puzzle pieces instead of one piece. This attribute, which many Bible prophecy verses possess, means that the Bible has more pieces than the world's largest jigsaw puzzle!

Another complication comes when gauging which verses can help us learn about the future. This is not an easy task. Many verses found outside of the prophetic books can help us gain a better understanding of God's plan.

This process can also be challenging because some Bible prophecy verses can relate to the past and to the future. For instance, Malachi 4 states that Elijah the prophet will come before the Day of the Lord, a critical period that I will discuss in the coming chapters:

(5) Behold, I will send you Elijah the prophet before the coming of the great and dreadful day of the Lord: (6) And he shall turn the heart of the fathers to the children, and the heart of the children to their fathers, lest I come and smite the earth with a curse. (Mal 4:5-6)

Matthew 17:10-13 suggests that the coming of John the Baptist fulfilled Malachi 4. However, many expect to see Malachi 4:5-6 to apply when Elijah serves as one of the Two Witnesses of God (see chapter nine). This means a fulfilled passage can also relate to the future.

Daniel 12:4 tells us that knowledge will increase. Gaining knowledge is an ongoing process that involves the constant study of the Bible. The more a person studies the Bible to see how pieces of this puzzle can be assembled the more opportunity he or she will have to learn about which verses help explain certain future events.

I hope you appreciate how difficult it truly is to understand Bible prophecy. I do not claim this book is perfect or reflects my final positions on various end time events. Gaining new knowledge is an ongoing process. However, what I present to you is an honest attempt to solve much of the puzzle.

Some positions I present in this book are unpopular but find support from the many pieces of the puzzle I have assembled over the years.

IT SOUNDS COMPLICATED! HOW DO I EVEN START?

Great question! For best results, always begin with prayer. Ask God to provide you with discernment, understanding, and patience as you study.

Do not feel discouraged if you do not understand what you read right away. There have been times in my life when I struggled to understand certain Bible prophecy concepts. I never gave up, and by the grace of God, I can present what I learned to you in this book.

HOW TO INTERPRET PROPHECY

Some Bible prophecy writers fall into the trap of interpreting a verse subjectively so that they can claim the verse supports their beliefs. The human mind is prone to error, but the Word of God is inerrant. We must let the Bible interpret itself because the sum of God's Word is the truth (Ps 119:160). Thus, I try to base my interpretation of each verse on evidence provided by other verses.

However, we cannot overlook the possibility of a nuance to be lost in the translation. As a result, we may have to dig deeper into the original language of a verse to find its exact meaning at times.

One slight caveat to our method of interpretation. Some verses use so much symbolic language that it makes a non-literal interpretation unavoidable. For instance, Revelation 12:4 depicts a third of the stars of Heaven being cast to the earth:

> And his tail drew the third part of the stars of heaven, and did cast them to the earth: and the dragon stood before the woman which was ready to be delivered, for to devour her child as soon as it was born.

As I will mention later in this book, this verse cannot refer to actual stars. Real stars would incinerate the earth. However, Revelation 1:20 tells us that a star can represent an angel.

Therefore, you should avoid seeking a non-literal or spiritualized interpretation of a particular verse unless it becomes unavoidable, and if that occurs, you should strive to find biblical clues to explain what the symbolism may mean.

Finally, we must be aware that the prophets of the Bible often wrote their prophecies so that their immediate audience could comprehend what they wrote even though they described an event or series of events that pertained to the future.

For example, Micah wrote his book in the eighth century B.C. when the Assyrian Empire controlled the Mideast. Micah 5 pertains to a time well beyond his day. It alludes to the birth of the Messiah (5:2) and the defeat of Israel's enemies by Him during the end times (5:5-6). Despite looking ahead in time, Micah depicted the seriousness of the future threat to Israel as an Assyrian attack against them.

Many now look at Micah 5 and posit that Israel will face a powerful foe in the future, but the enemy may not originate from Assyria.

PROPHECY IS ABOUT MUCH MORE THAN THE RAPTURE

Many people are mainly interested in learning about the Rapture and have little idea of what else will take place in the future. Bible prophecy covers many topics besides the Rapture. Here are just some of the other events that will take place:

- The destruction of the political and economic capital of the world.
- The unleashing of a supernatural locust plague.
- The return of the Prophet Elijah.
- The release of four angels imprisoned at the Euphrates River.

An incredible list, yet it is only a small sample of what we can find! Although amazing, the events described in the Book of Revelation and elsewhere do not originate from man's imagination, but from God, for our benefit. The questions we ought to ask ourselves are "Why?" and "When will these events take place?"

THE FLOW OF EVENTS IN THE BOOK OF REVELATION

One key to properly understanding Bible prophecy is to understand the relationship between:

- The breaking of the seven seals (Rev 6:1-17, 8:1).
- The sounding of the seven trumpets (Rev 8:2-13, 9:1-21, 11:15-19).
- The pouring of the seven bowls (or vials) (Rev 16).

The telescopic view is the most popular way to see the progression of the seven seals, the seven trumpets, and the seven bowls. This view follows mostly a linear chronology:

- The breaking of the seven seals come before the sounding of the seven trumpets.
- The seven trumpets sound before the pouring of the seven bowls.
- The seventh seal contains the seven trumpets, and the seventh trumpet contains the seven bowls.

This view is intuitive for many of us accustomed to having a story told in chronological order. For instance, here is the transition from the seventh seal to the seven trumpets:

(1) And when he had opened the seventh seal, there was silence in heaven about the space of half an hour. (2) And I saw the seven angels which stood before God; and to them were given seven trumpets. (Rev 8:1-2)

The view that the seventh seal leads to the seven trumpets is intuitive based on how the passage appears in Revelation 8. This passage will be discussed more in-depth shortly.

The telescopic view was so intuitive for me that I did not question it for many years. However, the more I studied, the more I realized we can challenge the theory.

The telescopic view assumes a strict chronology. But the Book of Revelation does not describe events this way. The book's chronology stops at various points to give details about events alluded to earlier in the book. Here are two examples where this is the case:

- Revelation 14:8 and Revelation 16:19 allude to the fall of Babylon the Great, but Babylon the Great is not fully discussed until Revelation 17-18.

- Revelation 12 begins a new series of visions that add details about a period discussed in earlier chapters.

This non-linear flow of events is consistent with what we find in the other prophetic books of the Bible. For instance, Daniel referred to the empire of the Antichrist in chapter two and again in chapter seven. Between those chapters, he recorded events and visions that pertained to his time.

Despite knowing this, I was uncomfortable with the thought that the breaking of the seven seals, the sounding of the seven trumpets, and the pouring of the seven bowls may occur in a non-linear order. However, the more I studied, the more I became convinced these events will progress in a non-linear order.

The turning point came after I compared the sixth seal with the seventh trumpet and the seventh bowl. After examining passages about these events (see Figure 1.1), it became hard for me to dismiss the possibility that these passages may cover the same time frame:

Figure 1.1: The 6th Seal, 7th Trumpet, and 7th Bowl

- **Great Earthquake**

- *The Wrath Is Come*

- <u>**Great Hail**</u>

Rev 6:15-17 (6th Seal): (15) And the kings of the earth, and the great men, and the rich men, and the chief captains, and the mighty men, and every bondman, and every free man, hid themselves in the dens and in the rocks of the mountains; (16) And said to the mountains and rocks, *Fall on us, and hide us from the face of him that sitteth on the throne, and from the wrath of the Lamb:* (17) *For the great day of his wrath is come; and who shall be able to stand?*

Rev 11:18-19 (7th Trumpet): (18) And the nations were angry, *and thy wrath is come*, and the time of the dead, that they should be judged, and that thou shouldest give reward unto thy servants the prophets, and to the saints, and them that fear thy name, small and great; and shouldest destroy them which destroy the earth. (19) And the temple of God was opened in heaven, and there was seen in his temple the ark of his testament: and there were lightnings, and voices, and thunderings, **and an earthquake, <u>and great hail</u>**.

Rev 16:18-21 (7th Bowl): (18) And there were voices, and thunders, and lightnings; **and there was a great earthquake, such as was not since men were upon the earth, so mighty an earthquake, and so great.** (19) And the great city was divided into three parts, and the cities of the nations fell: and great Babylon came in remembrance before God, to give unto her the cup of the wine of *the fierceness of his wrath.* (20) And every island fled away, and the mountains were not found. (21) And there fell upon men a great hail out of heaven, every stone about the weight of a talent: and men blasphemed God because of the **<u>plague of the hail; for the plague thereof was exceeding great</u>**.

I also resisted the idea that the seals, trumpets, and bowls may occur in a non-linear order because the introduction of the seven trumpets follows the breaking of the seventh seal in Revelation 8:

(1) And when he had opened the seventh seal, there was silence in heaven about the space of half an hour. (2) And I saw the seven angels which stood before God; and to them were given seven trumpets. (Rev 8:1-2)

However, my hesitancy went away when I reflected on how the chapter divisions in the Bible were made more than a thousand years after Revelation's writing. The choice to place the seventh seal at the start of chapter eight instead of at the end of chapter seven came from man.

Imagine how different things would be if the seventh seal was shown as "Revelation 7:18". Far fewer people would believe in the telescopic view. Many would interpret a chapter division between the breaking of the seventh seal and the introducing of the seven trumpets as evidence that these events are unrelated.

In the end, I realized that the telescopic view might not be the best way to see the progression of the seven seals, the seven trumpets, and the seven bowls. The non-linear flow of events in the Book of Revelation means we should look at a chronology that has the seals, trumpets, and bowls progress in a non-linear order.

The non-linear progression of the seals, trumpets, and bowls may not be intuitive for many of us accustomed to reading the events of a story in chronological order, but remember that God's ways and thoughts are above our ways and thoughts (Isa 55:8-9).

There are various ways to view the progression of the seals, trumpets, and bowls in a non-linear manner. For instance:

- Some believe that the breaking of the first seal, the sounding of the first trumpet, and the pouring of the first bowl will occur at the same time (some even claim that each respective seal, trumpet, and bowl represent the same event).

- Another view places the sounding of the trumpets during the breaking of the seals but delays the pouring of the bowls until after the breaking of the seventh seal and the sounding of the seventh trumpet.

- A third view puts the sounding of the trumpets and the pouring of the bowls some time during the breaking of the seals.

The chronology of prophetic events presented in this book proposes:

- The sounding of the seven trumpets and the pouring of the seven bowls will take place during the breaking of the seven seals.

- The seven seals, the seven trumpets, and the seven bowls are distinct events, but they share a common ending.

- The breaking of the sixth seal and the seventh seal will occur approximately at the same time as the sounding of the seventh trumpet and the pouring of the seventh bowl.

Don't worry if this does not make much sense to you now. This timeline will become clearer later in the book.

Finally, I believe Revelation 17-19 gives us more detail on things alluded to in earlier parts of the book. Revelation 20-22 picks up the chronology from the Millennium to the eternal state (see chapters twenty-four and twenty-five).

DEFINING THE END TIMES

The definition of the "end times" can vary by the person. Some teach we already live in the end times, but fail to provide a precise definition of the term "end times" to their audience. I do not want to confuse you, so I will provide you with a working definition of the "end times".

I define the end times *as the period spanning the start of the seventieth week of Daniel (commonly known as the tribulation) to the beginning of the Millennium, a thousand-year period when Christ will rule the earth.* This period is the focus of this book, but we will also look at past events and events that will take place after the start of the Millennium in this book.

LET'S PAUSE FOR A MOMENT

I know this chapter had a lot of information for you to process. Do not be overwhelmed! I encourage you to reflect on what you have read and to reread any parts that might have been difficult to understand before continuing to the next chapter. You can do this!

CHAPTER 2.

THE SEVEN CHURCHES OF REVELATION

The significance of the seven churches of the Book of Revelation is a topic of much speculation:

- Some believe they represent seven distinct ages of Church History.

- Others believe they represent seven different types of individuals or churches.

- A third group believes they carry no significance beyond being seven churches that existed in the first century A.D.

We will look at the significance of these churches in this chapter.

THE DIVISIONS OF THE CHURCH

The Apostle Paul taught that the Church is one body under Christ's leadership. The body of Christ is a spiritual body uniting all believers no matter who they are:

> (12) For as the body is one, and hath many members, and all the members of that one body, being many, are one body: so also is Christ. (13) For by one Spirit are we all baptized into one body, whether we be Jews or Gentiles, whether we be bond or free; and have been all made to drink into one Spirit. (14) For the body is not one member, but many. (1Cor 12:12-14)

Although there is one body of Christ, it is practically impossible for every Christian to gather at one place because of geographic distance. As a result, churches exist across the world so that Christians living in a particular area can have a place to assemble. This helps to make each church unique. They each have:

- Different leadership.
- Different people within its congregation.
- Different culture.
- Different doctrines.

THE SEVEN CHURCHES

Revelation 2 and Revelation 3 contain messages addressed to seven churches in western Asia Minor (modern day Turkey) in the first century A.D. Each church received a different message as each church adhered to the Christian faith differently. Christ assessed each church's strengths and weaknesses in these messages. Figure 2.1 summarizes the seven churches:

Figure 2.1: The Seven Churches

Ephesus (Rev 2:1-7): A former great church that deviated from the Christian faith.

Smyrna (Rev 2:8-11): Spiritually rich as they endure hardship, including financial hardship.

Pergamos (Rev 2:12-17): Holds onto the faith despite living in the heart of enemy territory. Not perfect because they uphold some condemnable practices.

Thyatira (Rev 2:18-29): Has performed good works, service, and deeds but tolerates some detestable practices.

Sardis (Rev 3:1-6): Spiritually dead.

Philadelphia (Rev 3:7-13): Kept Christ's word and remained patient.

Laodicea (Rev 3:14-22): So well-off they have grown spiritually complacent. They do not know their complacency has left them spiritually impoverished.

The messages given to the seven churches obviously have historical significance, but they may also apply beyond the first century A.D. for a couple of reasons.

Each church's assessment ends with the statement: "He that hath an ear, let him hear what the Spirit saith unto the churches." The frequency that this statement appears suggests it is a call for people unaffiliated with these historical churches to take heed of the messages given to them. In other words, the receptive readers of Revelation are called to hear the messages given to all the churches.

The end of each church's message also contains a promise of rewards for those that overcome (i.e., remain faithful through trying times). Thyatira's promise is especially intriguing because it encourages people to overcome and stay obedient to the *end*:

> And he that overcometh, and keepeth my works unto the end, to him will I give power over the nations: (Rev 2:26)

The message to overcome and stay obedient to *the end* eliminates the possibility that Thyatira's message only applies to those living in the first century A.D.

I believe the seven churches reflect the spiritual conditions of seven types of churches that have existed throughout history-not seven types of individuals. The main reason stems from Revelation 2:24. Christ recognized how some in Thyatira did not follow of one of the church's bad doctrines:

> But unto you I say, and unto the rest in Thyatira, as many as have not this doctrine, and which have not known the depths of Satan, as they speak; I will put upon you none other burden. (Rev 2:24)

If we say that the church of Thyatira reflected a particular type of person, how can we account for the fact that not everyone in Thyatira is like how Christ characterized the church to be?

- An individual who did not approve of Thyatira's doctrine would not belong in the Thyatira category if the seven churches reflected seven different types of people.

- The person would belong to another classification (i.e. Philadelphia).

Essentially, you can have exceptions when categorizing groups of people like churches, but you cannot have exceptions when classifying individuals.

THE CALL TO OVERCOME

The most striking theme in Revelation 2 and Revelation 3 is the call to overcome. It does not matter that a person is from a spiritually dead church or a faithful church; he or she will have eternal life if he or she overcomes.

The messages directed to the church of Philadelphia (the faithful church) and to the church of Sardis (the dead church) provide the best example of this. The spiritual states of these two churches are on opposite ends of the spectrum. Here are excerpts from each church's message:

> **Sardis (Dead Church):** (4) Thou hast a few names even in Sardis which have not defiled their garments; and they shall walk with me in white: for they are worthy. (5) He that overcometh, the same shall be clothed in white raiment; and I will not blot out his name out of the book of life, but I will confess his name before my Father, and before his angels. (Rev 3:4-5)

> **Philadelphia (Faithful Church):** Him that overcometh will I make a pillar in the temple of my God, and he shall go no more out: and I will write upon him the name of my God, and the name of the city of my God, which is new Jerusalem, which cometh down out of heaven from my God: and I will write upon him my new name. (Rev 3:12)

It is crucial for Christians to stay faithful during trying times, and we will see in coming chapters that many trying times lie ahead.

LET'S PAUSE FOR A MOMENT

The seven churches of the Book of Revelation help us to understand the spiritual conditions of seven types of churches that have existed throughout history. Christ encouraged each believer to overcome because an eternal reward awaits those who overcome.

Learning about Bible prophecy is a wonderful way to help you and help others navigate and overcome the trying times ahead. Therefore, do not give up if you already feel bogged down by this. You can do so much good if you do not give up!

CHAPTER 3.

AN OVERVIEW OF THE ONGOING SPIRITUAL CONFLICT

Human activity takes place amid a great spiritual war. The battle between the spiritual forces of evil and the spiritual forces of good rages on at all times. Understanding this war is essential to fathom what is taking place now and to forecast what may happen in the future.

However, most people know little about the spiritual war or are aware that one is underway. As a result, we will focus on this conflict that affects our lives and the world around us in this chapter.

SATAN'S GOAL

Satan desires to replace God as everyone's object of worship. This desire helped lead to his fall and will lead to his demise (Ezek 28:13-15, 17, Isa 14:12-14). Regardless of how hard Satan strives to become everyone's object of worship, he will never fully succeed. God will stop Satan before he meets his goal.

Nevertheless, Satan is working to achieve his goal by attempting to turn people away from God and bring people to himself. Satan also faces eternity in the lake of fire. Obviously, Satan does not want this outcome, so he is working to thwart God's plans any way he can in a futile effort to change the outcome.

Next, I will highlight some of the key activities Satan has engaged in or is engaging in while striving to thwart God's plans and turn people away from God. Afterward, I will briefly summarize what Satan plans for the future.

THE FALL OF MAN

Satan has been working to turn people away from God since the moment God created man. Satan, the serpent, instigated the fall of man in the Garden of Eden by deceiving Eve into eating from the tree of the knowledge of good and evil (Gen 3:1-7). This act of deception corrupted man with sin, and as a result, has adversely affected the relationship between man and God since that time.

THE PERSECUTION OF THE PEOPLE OF ISRAEL

After the fall of man, God warned Satan, the serpent, that the seed (or offspring) of the woman will one day bruise his head (Gen 3:15). Since that time, Satan sought to prevent the coming of the seed that will bruise his head (Jesus Christ).

The people of Israel (i.e. the descendants of Jacob, the "children of Israel" of the Bible) became Satan's primary target when he realized they were God's chosen people and from where the seed of the woman would eventually arise.

In chapter six, I will detail how Satan has used some of the history's most infamous rulers and empires to wage war against the people of Israel.

THE TEMPTATION AND CRUCIFIXION OF CHRIST

Satan sought to prevent Christ from fulfilling His mission after he failed to stop Christ's birth. Satan tried to tempt Christ and even offered Christ control over the whole world if He worshiped him:

> (8) Again, the devil taketh him up into an exceeding high mountain, and sheweth him all the kingdoms of the world, and the glory of them; (9) And saith unto him, All these things will I give thee, if thou wilt fall down and worship me. (Matt 4:8-9)

If Satan had succeeded, the redemption of humankind through Christ might not have happened. Fortunately, Christ turned down the offer and sent Satan away by quoting scripture (Matt 4:10-11).

Later, Satan sought to destroy Christ. He possessed Judas Iscariot and had him betray Christ by turning Him over to those that sought to kill Him. However, Satan's strategy failed when Christ rose from the dead after His crucifixion and ascended to Heaven.

THE BATTLEGROUND OF THE MIND

The human mind is a critical battleground of the ongoing spiritual conflict. Satan tries to attack the minds of people by placing ungodly thoughts and lies in their minds. The Bible instructs us to reject these thoughts:

> (3) For though we walk in the flesh, we do not war after the flesh: (4) (For the weapons of our warfare are not carnal, but mighty through God to the pulling down of strong holds;) (5) Casting down imaginations, and every high thing that exalteth itself against the knowledge of God, and bringing into captivity every thought to the obedience of Christ; (6) And having in a readiness to revenge all disobedience, when your obedience is fulfilled. (2Cor 10:3-6)

Satan will try to tempt people in areas where they are weak and often when they are feeling weak. For example, Satan sought to tempt Christ to turn stones into bread when He was hungry after forty days of fasting. He failed when Christ quoted Scripture:

> (1) Then was Jesus led up of the Spirit into the wilderness to be tempted of the devil. (2) And when he had fasted forty days and forty nights, he was afterward an hungred. (3) And when the tempter came to him, he said, If thou be the Son of God, command that these stones be made bread. (4) But he answered and said, It is written, Man shall not live by bread alone, but by every word that proceedeth out of the mouth of God. (Matt 4:1-4)

Satan will also attack people when they face difficult trials. Peter warned that Satan is like a roaring lion to those who are dealing with hard times:

> (8) Be sober, be vigilant; because your adversary the devil, as a roaring lion, walketh about, seeking whom he may devour: (9) Whom resist stedfast in the faith, knowing that the same afflictions are accomplished in your brethren that are in the world. (1Pet 5:8-9)

Satan is particularly vicious to unsaved people when they hear the

Word of God. Christ warned that Satan tries to take the Word of God out of unsaved people's hearts to prevent them from believing it and becoming saved:

> (5) A sower went out to sow his seed: and as he sowed, some fell by the way side; and it was trodden down, and the fowls of the air devoured it.... (11) Now the parable is this: The seed is the word of God. (12) Those by the way side are they that hear; then cometh the devil, and taketh away the word out of their hearts, lest they should believe and be saved. (Luke 8:5, 11-12)

Satan is not a foe to underestimate. He is working to undermine Christians' faith and working to stop unsaved people from believing in Christ.

FALSE RELIGIOUS TEACHINGS

Satan uses fallen angels to give people deceptive messages and false teachings that cause them to turn away from God. The Apostle Paul warned that seducing spirits will cause some to depart from the faith with ungodly teachings:

> (1) Now the Spirit speaketh expressly, that in the latter times some shall depart from the faith, giving heed to seducing spirits, and doctrines of devils; (2) Speaking lies in hypocrisy; having their conscience seared with a hot iron; (3) Forbidding to marry, and commanding to abstain from meats, which God hath created to be received with thanksgiving of them which believe and know the truth. (1Tim 4:1-3)

Fallen angels can hide their true nature from those who lack discernment. As a result, they can readily provide their false teachings to unsuspecting people. In fact, Paul warned that satanic representatives like fallen angels can transform or masquerade themselves as ministers of righteousness:

> (13) For such are false apostles, deceitful workers, transforming themselves into the apostles of Christ. (14) And no marvel; for Satan himself is transformed into an angel of light. (15) Therefore it is no great thing if his ministers also be transformed as the ministers of righteousness; whose end shall be according to their works. (2Cor 11:13-15)

Furthermore, the Bible suggests that angels can take on other physical forms. For instance, the Book of Hebrews suggests angels can look like people when they interact with them:[1]

> Be not forgetful to entertain strangers: for thereby some have entertained angels unawares. (Heb 13:2)

Fallen angels' ability to masquerade their true nature to those who lack discernment makes them extremely dangerous.

THE FUTURE

The Coming Strong Delusion

Satan will try to thwart Christ again during the end times. He will try to convert everyone on Earth into a follower of his. He will seek to persuade unsuspecting people to follow him, primarily using lying signs and wonders.

Satan will give lying signs and wonders mainly through false Christs, including the Antichrist, and through false prophets, including the False Prophet. The lying signs and wonders will be so convincing that they would deceive the elect (those chosen by God to be saved) if it were possible (Matt 24:24).

While Satan will use lying signs and wonders for his selfish purposes, he will inadvertently help fulfill God's plan. God will allow Satan to unleash all sorts of lying signs and wonders to sift out those who do not believe the truth of His Word:

> (9) him [Antichrist], whose coming is after the working of Satan with all power and signs and lying wonders, (10) And with all deceivableness of unrighteousness in them that perish; because they received not the love of the truth, that they might be saved. (11) And for this cause God shall send them strong delusion, that they should believe a lie. (12) That they all might be damned who believed not the truth, but had pleasure in unrighteousness. (2Thess 2:9-12)

Antichrist and Armageddon

The spiritual conflict will reach its climax during the end times. Satan and his angels will be expelled from Heaven and relegated to Earth after losing a war against the Archangel Michael and his angels (Rev 12:7-9).

After his banishment, Satan will empower his representative: the Antichrist (Rev 13:2). Many opponents of Satan and the Antichrist will lose their lives, but those who succumb to them will suffer for eternity in the lake of fire (Rev 14:10, Rev 20:15).

The war of Armageddon will be Satan's last-ditch effort to stop Christ during this age. Satan, the Antichrist, and the False Prophet will gather the armies of Earth to fight Christ, His forces, and His people. The war will end in a complete rout of the wicked and the incarceration of Satan for a thousand years.

Satan will have a last opportunity to stop Christ after his release, but he will fail again.

LET'S PAUSE FOR A MOMENT

We are nearing the end of an age-long spiritual conflict. The future will be full of many dangers for Christians and the people of Israel.

Many will fall away from the faith to follow false religious teachings and succumb to Satan's lying signs and wonders. Therefore, it is important for you to learn about what lies ahead so that you and your loved ones will not be a casualty of this conflict.

Notes

1. Gen 19:1-5 describes a time when the people of Sodom mistaken angels for humans that attracted them:

CHAPTER 4.

A SPOTLIGHT ON ISRAEL

The people of Israel are at the center of the spiritual conflict that affects our world. Satan wants to destroy Israel's relationship with God, while God wants His people to be obedient.

Before the Israelites entered the Promised Land, they had a choice. They could stay faithful to the Lord or disobey the Lord. Obedience would lead to blessings, while disobedience would lead to curses.

THE BLESSINGS

Israel would receive many blessings for its obedience to God. Figure 4.1 lists some of the benefits Israel would receive for their obedience:

Figure 4.1: Blessings for Remaining Obedient to God[1]

- Timely Rain (Lev 26:4)
- Plentiful Food and Bumper Crops (Lev 26:4-5)
- Peace and Protection from Enemies (Lev 26:6-7)
- Healthy Population Growth (Lev 26:9)
- Having God's Presence in the Land (Lev 26:11-12)

THE CURSES

In contrast, Israel would face punishment if they disobeyed God. Figure 4.2 lists *just* some of the curses Israel would receive if they disobeyed God. Israel would not face every curse at the same time, but they would chastised each time they disobeyed God:

Figure 4.2: Curses for Disobeying God[2]

- Enemies Will Pillage Israel's Food Supply (Lev 26:16-17)
- Poor Crop Yields and Famine (Lev 26:18-20)
- Wild Animal Attacks (Lev 26:22)
- Pestilence and Devastating Enemy Attacks (Lev 26:25-26)
- Expulsion from the Land of Israel (Lev 26:38-39)

The people of Israel received many warnings to repent and change their ways and faced punishment when they ignored the warnings. Despite all the punishment the people of Israel endured, they continued to disobey God.

As a result, the people of Israel received the final curse. This curse called for them to be expelled from their land and scattered across the world (Lev 26:38-39, Deut 28:63-68). This expulsion came in 70 A.D. after the people of Israel rejected the true Messiah: Jesus Christ (Matt 23:37-39, Luke 19:41-44).

The Hardening

Their rejection of the true Messiah had another adverse consequence. The Apostle Paul taught that Israel stumbled when they did not seek righteousness by faith in Jesus Christ:

> (30) What shall we say then? That the Gentiles, which followed not after righteousness, have attained to righteousness, even the righteousness which is of faith. (31) But Israel, which followed after the law of righteousness, hath not attained to the law of righteousness. (32) Wherefore? Because they sought it not by faith, but as it were by the works of the law. For they stumbled at that stumblingstone; (Rom 9:30-32)

Instead of seeking righteousness by faith in Jesus Christ, Israel sought its own righteousness:

(1) Brethren, my heart's desire and prayer to God for Israel is, that they might be saved. (2) For I bear them record that they have a zeal of God, but not according to knowledge. (3) For they being ignorant of God's righteousness, and going about to establish their own righteousness, have not submitted themselves unto the righteousness of God. (4) For Christ is the end of the law for righteousness to every one that believeth. (Rom 10:1-4)

Paul noted that God always preserves a faithful remnant of His people and did so again when Israel rejected Christ. However, the hearts of many others were blinded (hardened) against Jesus:

(1) ...Hath God cast away his people? God forbid. For I also am an Israelite, of the seed of Abraham, of the tribe of Benjamin. (2) God hath not cast away his people which he foreknew.... (7) What then? Israel hath not obtained that which he seeketh for; but the election hath obtained it, and the rest were blinded. (8) (According as it is written, God hath given them the spirit of slumber, eyes that they should not see, and ears that they should not hear;) unto this day. (Rom 11:1-2, 7-8)

The hardening that affects a portion of Israel remains today. Much of Israel still fails to recognize Christ as the true Messiah. As we will see later, this hardening will not end until after the people of Israel endure many future hardships.

AFTER THE FINAL CURSE

The final curse, which led to the expulsion of the people of Israel from their land and their scattering across the world, is not permanent. After the lifting of the final curse, the people of Israel will be gathered from the places from where they are scattered. They will live prosperously in the land of their ancestors:

(1) And it shall come to pass, when all these things are come upon thee, the blessing and the curse, which I have set before thee, and thou shalt call them to mind among all the nations, whither the LORD thy God hath driven thee, (2) And shalt return unto the LORD thy God, and shalt obey his voice according to all that I command thee this day, thou and thy children, with all thine heart, and with all thy soul; (3) That then the LORD thy God will turn thy captivity, and have compassion

upon thee, and will return and gather thee from all the nations, whither the LORD thy God hath scattered thee. (4) If any of thine be driven out unto the outmost parts of heaven, from thence will the LORD thy God gather thee, and from thence will he fetch thee: (5) And the LORD thy God will bring thee into the land which thy fathers possessed, and thou shalt possess it; and he will do thee good, and multiply thee above thy fathers. (Deut 30:1-5)

Some conclude (as I once did) that the creation of the state of Israel in 1948 marked the end of the final curse.[3] However, a review of Deuteronomy 30 shows that the conditions of the passage are unmet.

Verses 2-3 tell us that the people of Israel will be ready to obey the Lord's voice and will follow the Lord with all their heart and with all their soul when they return from the nations. We can see that this condition remains unmet by examining Joel 2:12-13. This is an end time passage that describes the people of Israel being urged to turn to the Lord with all their heart at that time:

(12) Therefore also now, saith the LORD, turn ye even to me with all your heart, and with fasting, and with weeping, and with mourning: (13) And rend your heart, and not your garments, and turn unto the LORD your God: for he is gracious and merciful, slow to anger, and of great kindness, and repenteth him of the evil. (Joel 2:12-13)

Verses 3-4 mention that the Lord will have compassion for the people of Israel when He gathers them from the nations. Isaiah 49 shows that the Lord will have this compassion for His people after the hardships they will endure during the end times:[4]

(8) Thus saith the LORD, In an acceptable time have I heard thee, and in a day of salvation have I helped thee: and I will preserve thee, and give thee for a covenant of the people, to establish the earth, to cause to inherit the desolate heritages;... (12) Behold, these shall come from far: and, lo, these from the north and from the west; and these from the land of Sinim. (13) Sing, O heavens; and be joyful, O earth; and break forth into singing, O mountains: for the LORD hath comforted his people, and will have mercy upon his afflicted. (14) But Zion said, The LORD hath forsaken me, and my Lord hath forgotten me. (15) Can a woman forget her sucking child, that she should not have compassion on the son of her womb? yea, they may forget, yet will I not forget thee. (Isa 49:8, 12-15)

Moreover, verse 5 mentions that the people of Israel will inherit the land of their ancestors and prosper. This promise appears in passages that pertain to the time just before the start of the Millennium. Jeremiah 3:18, 16:14-15, 30:3 and Ezekiel 20:41-42, 36:27-29, 37:24-36 are some of these passages.

The following is a comparison between Deuteronomy 30:5, Jeremiah 3:18, and Ezekiel 36:27-29, and together these passages show that Deuteronomy 30:5 cannot refer to the gathering of people after the creation of the state of Israel in 1948. They refer to events that have not happened yet:

> **And the LORD thy God will bring thee into the land which thy fathers possessed, and thou shalt possess it**; and he will do thee good, and multiply thee above thy fathers. (Deut 30:5)

> In those days the house of Judah shall walk with the house of Israel, and they shall come together out of the land of the north to the land that **I have given for an inheritance unto your fathers**. (Jer 3:18)

> (27) And I will put my spirit within you, and cause you to walk in my statutes, and ye shall keep my judgments, and do them. (28) **And ye shall dwell in the land that I gave to your fathers**; and ye shall be my people, and I will be your God. (29) I will also save you from all your uncleannesses: and I will call for the corn, and will increase it, and lay no famine upon you. (Ezek 36:27-29)

Finally, the conditions described in Deuteronomy 30:6-7 will be met when the people of Israel gather in the land of Israel just before the start of the Millennium:[5]

> (6) And the LORD thy God will circumcise thine heart, and the heart of thy seed, to love the LORD thy God with all thine heart, and with all thy soul, that thou mayest live. (7) And the LORD thy God will put all these curses upon thine enemies, and on them that hate thee, which persecuted thee. (Deut 30:6-7)

Thus, the creation of the state of Israel in 1948 did not mark the end of the final curse for the people of Israel. However, the Lord plans to get His people to follow Him with all their heart, and the time to finish the implementation of His plan is approaching.

LET'S PAUSE FOR A MOMENT

We focused on the people of Israel and their global scattering in this chapter. We saw that a long-standing prophecy about the return of the people of Israel to the land of Israel remains unfulfilled despite the creation of the state of Israel in 1948.

I encourage you to reflect on what you have read and to reread any parts that might have been difficult to understand before continuing to the next chapter.

Notes

1. Also see Deut 28:1-14.

2. Also see Deut 28:15-68.

3. Some believe the creation of the state of Israel in 1948 fulfilled the Valley of Dry Bones prophecy of Ezekiel 37. See the article on my website titled "Is the Valley of Dry Bones Prophecy Fulfilled?" for a critique of this view.

4. A comparison between Deut 30:3, Mic 7:18-20, Zech 10:5-6, Ps 106:44-48, Ezek 39:24-25, Jer 30:17-18, Isa 14:1-2, 54:7-11 further shows that the Lord will have compassion for the people of Israel after the hardships they will endure during the end times.

5. Deut 30:6-7 states that the Lord will circumcise His people's heart, which implies that He will cleanse them from sin, and will punish those who persecuted them.

   Jer 32:37-39, Ezek 36:24-27, and Ezek 11:17-19 suggest the heart transformation will mainly take place when the people of Israel gather in the land of Israel just before the start of the Millennium (see chapter twenty-three).

   Meanwhile, several verses about Israel's homecoming near the start of the Millennium refer to the reversal of fortune for Israel's enemies (Jer 30:16-18, Isa 14:1-3, 41:10-13).

CHAPTER 5.

THE SEVENTY WEEKS OF DANIEL

The seventy weeks of Daniel is an important timeline to learn about. Learning this timeline will help you a lot. You will gain critical knowledge about the end times. You will also gain an appreciation of how powerful and precise Bible prophecy is.

In this chapter, I show how Daniel's first sixty-nine weeks have already transpired and I outline the upcoming seventieth week of Daniel.

THE VISION

The Angel Gabriel appeared to the Prophet Daniel as he prayed to God. Gabriel told Daniel that seventy weeks were given to the people of Israel and the city of Jerusalem to bring about several developments:

> Seventy weeks are determined upon thy people and upon thy holy city, to finish the transgression, and to make an end of sins, and to make reconciliation for iniquity, and to bring in everlasting righteousness, and to seal up the vision and prophecy, and to anoint the most Holy. (Dan 9:24)

Here is an overview of the developments that will begin to be brought about at the completion of the seventieth week of Daniel:

- **Finish the Transgression:** The Hebrew word for "transgression" (*pesha*) implies "revolt" or "rebellion" at a national level.[1] The idea is that Israel's national rebellion against the Lord will come to an end.

- **Make an End of Sins:** The Hebrew word for "end" (*chatham*) implies "to close up" or "to seal".[2] The idea is not that all sin will be put to an end so that no one will ever sin again after the seventieth week of Daniel. The idea is that Israel's sins will be removed from sight or concealed.

- **Make Reconciliation for Iniquity:** The Hebrew word for "reconciliation" (*kaphar*) implies atonement.[3] The idea is Israel's iniquity will be atoned for.

- **Bring in Everlasting Righteousness:** Everlasting righteousness will begin with the establishment of God and Christ's eternal reign (Dan 7:27, Rev 11:15-18).

- **Seal Up Vision and Prophecy:** The Hebrew word *chatham* appears again here, which suggests that something will be closed up or sealed. In this context, the vision and prophecy will be preserved through time.[4]

- **Anoint the Most Holy:** This likely refers to the crowning of Christ as the King of the earth (Rev 11:15-18) or the consecration of a temple that Christ will reign from (Zech 6:13).

THE FIRST SIXTY-NINE WEEKS OF DANIEL

Gabriel gave Daniel details about the first sixty-nine weeks:

- The first week begins with a call to restore and build Jerusalem.

- The restoration and building process would last for seven weeks, and after that, there would be an additional sixty-two weeks ending when the Messiah (Christ) is "cut off".

This sixty-nine week time frame saw its fulfillment nearly 2,000 years ago with Christ's crucifixion and ascension to Heaven:

(25) Know therefore and understand, that from the going forth of the commandment to restore and to build Jerusalem unto the Messiah the Prince shall be seven weeks, and threescore and two weeks: the street

shall be built again, and the wall, even in troublous times. (26) And after threescore and two weeks shall Messiah be cut off, but not for himself:… (Dan 9:25-26)

Jerusalem was in ruins long before the time Daniel received the vision in the sixth century B.C. The call to restore Jerusalem that Gabriel spoke of came in the Hebrew month of Nisan during Artaxerxes's twentieth year of the reign (Neh 2:1, 5)

Most scholars agree that the twentieth year of Artaxerxes was in 445 or 444 B.C. while Christ's crucifixion occurred between 26 and 36 A.D.-corresponding to the rule of Pontius Pilate.

The Prophetic Week

Gabriel did not speak of seventy weeks where each week is seven days long. The Hebrew rendering of the word "week" in Daniel is *shabuwa`*, which means "seven".[5] Therefore, we can also refer to Daniel's prophecy as "the seventy sevens".

We can derive the length of a prophetic week by analyzing the structure of the seventieth week of Daniel. Daniel's seventieth week has two distinct halves.

The Antichrist will confirm a covenant with many at the start of the week, but will halt the daily sacrifice midway through the week:

And he shall confirm the covenant with many for one week: and in the midst of the week he shall cause the sacrifice and the oblation to cease, and for the overspreading of abominations he shall make it desolate, even until the consummation, and that determined shall be poured upon the desolate. (Dan 9:27)

The second half of the week will be a period of severe persecution. This period will last for "a time, times, and an half" according to Daniel 12:7: "… it shall be for a time, times, and an half; and when he shall have accomplished to scatter the power of the holy people, all these things shall be finished."

The word "time" is translated from the Hebrew word *mow`ed*, which can mean "a year".[6] Most commentators that analyze Daniel's seventy weeks prophecy correctly agree that "a time, times, and an half" represents 3.5 years. Therefore, a prophetic week is a 7-year period with dual 3.5-year halves.

We learn that 3.5 prophetic years (or half of a prophetic week) is equivalent to 1,260 days by comparing Revelation 12:14 and 12:6, and if we divide 1,260 days by 3.5 years, we find that a prophetic year is 360 days long:

> And to the woman were given two wings of a great eagle, that she might fly into the wilderness, into her place, where she is nourished **for a time, and times, and half a time, from the face of the serpent**. (Rev 12:14)

> And the woman fled into the wilderness, where she hath a place prepared of God, that they should feed her there **a thousand two hundred and threescore days**. (Rev 12:6)

Given that one-half of a prophetic week is 1,260 days, we can conclude that a whole prophetic week is 2,520 days.

Attempts to Verify the Prophecy

Many have tried to show the precision of the first sixty-nine weeks of the prophecy. Sir Robert Anderson and Harold Hoehner wrote two of the most famous efforts to verify the prophecy.

Sir Robert Anderson

Sir Robert Anderson wrote about the coming of Christ in his book *The Coming Prince*. He gave great insight about the seventy weeks prophecy and showed us how to calculate a prophetic year.

He set March 14, 445 B.C. on the Julian calendar (March 9, 445 B.C. on our calendar) as the start date of the first week of Daniel and April 6, 32 A.D. on the Julian calendar (April 4, 32 A.D. on our calendar and Palm Sunday) as the end date of the sixty-ninth week of Daniel. Anderson claimed that 32 A.D. was likely the termination year since Passover occurred on a Thursday.

Anderson's timeline was flawed since Passover fell on a Monday in 32 A.D., a day of the week that would not work as the crucifixion date. Despite this issue, Anderson's work paved the way for others.

Harold Hoehner

Harold Hoehner wrote the acclaimed book *Chronological Aspects of the Life of Christ.* Hoehner knew that Anderson's end date did not work, so he aimed for 33 A.D.

Hoehner's proposed sixty-nine week time frame has March 5, 444 B.C. on the Julian calendar (February 28, 444 B.C. on our calendar) as the start of the first week of Daniel and March 30, 33 A.D. on the Julian calendar (March 28, 33 A.D. on our calendar) as the end date of Daniel's sixty-ninth week.

Hoehner's study has two major flaws. First, his start date for Daniel's first week is impossible:

- The only source that Hoehner cited to support his start date was Herman H. Goldstine's *New and Full Moons, 1001 B.C. to A.D. 1651,* which listed the dates when a new moon was present. The issue with this source is that although a Hebrew month begins at the appearance of the new moon, Goldstine did not indicate which Hebrew month it was when each new moon appeared. March 5, 444 B.C. occurred in the early portion of the Hebrew month of Adar II since 444 B.C. had an additional month due to it being a leap year on the Hebrew calendar.

Second, the sixty-nine week timeline Hoehner proposed does not span the total length of sixty-nine prophetic weeks.

My Attempt to Verify the Prophecy

I used a calendar converter found at Abdicate.net to find the start date and end date of Daniel's first sixty-nine weeks.[7] The calendar gives dates for:

- The Jewish (Hebrew) calendar
- The Gregorian calendar: The calendar system we use today.
- The Julian calendar: A calendar system used by astronomers to perform arithmetic with dates.

The calendar converter also accounts for the absence of a year 0 in history and can calculate the difference between dates.

Before I show the results, here are the conditions that the proposed sixty-nine weeks of Daniel time frame must meet:

- The start of the first week must be in the month of Nisan in either 445 or 444 B.C.

- The year of Christ's crucifixion must occur between 26-36 A.D.

- Christ's crucifixion date must fall on the 14th of Nisan (eve of Passover) and fall on a Friday.[8]

- The end of the sixty-ninth week took place at the ascension of Christ rather than the crucifixion of Christ since His removal from the world occurred at His ascension.[9]

- Christ rose from the dead on Sunday and spent 40 days on Earth before He ascended to Heaven (Acts 1:1-3, 9-11).

33 A.D. is the only year among the three years from 26 to 36 A.D. that had Nisan 14 on a Friday (26, 33, and 36 A.D.) and could comply with the conditions set:

- Nisan 14, 33 A.D. occurred on April 1 of the Gregorian calendar.

- Sunday, April 3, or Nisan 16 was the date of Christ's resurrection.

- Christ's ascension date (the end of the sixty-ninth week) occurred 40 days later (counting the resurrection date as the first day) on May 12, 33 A.D.

I converted sixty-nine prophetic weeks into days to begin the search for the start of the first week of Daniel. I did this by turning sixty-nine prophetic weeks into prophetic years and then prophetic years into days:

- One Prophetic Week = 7 Prophetic Years

- 69 Weeks of 7 Prophetic Years = 483 Prophetic Years

- One Prophetic Year = 360 Days

- 483 Prophetic Years x 360 Days in a Prophetic Year = 173,880 Days

According to the calendar converter, 173,380 days from May 12, 33 A.D. was April 18, 444 B.C. The key dates of this proposed time frame are in Figure 5.1:

Figure 5.1: The Sixty-Nine Weeks Time Frame

Crucifixion: April 1, 33 A.D. or

Nisan 14, 3793 (Hebrew) or April 3, 33 A.D. (Julian)

Resurrection: April 3, 33 A.D. or

Nisan 16, 3793 (Hebrew) or April 5, 33 A.D. (Julian)

Ascension: May 12, 33 A.D. or

Iyyar 25, 3793 (Hebrew) or May 14, 33 A.D. (Julian)

The Start of the 1st Week: April 18, 444 B.C.

Nisan 22, 3317 (Hebrew) or April 23, 444 B.C. (Julian)

Therefore, Christ was "cut off" on May 12, 33 A.D., which was 483 prophetic years or exactly sixty-nine prophetic weeks after the decree came to restore Jerusalem on April 18, 444 B.C.

Thus, Daniel's sixty-nine week time frame complies with Scripture when Christ's ascension marks the end of the sixty-ninth week instead of His crucifixion. This leads to a bittersweet trade-off:

- We cannot claim that Daniel 9 predicted that Christ, the Messiah, would be crucified at the end of Daniel's sixty-ninth week.

- However, we can still proclaim that Jesus Christ is the Messiah because the prophecy referred to Him as having that role.

- Also, we gain precision that reveals Christ's likely crucifixion date and precision that helps us to dispel critics about this prophecy.

THE REST OF THE PROPHECY

The prophecy next called for the destruction of Jerusalem and the Second Temple. Both events occurred in 70 A.D.:

And after threescore and two weeks shall Messiah be cut off, but not for himself: and the people of the prince that shall come shall destroy the city and the sanctuary; and the end thereof shall be with a flood, and unto the end of the war desolations are determined. (Dan 9:26)

THE SEVENTIETH WEEK OF DANIEL

The seventieth week of Daniel will be a key time when many end time events will transpire. This final seven year period (also known as "the tribulation") will start when a covenant with many is confirmed. However, halfway through the week (3.5 years thru) the Antichrist will stop the daily sacrifice in the future Third Temple. He will also set up an abomination of desolation, an object affront to God, in the temple:

> And he shall confirm the covenant with many for one week: and in the midst of the week he shall cause the sacrifice and the oblation to cease, and for the overspreading of abominations he shall make it desolate, even until the consummation, and that determined shall be poured upon the desolate. (Dan 9:27)

Christ warned that a time of great tribulation will begin after the abomination of desolation is set up (Matt 24:15-21). Indeed, Daniel was told how the people of Israel will face unprecedented trouble for 3.5 years, or a time (year), times (two years), and half a time (half a year):

> (1) And at that time shall Michael stand up, the great prince which standeth for the children of thy people: and there shall be a time of trouble, such as never was since there was a nation even to that same time: and at that time thy people shall be delivered, every one that shall be found written in the book.... (6) And one said to the man clothed in linen, which was upon the waters of the river, How long shall it be to the end of these wonders? (7) And I heard the man clothed in linen, which was upon the waters of the river, when he held up his right hand and his left hand unto heaven, and sware by him that liveth for ever that it shall be for a time, times, and an half; and when he shall have accomplished to scatter the power of the holy people, all these things shall be finished. (Dan 12:1, 6-7)

Therefore, the second half of the seventieth week of Daniel will be a time of great persecution.

LET'S PAUSE FOR A MOMENT

It is important to pause here and allow what you just read to sink in. The seventy weeks of Daniel prophecy (recorded hundreds of years before the birth of Christ) contains absolute proof that Jesus Christ is the Messiah! We can use this prophecy to prove that what the Bible says is true, including the things it says about Jesus.

Bible prophecy is an incredible topic. Not only can it help us understand what is to come but also why certain historical events have occurred. The next chapter provides insight into some of the history's most powerful empires.

Notes

1. Strong, James. "pesha`". *Strong's Exhaustive Concordance of the Bible*. New York, Cincinnati, Eaton & Mains; Jennings & Graham, 1890. H6588.

2. Ibid. "chatham". H2856.

3. Ibid. "kaphar". H3722.

4. Some argue that sealing up vision and prophecy implies that all prophecy will be confirmed to be true or that vision and prophecy will no longer be needed. However, I am skeptical of this view. The reason is that the young people of Israel will have visions and prophesy after the Lord pours out His Spirit on all flesh (Joel 2:26-28). This will take place after they gather in the land of Israel following the end of the war of Armageddon.

5. Strong, James. "shabuwa`". *Strong's Exhaustive Concordance of the Bible*. New York, Cincinnati, Eaton & Mains; Jennings & Graham, 1890. H7620.

6. Ibid. "mow`ed". H4150.

7. "Jewish Calendar, Gregorian Calendar, and Julian Calendar Converter." *The Shepherd's Page*. 2021. Web. 19 Dec. 2021. http://abdicate.net/cal.aspx.

8. Some believe the crucifixion of Christ took place on a Wednesday instead of a Friday. I have studied both dates, and after studying the issue, I believe the crucifixion most likely took place on a Friday.

The Bible states that the crucifixion of Christ took place on the "day of preparation", a term directly connected to Friday-the day before the weekly Sabbath (Mark 15:42, Luke 23:54, John 19:31).

Nevertheless, Wednesday proponents will argue that Christ's crucifixion could not occur on a Friday because Christ said He would spend "three days and three nights in the heart of the earth" (Matt 12:40).

However, the term "three days and three nights" was not a phrase that signified 72 hours. The term was an idiom whose basic meaning in New Testament days is the same as the "day after tomorrow" nowadays.

We can see that "three days and three nights" does not equate to a literal 72-hour period by looking at a comparable term: "the third day". Christ told His followers that He would rise from the dead on "the third day":

(33) Saying, Behold, we go up to Jerusalem; and the Son of man shall be delivered unto the chief priests, and unto the scribes; and they shall condemn him to death, and shall deliver him to the Gentiles: (34) And they shall mock him, and shall scourge him, and shall spit upon him, and shall kill him: and the third day he shall rise again. (Mark 10:33-34)

The "third day" is equal to "three days and three nights" because they both represent the amount of time that Christ would be dead. "The third day" is not a literal 72-hour period. In fact, Luke 13:32 strongly implies that "the third day" covers a span of time equal to the day after tomorrow:

And he said unto them, Go ye, and tell that fox, Behold, I cast out devils, and I do cures to day and to morrow, and the third day I shall be perfected. (Luke 13:32)

Given all this, we can conclude that the term "three days and three nights" is equivalent to the day after tomorrow.

9. It would be great to prove that Daniel's sixty-ninth week finished on the exact date of Christ's crucifixion. However, this is problematic since subtracting 173,880 days from the crucifixion of Christ will not place the start date of the first week of Daniel in the month of Nisan. Given this, we must look for another way to make the time frame fit between Nisan of Artaxerxes's 20th year and the date that the Messiah was "cut-off".

Many believe the term "cut-off" in Daniel 9:26 refers to Christ's crucifixion. This is why most attempts to show the precision of Daniel's sixty-nine week timeline focus on Christ's crucifixion date. However, I believe the term "cut-off" refers to Christ temporarily being taken away without His kingdom when He ascended to Heaven.

According to Keil and Delitzsch, the term "cut-off" (Hebrew: יכרת) does not necessarily refer to the death of the Messiah:

"... יכרת does not denote the putting to death, or cutting off of existence, but only the annihilation of His place as *Maschiach* among His people and in His kingdom. For if after His "cutting off" He has not what He should have, it is clear that annihilation does not apply to Him personally, but only that He has lost His place and function as the *Maschiach*." (Delitzsch, Franz, and Carl F. Keil. *Biblical Commentary on the Old Testament*. The Book of the Prophet Daniel. Translated by M.G. Easton. Edinburgh: T. & T. Clark, 1884. 361-362.)

Many Jews view the Messiah as a leader who will bring world peace, gather the people of Israel back to the land of Israel, and restore the Kingdom of Israel. Christ said just before His ascension that it was not yet time for Him to set up the Messianic Kingdom of Israel:

(6) When they therefore were come together, they asked of him, saying, Lord, wilt thou at this time restore again the kingdom to Israel? (7) And he said unto them, It is not for you to know the times or the seasons, which the Father hath put in his own power. (Acts 1:6-7)

Therefore, Christ was not meant to serve as a messianic ruler in His first coming. He will reign in the future since Gabriel called Him the Messiah.

The notion that the Messiah would temporarily go away without His kingdom is not blasphemy!!! In fact, Revelation described Christ, the future ruler of all the nations, being taken up to Heaven:

And she brought forth a man child, who was to rule all nations with a rod of iron: and her child was caught up unto God, and to his throne. (Rev 12:5)

Finally, the interpretation of "cut off" that I present makes further sense when you consider the next phrase in Daniel 9:26. The next phrase reads "...but not for himself". This phrase relates to the fact that Christ left Earth without His messianic kingdom.

With "cut-off" not referring to Christ's crucifixion, we can reference His ascension date as the date when He was cut-off.

CHAPTER 6.

FORERUNNERS OF THE ANTICHRIST

Revelation 17 is among the most difficult chapters in the Bible to understand because it is full of symbolism. Unsurprisingly, many different views of the chapter exist. I explain why I believe Revelation 17 accounts for many of history's most powerful empires and most infamous leaders in this chapter.

THE VISION

Revelation 17 begins with a vision of a woman riding on a beast with seven heads and ten horns:

(1) And there came one of the seven angels which had the seven vials, and talked with me, saying unto me, Come hither; I will shew unto thee the judgment of the great whore that sitteth upon many waters: (2) With whom the kings of the earth have committed fornication, and the inhabitants of the earth have been made drunk with the wine of her fornication. (3) So he carried me away in the spirit into the wilderness: and I saw a woman sit upon a scarlet coloured beast, full of names of blasphemy, having seven heads and ten horns. (Rev 17:1-3)

Although John noticed the woman, I focus solely on the beast in this chapter. The beast is symbolic because the angel that accompanied John had to reveal what it represents. The angel provided details about the beast in verse 8, including that the beast is from the bottomless pit (or the abyss), a place where wicked souls remain until their final judgment:

(7) And the angel said unto me, Wherefore didst thou marvel? I will

tell thee the mystery of the woman, and of the beast that carrieth her, which hath the seven heads and ten horns. (8) The beast that thou sawest was, and is not; and shall ascend out of the bottomless pit, and go into perdition: and they that dwell on the earth shall wonder, whose names were not written in the book of life from the foundation of the world, when they behold the beast that was, and is not, and yet is. (9) And here is the mind which hath wisdom. The seven heads are seven mountains, on which the woman sitteth. (Rev 17:7-9)

The seven heads of the beast, which equate to seven mountains, are often thought of representing Rome. Rome has seven hills, and some Bible versions even replace the word "mountains" with "hills" in verse 9. However, this interpretation is incorrect because these seven mountains relate to seven kings in verse 10.

Five kings came before John's time. One king was in power during John's time, and another had not yet appeared on Earth. Revelation 17:11 reveals the importance of these seven kings, which is that one of the kings will serve again as an eighth king:

(10) And there are seven kings: five are fallen, and one is, and the other is not yet come; and when he cometh, he must continue a short space. (11) And the beast that was, and is not, even he is the eighth, and is of the seven, and goeth into perdition. (Rev 17:10-11)

Some take an additional step by equating the seven mountains with seven kingdoms. This step is reasonable because mountains can symbolize kingdoms in Bible prophecy. For instance, Daniel compares the kingdom of God to a stone that grows to the size of a mountain that fills the whole earth (Dan 2:34-35, 44-45).

The implication of taking this added step is that seven heads can represent seven kings or kingdoms. This interchangeability is feasible given that the terms "kingdom" and "kings" are used interchangeably in Daniel 7:17 and 7:23:

These great beasts, **which are four, are four kings**, which shall arise out of the earth. (Dan 7:17)

Thus he said, **The fourth beast shall be the fourth kingdom** upon earth, which shall be diverse from all kingdoms, and shall devour the whole earth, and shall tread it down, and break it in pieces. (Dan 7:23)

This interchangeability did not occur because translators subjectively chose the words "king" in verse 17 and "kingdom" in verse 23:

- The word *melek* is used in verse 17, and *melek* in Chaldee (a form of Aramaic and the original language of verse 17 and some other parts of the Book of Daniel) means "king".[1]

- The word *malkuw* is used in verse 23, and *malkuw* in Chaldee can mean "dominion" or "kingdom".[2]

The interchangeability between king and kingdom indicates that each king represents a particular kingdom.

THE SEVEN KINGS AND KINGDOMS

The Dragon

The beast from the abyss is one of three entities in the Book of Revelation that possess seven heads. The dragon of Revelation 12 and Revelation 13's beast from the sea are the other two entities.

We will look at dragon in this section since it will help us learn about the affiliation of these seven kingdoms/kings.

Revelation 12 summarizes the longstanding conflict between the dragon and the remnant of Israel (the woman).[3] Verses 3-4 describe the dragon-later identified as Satan in verse 9-casting a third of the stars to the earth:

> (3) And there appeared another wonder in heaven; and behold a great red dragon, having seven heads and ten horns, and seven crowns upon his heads. (4) And his tail drew the third part of the stars of heaven, and did cast them to the earth: and the dragon stood before the woman which was ready to be delivered, for to devour her child as soon as it was born. (Rev 12:3-4)

Literal stars did not fall to the earth given that they would incinerate the earth. Most Bible scholars agree these stars represent angels because stars represent angels elsewhere in Revelation (Rev 1:20, 9:1-11). This interpretation is consistent with the widespread belief that Satan led a fallen angel revolt against God.

The dragon in the vision is Satan (Rev 12:9). Each king/kingdom is associated with Satan since each head helps to describe him:

And there appeared another wonder in heaven; and behold a great red dragon, having seven heads and ten horns, and seven crowns upon his heads. (Rev 12:3)

Satan has used these kingdoms/kings in an effort to prevent the birth and *eventual eternal reign* of the special child, Christ. He has used them to persecute and to wage war against the people of Israel:

(4) And his tail drew the third part of the stars of heaven, and did cast them to the earth: and the dragon stood before the woman which was ready to be delivered, for to devour her child as soon as it was born. (5) And she brought forth a man child, who was to rule all nations with a rod of iron: and her child was caught up unto God, and to his throne. (Rev 12:4-5)

This interpretation implies that these kings have arisen over the course of history instead of one empire. This implication is important, as it helps our effort to identify these kings.

Nebuchadnezzar's Statue & the Four Beasts

The Book of Daniel provides clues that enable us to identify four of the seven kingdoms. Daniel 2 tells us that King Nebuchadnezzar of Babylon dreamed of a giant statue. Daniel described the statue and explained its significance to the king. He described a statue made of several different components:

(31) Thou, O king, sawest, and behold a great image. (32) This great image, whose brightness was excellent, stood before thee; and the form thereof was terrible. This image's head was of fine gold, his breast and his arms of silver, his belly and his thighs of brass, (33) His legs of iron, his feet part of iron and part of clay. (Dan 2:31-33)

Each component represents a different kingdom. For instance, Nebuchadnezzar's Babylonian Empire is the head of gold:

(37) Thou, O king, art a king of kings: for the God of heaven hath given thee a kingdom, power, and strength, and glory. (38) And wheresoever the children of men dwell, the beasts of the field and the fowls of the heaven hath he given into thine hand, and hath made thee ruler over them all. Thou art this head of gold. (Dan 2:37-38)

Most agree that the next two kingdoms represent the Medo-Persian Empire (the chest and arms of silver) and the Grecian/Seleucid Empire (the thighs of brass):

> And after thee shall arise another kingdom inferior to thee, and another third kingdom of brass, which shall bear rule over all the earth. (Dan 2:39)

Nearly everyone views the fourth kingdom (the legs of iron) as the Roman Empire, the kingdom of John's time:

> And the fourth kingdom shall be strong as iron: forasmuch as iron breaketh in pieces and subdueth all things: and as iron that breaketh all these, shall it break in pieces and bruise. (Dan 2:40)

Daniel 7 records a vision of four beasts that emerge from a sea. Most agree that the first three beasts described in Daniel 7 are kingdoms that have already come:

- The lion is the Babylonian Empire (Dan 7:4)
- The bear is the Medo-Persian Empire (Dan 7:5)
- The leopard is the Grecian/Seleucid Empire (Dan 7:6)

> (2) Daniel spake and said, I saw in my vision by night, and, behold, the four winds of the heaven strove upon the great sea. (3) And four great beasts came up from the sea, diverse one from another. (4) The first was like a lion, and had eagle's wings: I beheld till the wings thereof were plucked, and it was lifted up from the earth, and made stand upon the feet as a man, and a man's heart was given to it. (5) And behold another beast, a second, like to a bear, and it raised up itself on one side, and it had three ribs in the mouth of it between the teeth of it: and they said thus unto it, Arise, devour much flesh. (6) After this I beheld, and lo another, like a leopard, which had upon the back of it four wings of a fowl; the beast had also four heads; and dominion was given to it. (Dan 7:2-6)

Most rightly view the fourth beast of Daniel 7 and the feet of the statue as the empire of the Antichrist (the subject of chapter ten).

Thus, we can conclude that *four of the kings mentioned in Revelation 17 come from the Babylonian Empire, the Medo-Persian Empire, Grecian/ Seleucid Empire, and the Roman Empire.* The identity of the seven kings of Revelation 17 is the topic of the next section.

Nebuchadnezzar II

Nebuchadnezzar was the king of the Babylonian Empire from circa 605 B.C. to circa 562 B.C. Daniel identified him as the first king in a series of powerful kings/kingdoms (Dan 2:37-38). Nebuchadnezzar plundered Solomon's Temple multiple times before destroying it (2Chr 36:6-7, 18-19, 2Kgs 24:13, 25:13-17). He also had the city of Jerusalem destroyed (2Kgs 25:8-9) and had the city's residents deported (Jer 52:28-30).

Haman

Relatively little is known about Haman the Agagite, but Jews remember his evil deeds each year on the Jewish holiday of Purim. The only biblical description of Haman is in the Book of Esther.

Esther 3:2 reports that Haman received adoration from everyone in the King Ahasuerus's (Xerxes's I) court except for Mordecai. Haman became determined to destroy the Jews when he learned Mordecai was a Jew (Esth 3:6). Haman persuaded the king to give him the authority to persecute the Jews and then used it to issue an order to kill the Jews (Esth 3:12-14).

Although Haman was not the actual king of Medo-Persia, Ahasuerus made Haman de facto ruler when he elevated Haman above all princes of the kingdom (Esth 3:1) and gave Haman all the empire's resources to persecute the Jews.

Antiochus Epiphanes IV

Alexander the Great built one of the largest empires in world history. However, his vast empire was divided amongst four generals after his death. Daniel 11 predicted this development (Dan 11:3-4).

Seleucus I, one of the four generals, founded an empire that spanned many areas of the Mideast. Greek culture dominated this empire as many Greeks emigrated to build new cities and settlements. This empire became known as the Seleucid Empire.

One of Seleucus's descendants was Antiochus Epiphanes IV ("God Manifest" in Greek), who developed into a powerful leader after his ascension in 175 B.C. Daniel 8 prophesied his rise. He is the "little horn" which became great in verse 9:

> And out of one of them came forth a little horn, which waxed exceeding great, toward the south, and toward the east, and toward the pleasant land. (Dan 8:9)

Antiochus strove to Hellenize the Jews, but many Jews resisted his efforts. This resistance angered Antiochus.

He stormed the Second Temple of Jerusalem in 167 B.C. and set up a statue dedicated to Zeus in the Holy of Holies. Besides defiling the temple, he banned the practice of Judaism and had anyone who dared to practice it executed.

Daniel 8 and Daniel 11 cover much of his career. Many see him as a preview of the Antichrist. Several parallels between what he did and what Antichrist will do exist. For instance, both persecute others for their religious beliefs and desecrate a temple in Jerusalem.

The Roman Caesar of John's Time

Recall that the fourth kingdom of Daniel 2 was the Roman Empire and that the angel of Revelation 17 told John that one of the six kings was alive ("one is"). Most scholars believe John wrote the Book of Revelation around 96 A.D. while others believe he wrote it in 70 A.D. This means the sixth king of Revelation 17:10 was:

- Vespasian, if John wrote the Book of Revelation in 70 A.D.

- Domitian, if John wrote the Book of Revelation around 96 A.D.

Beyond the Book of Daniel

We've identified four of the kings and kingdoms, with the Roman Empire serving as the sixth kingdom and the Caesar of John's time serving as the sixth king. Therefore, we still need to identify two other kings and kingdoms before the rise of the Roman Empire.

Three kingdoms identified in Daniel came in succession before the rise of the Roman Empire. Therefore, we must look before the time of the Babylonian Empire for the identities of the two unidentified kings and kingdoms.

Interestingly, the Bible speaks of two other strong kingdoms that oppressed the people of Israel: Egypt and Assyria.

Pharaoh of Exodus Chapter 1

The name of the Pharaoh is unknown. However, we know he enslaved the children of Israel and twice ordered the killing of all their newborn males (Exod 1:8-22).

Sennacherib

Sennacherib was the king of Assyria during a time of great distress in the land of Israel. Israel was reeling after Shalmaneser V and Sargon II squashed a revolt in Northern Israel and deported ten of the twelve tribes of Israel. He launched an offensive against Judah, and his forces defeated several fortified cities in Judah before setting their sights on Jerusalem.

After the Assyrian army arrived outside of Jerusalem, a representative from the army tried to persuade the inhabitants to turn against King Hezekiah of Judah, stop trusting the Lord, and to follow Sennacherib (2Kgs 18:28-35).

Sennacherib promised the inhabitants of Jerusalem a new life, much like life described in messianic prophecies (2Kgs 18:31-32). His arrogance and blasphemy angered the Lord. The Lord promised Hezekiah that He would defend Jerusalem, which He did when He sent the Angel of the Lord to smite 185,000 troops (2Kgs 19:20-36).

The Seventh King

The identity of the seventh king is subject to much debate. The seventh king is the leader of an empire that had not yet appeared when John was alive. Some argue that the seventh king has already come while others argue that he is a leader who is yet to come.[4]

The defining characteristic of the seventh king is that he will be in power for only a short time, according to Revelation 17:10:

And there are seven kings: five are fallen, and one is, and the other is not yet come; and when he cometh, he must continue a short space.

We will discuss him in more detail in a couple of chapters.

LET'S PAUSE FOR A MOMENT

I appreciate your patience as you read about historical figures and events in the past several chapters. Do not hesitate to reread this chapter or any of the previous chapters.

Make sure you have a firm grasp of the things we have discussed, because we will start focusing on future events in the next chapter.

Notes

1. Strong, James. "melek". *Strong's Exhaustive Concordance of the Bible*. New York, Cincinnati, Eaton & Mains; Jennings & Graham, 1890. H4430.

2. Ibid. "malkuw". H4437.

3. The identity of the woman of Rev 12 is subject to debate. The woman clearly relates to the nation of Israel since she relates to Jacob, Rachel, and the twelve tribes of Israel in her imagery (Rev 12:1, Gen 37:9).

   However, the woman is not the entire nation of Israel because a significant portion of Israel will not receive divine protection during the end times (see chapter eleven).

   Also, the woman is not the 144,000 because they were not around when Christ was born. Furthermore, the 144,000 consist of strictly male virgins, which is inconsistent with the imagery of a woman who has given birth.

   The woman likely represents the portion of Israel that the Lord spares throughout His people's history (Rom 11:1-7). In an end time context, the woman probably comprises a group of unsaved Israel who will find refuge in the wilderness areas of Edom, Moab, and Ammon (modern day Jordan).

4. If the seventh king is a past leader, I believe Adolf Hitler is likely him. Hitler's Third Reich only lasted for twelve years, so he (and his empire) reigned for a short time. His regime murdered six million Jews, which was about two-thirds of the European Jewish population at the time. Also, his regime planned to eradicate Christianity and replace it with a new religion.

CHAPTER 7.

EVENTS LEADING TO THE ANTICHRIST'S RISE

The world will go through much turmoil and will see many false doctrines permeate as the end of the age approaches.

The first half of the tribulation will be eventful as the Antichrist gains power through political and military means. It will be a time of relative peace in Israel but a time of chaos elsewhere in the world.

This chapter describes what to expect between now and the midpoint of the tribulation.

BIRTH PAINS

Christ described a chaotic period that will precede His coming at the end of the age (or end of the world). He said the world will see:

- False Christs arise (Matt 24:5, Mark 13:6, Luke 21:8)
- Wars and rumors of wars (Matt 24:6, Mark 13:7, Luke 21:9)
- Ethnic conflict (Matt 24:7, Mark 13:8, Luke 21:10)
- Pestilences and famines (Matt 24:7, Mark 13:8, Luke 21:11).
- Great earthquakes in many places (Matt 24:7, Mark 13:8, Luke 21:11)
- Political Instability (Luke 21:9)

Christ characterized these events as the beginning of sorrows or birth pains (Matt 24:8).

Some believe birth pains will not take place until the tribulation.

They think the conditions Christ described are the events related to the seals of Revelation 6, which I will introduce shortly.

I disagree with the view that we won't see birth pains until the start of the tribulation. This idea contradicts the fact that the world already has seen false Christs, devastating world wars, famines, earthquakes, and major plagues.

Beyond that, I do not believe the parallels between the birth pains conditions and the seals of Revelation 6 are strong with regards to the first seal and the fourth seal.[1] [2]

Furthermore, Christ stressed that people should not be startled when these events transpire since they are preordained to occur before the end of the age. In fact, Christ qualified His statement by stating, "but the end is not yet." (Matt 24:6) when these events (false Christs, wars, rumors of war, etc.) take place.

The message to remain calm when birth pains occur suggests that they will not occur only during the end times. Their occurrence should not be a reason to reach drastic conclusions about the proximity to the end of the age.

Nonetheless, the birth pains analogy is important to understand. It may give us a sense of how bad conditions may get in the future:

- Birth pains start with initial pain followed by a period of relative calm. However, the frequency that pain is felt increases as time progresses.

- Therefore, the frequency of the events that Christ described may increase on Earth as we approach the end times. The frequency of war may increase, the frequency of revolutions may increase, etc.

THE FALLING AWAY

False doctrines will become more prevalent, and a growing number of people will adhere to these false doctrines as the end times nears. In fact, the Apostle Paul warned that some will even depart from the faith in the "latter times"-a period that may aptly describe modern times:

(1) Now the Spirit speaketh expressly, that in the latter times some shall depart from the faith, giving heed to seducing spirits, and doctrines of

devils; (2) Speaking lies in hypocrisy; having their conscience seared with a hot iron; (3) Forbidding to marry, and commanding to abstain from meats, which God hath created to be received with thanksgiving of them which believe and know the truth. (1Tim 4:1-3)

Paul also warned a time will come when people will seek teachers who will tell them what they want to hear instead of telling them the truth:

(2) Preach the word; be instant in season, out of season; reprove, rebuke, exhort with all longsuffering and doctrine. (3) For the time will come when they will not endure sound doctrine; but after their own lusts shall they heap to themselves teachers, having itching ears; (4) And they shall turn away their ears from the truth, and shall be turned unto fables. (2Tim 4:2-4)

Paul also warned that apostasy (a falling away) will precede the coming of Christ and the unveiling of the Antichrist:

(1) Now we beseech you, brethren, by the coming of our Lord Jesus Christ, and by our gathering together unto him, (2) That ye be not soon shaken in mind, or be troubled, neither by spirit, nor by word, nor by letter as from us, as that the day of Christ is at hand. (3) Let no man deceive you by any means: for that day shall not come, except there come **a falling away** first, and that man of sin be revealed, the son of perdition; (2Thess 2:1-3)

The apostasy may already be underway with the decline of moral values and with fewer churches and individuals teaching from the Bible as time goes on.

The decline in spiritual conditions will lead to a world full of evil in the last days. Many will act ungodly and chide Christians for expecting the coming of Christ:

(3) Knowing this first, that there shall come in the last days scoffers, walking after their own lusts, (4) And saying, Where is the promise of his coming? for since the fathers fell asleep, all things continue as they were from the beginning of the creation. (2Pet 3:3-4, also see Jude 1:18)

(1) This know also, that in the last days perilous times shall come. (2) For men shall be lovers of their own selves, covetous, boasters, proud, blasphemers, disobedient to parents, unthankful, unholy, (3) Without natural affection, trucebreakers, false accusers, incontinent, fierce, despisers of those that are good, (4) Traitors, heady, highminded,

lovers of pleasures more than lovers of God; (5) Having a form of godliness, but denying the power thereof: from such turn away. (6) For of this sort are they which creep into houses, and lead captive silly women laden with sins, led away with divers lusts, (2Tim 3:1-6)

Unfortunately, the world will become a worse place and more difficult place to live in as we approach the end times. However, we must remember that these developments must take place.

THE EMERGENCE OF THE ANTICHRIST

Daniel 7:7 onward covers the rise of the Antichrist and suggests that he will start his political career from relatively humble beginnings. The ten kingdoms that will later comprise his empire will be in place as a political unit before he rises to power:

> After this I saw in the night visions, and behold a fourth beast, dreadful and terrible, and strong exceedingly; and it had great iron teeth: it devoured and brake in pieces, and stamped the residue with the feet of it: and it was diverse from all the beasts that were before it; and it had ten horns. (Dan 7:7)

Daniel described the Antichrist as a little horn when he begins his rise to power. The little horn will arise *after* ten horns are in place. The statement that the little horn will arise "among them" suggests that the Antichrist will be someone who originates from within the borders of this ten kingdom political unit. However, the distinction between the little horn and the ten horns suggests the Antichrist will be unaffiliated with the political unit's ten kings at the start:

> (8) I considered the horns, and, behold, there came up among them another little horn, before whom there were three of the first horns plucked up by the roots: and, behold, in this horn were eyes like the eyes of man, and a mouth speaking great things.... (24) And the ten horns out of this kingdom are ten kings that shall arise: and another shall rise after them; and he shall be diverse from the first, and he shall subdue three kings. (Dan 7:8, 24)

Also, the characterization of the Antichrist as a little horn vis-à-vis the ten horns indicates that he will be viewed initially as a leader of lesser stature than the ten kings. However, we shall soon see that this will change quickly.

THE SCROLL & ITS SEVEN SEALS

Revelation 5 describes a scene in Heaven shortly before the breaking of the seven seals located outside of a scroll.[3] This scroll needs to have every seal broken before it can be opened. Christ will open the seven seals and the scroll as He is the only one worthy to open them (Rev 5:6-9).

Some believe the scroll contains the judgments of God, while others believe the scroll represents the title deed of the planet Earth. I lean towards the position that it represents the title deed of Earth.

The position posits that humankind lost its authority over Earth to Satan when it fell into sin.[4] Christ is our kinsman redeemer, the One who became a man to pay the price of redemption that humankind could not pay (the payment of our sin debt) when He died on the cross.[5] [6] Christ's sacrifice on the cross makes Him eligible or worthy to redeem the title deed of Earth at the appointed time.

The time to redeem the planet will be near when Christ prepares to break the seven seals at the start of the tribulation. The seven seals are associated with conditions that must occur on Earth before the scroll can be opened. The seven seals will be broken one at a time, and the breaking of each seal will be followed by a series of new events. However, the planet cannot be redeemed until all the seals are broken and until *all the conditions associated with the seals are fulfilled.*

The First Seal and the Covenant with Many

The breaking of the first seal by Christ marks the arrival of a rider on a white horse. The rider on the white horse is unlikely Christ because He is in Heaven as He opens the seals. Instead, the rider on the white horse probably represents a false Christ, the Antichrist, who will accumulate power rapidly:

(1) And I saw when the Lamb opened one of the seals, and I heard, as it were the noise of thunder, one of the four beasts saying, Come and see. (2) And I saw, and behold a white horse: and he that sat on him had a bow; and a crown was given unto him: and he went forth conquering, and to conquer. (Rev 6:1-2)

The Antichrist will help to confirm a "covenant with many" for one prophetic week or seven years. This event will usher in the start of the seventieth week of Daniel (the tribulation):

> And he shall confirm the covenant with many for one week: and in the midst of the week he shall cause the sacrifice and the oblation to cease, and for the overspreading of abominations he shall make it desolate, even until the consummation, and that determined shall be poured upon the desolate." (Dan 9:27)

Isaiah 28 refers to the covenant of many as "the covenant with death". This pact may include a firm security guarantee for Israel. Verse 15 tells us that Israel's leaders will have a false sense of security after they agree to the pact:

> (14) Wherefore hear the word of the LORD, ye scornful men, that rule this people which is in Jerusalem. (15) Because ye have said, We have made a covenant with death, and with hell are we at agreement; when the overflowing scourge shall pass through, it shall not come unto us: for we have made lies our refuge, and under falsehood have we hid ourselves: (Isa 28:14-15)

Meanwhile, the Antichrist may gain great stature in the international community. They may praise him as the man who helped to bring peace to a place that has seen little peace in recent history.

The Second Seal: Antichrist at War

Revelation 6:3-4 tells us that peace will be taken away from the earth after the breaking of the second seal:

> (3) And when he had opened the second seal, I heard the second beast say, Come and see. (4) And there went out another horse that was red: and power was given to him that sat thereon to take peace from the earth, and that they should kill one another: and there was given unto him a great sword. (Rev 6:3-4)

The Antichrist will likely be a major military player at this time of war on the earth. Daniel tells us that the Antichrist will destroy many unexpectedly when his opponents think they are at peace:

> "And through his policy also he shall cause craft to prosper in his hand;

and he shall magnify himself in his heart, and by peace shall destroy many:... (Dan 8:25)

His opponents won't expect him to be plotting against them. Most will perceive him as a peacemaker after he confirms the covenant with many. Nevertheless, even his most prepared foes will not be able to stop him.

Daniel 11:39 tells us that the Antichrist will defeat the strongest opponents, and reward those loyal to him with control over land:

> Thus shall he do in the most strong holds with a strange god, whom he shall acknowledge and increase with glory: and he shall cause them to rule over many, and shall divide the land for gain. (Dan 11:39)

This is perhaps the time when the Antichrist will subdue three kings, as predicted by Daniel:

> And the ten horns out of this kingdom are ten kings that shall arise: and another shall rise after them; and he shall be diverse from the first, and he shall subdue three kings. (Dan 7:24)

Although the focus has been on Antichrist, conflicts unrelated to the conquest of Antichrist could take place. Also, birth pains conditions may be prevalent during the end times, so things like widespread ethnic conflict and war cannot be ruled out (Matt 24:7, Mark 13:8, Luke 21:10).

The Third Seal: Famine

Widespread famine will also occur at that time. Food will be so scarce that a day's worth of wages will only be enough to buy a small amount of wheat or barley:

> (5) And when he had opened the third seal, I heard the third beast say, Come and see. And I beheld, and lo a black horse; and he that sat on him had a pair of balances in his hand. (6) And I heard a voice in the midst of the four beasts say, A measure of wheat for a penny, and three measures of barley for a penny; and see thou hurt not the oil and the wine. (Rev 6:5-6)

The Fourth Seal: Widespread Death

Conditions will worsen after the breaking of the fourth seal. Many will die from famine, plague, war, and other causes:

> And I looked, and behold a pale horse: and his name that sat on him was Death, and Hell followed with him. And power was given unto them over the fourth part of the earth, to kill with sword, and with hunger, and with death, and with the beasts of the earth. (Rev 6:8)

Death will not be limited to just one area covering one-fourth of the earth because conditions, such as famine, should be seen worldwide. Therefore, it is likely that one-fourth of the world's population will die.

THE START OF TEMPLE SACRIFICE

Daily temple sacrifice will take place during the tribulation (Dan 9:27). Its start will be a huge development since it has not taken place since the Romans destroyed the Second Temple in 70 A.D.

Although Scripture says nothing specific, the covenant with many could permit a new temple to be built and permit daily sacrifice to start.[7] Daniel 8 may provide a clue about when we may see the start of the daily sacrifice after the tribulation begins.

Daniel 8 contains a prophecy that concerns the time of Antiochus Epiphanes IV:

> (9) And out of one of them came forth a little horn, which waxed exceeding great, toward the south, and toward the east, and toward the pleasant land. (10) And it waxed great, even to the host of heaven; and it cast down some of the host and of the stars to the ground, and stamped upon them. (11) Yea, he magnified himself even to the prince of the host, and by him the daily sacrifice was taken away, and the place of his sanctuary was cast down. (12) And an host was given him against the daily sacrifice by reason of transgression, and it cast down the truth to the ground; and it practised, and prospered. (13) Then I heard one saint speaking, and another saint said unto that certain saint which spake, How long shall be the vision concerning the daily sacrifice, and the transgression of desolation, to give both the sanctuary and the host to be trodden under foot? (14) And he said unto me, Unto two thousand and three hundred days; then shall the sanctuary be cleansed. (Dan 8:9-14)

However, this prophecy is also about the end times. The Angel Gabriel told Daniel that the vision pertains to the time of the end:

(17) So he [Gabriel] came near where I stood: and when he came, I was afraid, and fell upon my face: but he said unto me, Understand, O son of man: **for at the time of the end shall be the vision.** (18) Now as he was speaking with me, I was in a deep sleep on my face toward the ground: but he touched me, and set me upright. (19) And he said, Behold, I will make thee know what shall be in the last end of the indignation: for at **the time appointed the end** shall be. (Dan 8:17-19)

Many believe Daniel 8:20-22 is about the period spanning from the rise of Alexander the Great to the division of his empire after his death. Daniel 8:23 onward is about the Antichrist in the end times:

(23) And in the latter time of their kingdom, when the transgressors are come to the full, a king of fierce countenance, and understanding dark sentences, shall stand up. (24) And his power shall be mighty, but not by his own power: and he shall destroy wonderfully, and shall prosper, and practise, and shall destroy the mighty and the holy people. (25) And through his policy also he shall cause craft to prosper in his hand; and he shall magnify himself in his heart, and by peace shall destroy many: he shall also stand up against the Prince of princes; but he shall be broken without hand. (26) And the vision of the evening and the morning which was told is true: wherefore shut thou up the vision; for it shall be for many days. (Dan 8:23-26)

The vision of the evening and the morning in verse 26 refers directly to the daily sacrifice and relates to a 2,300-day frame time of Verse 14. Daniel 8:13-14 indicates that the 2,300-days pertain to:

• The daily sacrifice

• The abomination of desolation

• The cleansing of the sanctuary

The 2,300 Day Timeline

We can use this information to glean much about the daily sacrifice timeline. Let's look at the end date of the 2,300-day prophecy and work backwards to find its start:[8]

- The daily sacrifice will cease and the abomination of desolation will be set up at the midpoint of the tribulation (Dan 9:27). Recall that this will take place 1,260 days after it begins (given that half a prophetic week is 1,260 days).

- The abomination of desolation will be in place for 1,290 days after the midpoint of the tribulation or until the 2,550th day after the tribulation starts:

  "And from the time that the daily sacrifice shall be taken away, and the abomination that maketh desolate set up, there shall be a thousand two hundred and ninety days. (Dan 12:11)

- Daniel 8:14 states that the cleansing of the temple will take place on the last day of the 2,300-day time frame. This means the end of the 2,300-day time frame will fall on the 2,550th day after the tribulation starts.

- Subtracting 2,300 days from the 2,550th day means the 2,300-day time frame will start on the 250th day after the tribulation begins.

- The first day of the 2,300-day prophecy concerns the daily sacrifice, so we can deduce that the daily sacrifice will start on the 250th day of the tribulation.

Figure 7.1 shows how the 2,300-day time frame fits into everything we have learned so far. Recall that "the tribulation" is a term to describe the seventieth week of Daniel:

Figure 7.1: Daniel's Timeline

Start of the Tribulation

- Confirmation of the Seven Year Covenant (Dan 9:27)

Daily Sacrifice Begins (Day 250)

- Start of the 2,300-Day Prophecy (Dan 8:13-14)

Midpoint of the Tribulation (Day 1,260)

- The Daily Sacrifice Stops (Dan 9:27)
- Abomination of Desolation is Set Up (Dan 9:27)

The End of the Tribulation (Day 2,520)

Abomination of Desolation Removal

- 1,290 Days Since the Midpoint (Dan 12:11)
- The 2,300-Day Prophecy Ends (Dan 8:13-14)

WAR IN HEAVEN & THE FALLEN ANGEL INVASION

A war in Heaven will take place near the midpoint of the tribulation. The war will pit the Archangel Michael and his angels against Satan and his angels.

Satan and his angels will lose the war. As a result, they will be cast out of Heaven and will be forced onto the earth:

(7) And there was war in heaven: Michael and his angels fought against the dragon; and the dragon fought and his angels, (8) And prevailed not; neither was their place found any more in heaven. (9) And the great dragon was cast out, that old serpent, called the Devil, and Satan, which deceiveth the whole world: he was cast out into the earth, and his angels were cast out with him. (Rev 12:7-9)

Satan's defeat will be good news for those in Heaven, but bad news for those living on the earth. Satan will be full of wrath while knowing he only has a short amount of time to inflict his wrath:

Therefore rejoice, ye heavens, and ye that dwell in them. Woe to the inhabiters of the earth and of the sea! for the devil is come down unto you, having great wrath, because he knoweth that he hath but a short time. (Rev 12:12)

THE ANTICHRIST'S RETURN TO JERUSALEM

The last stop before the Antichrist reveals his true nature to the world will likely be Jerusalem. The Antichrist will surround the city just before he sets up the abomination of desolation:

(20) And when ye shall see Jerusalem compassed with armies, then know that the desolation thereof is nigh. (21) Then let them which are in Judaea flee to the mountains; and let them which are in the midst of it depart out; and let not them that are in the countries enter thereinto. (Luke 21:20-21, also see Matt 24:15-16, Mark 13:14)

The Abomination of Desolation

The Antichrist will cease temple sacrifice to God in the middle of the tribulation and set up the abomination of desolation (Dan 9:27) We can perhaps glean more insight about what will happen when the Antichrist sets up the abomination of desolation. Paul wrote that the Antichrist will sit in the temple of God (in Jerusalem) and proclaim that he is God. The Antichrist's true identity as the man of sin shall be revealed at that moment:

(3) Let no man deceive you by any means: for that day shall not come, except there come a falling away first, and that man of sin be revealed, the son of perdition; (4) Who opposeth and exalteth himself above all that is called God, or that is worshipped; so that he as God sitteth in the temple of God, shewing himself that he is God. (2Thess 2:3-4)

Daniel 11:36-39 most likely describes the Antichrist when he sets up the abomination of desolation. The passage depicts him as someone who will exalt himself above all things:

(36) **And the king shall do according to his will; and he shall exalt himself, and magnify himself above every god,** and shall speak marvellous things against the God of gods, and shall prosper till the indignation be accomplished: for that that is determined shall be done. (37) **Neither shall he regard the God of his fathers, nor the desire of**

women, nor regard any god: for he shall magnify himself above all.
(Dan 11:36-37)

Although the Antichrist will magnify himself above God, Daniel 11:38 indicates that the Antichrist will honor an entity known as the god of forces, a god whom his forefathers did not know, with valuable riches:

> But in his estate shall he honour the God of forces: and a god whom his fathers knew not shall he honour with gold, and silver, and with precious stones, and pleasant things. (Dan 11:38)

Daniel 11:39 adds that this god will help the Antichrist defeat the strongest opponents during his rise to power:

> Thus shall he do in the most strong holds with a strange god, whom he shall acknowledge and increase with glory: and he shall cause them to rule over many, and shall divide the land for gain. (Dan 11:39)

Daniel 8 also indicates that the Antichrist will receive outside help during his rise to power. This help will give him immense power:

> **And his power shall be mighty, but not by his own power**: and he shall destroy wonderfully, and shall prosper, and practise, and shall destroy the mighty and the holy people. (Dan 8:24)

We may be able to find the identity of the god of forces with the help of Revelation 13. The chapter tells us that the dragon (Satan) will be the source of Antichrist's power during his reign. Interestingly, the people of earth will worship the beast of Revelation 13 (through the worship of the Antichrist) *and the dragon*:

> (2) And the beast which I saw was like unto a leopard, and his feet were as the feet of a bear, and his mouth as the mouth of a lion: and the dragon gave him his power, and his seat, and great authority. (3) And I saw one of his heads as it were wounded to death; and his deadly wound was healed: and all the world wondered after the beast. (4) And they worshipped the dragon which gave power unto the beast: and they worshipped the beast, saying, Who is like unto the beast? who is able to make war with him? (Rev 13:2-4)

Recall that Satan offered Christ the kingdoms of the earth and the glory that comes along with being the ruler of the world if He would worship Satan (Matt 4:8-9, Luke 4:5-7). Also recall that Christ rejected Satan's offer and rebuked him from tempting Him.

In contrast, Antichrist will accept Satan's offer. He will acknowledge Satan and compel the world to worship Satan alongside him.

Given all this, the god of forces is most likely Satan since he will be the one who gives Antichrist his power.[9] Thus, the Antichrist will likely honor the dragon/Satan when he sets up the abomination of desolation.

How Antichrist May Honor Satan

Many recognize the parallels between the careers of Antiochus Epiphanes IV and the Antichrist. The Book of Daniel described the careers of both men, including:

- The removal of the daily sacrifice
- The setting up of an abomination of desolation

Given the parallels, we may be able to envision how the Antichrist may honor Satan when he sets up the abomination of desolation:

- **Antiochus Epiphanes IV:** He defiled the Second Temple by setting up a statue of Zeus in the Holy of Holies, the most sacred area of the temple. He further defiled the temple by sacrificing a pig, an abominable animal in Judaism, to honor Zeus.

- **Antichrist:** The Antichrist may erect a dragon statue in the Holy of Holies. However, it does not appear that the Antichrist will sacrifice a pig on the altar of the temple. He will honor the god of forces/Satan with valuable riches (Dan 11:38).

As mentioned, the people of earth will finally see the Antichrist for who he truly is at that time. The next chapter will focus on the identity of the Antichrist.

LET'S PAUSE FOR A MOMENT

I will end most chapters from now on with a timeline that displays a probable sequence of events. This is meant to help you better understand the chronological order of events and how they relate.

Here is a look at where the key events discussed in this chapter fit in our timeline (events mentioned in the current chapter are in italics. This practice will continue in coming chapters):

Probable Sequence of Events: Ch.7

The Start of the Tribulation: Dan. 9:27 (Ch.5)

1st to 4th Seal: Rev 6:1-8 (Ch.7)

- *Start of Temple Sacrifice: Dan 8:13-19 (Ch.7)*
- *War in Heaven: Rev 12:7-12 (Ch.7)*

Midpoint of the Tribulation: Dan 9:27 (Ch.7)

- *Abomination of Desolation: Dan 9:27, Matt 24:15 (Ch.7)*

Do not be afraid of the events I am describing to you. If you are afraid, please ask God to remove your fear. I was terrified when I began to learn about Bible prophecy. God removed my fear, so I know He can remove any fears you may have about end time events.

Please continue to the next chapter as soon as you feel comfortable because I have more to tell you about the future.

Notes

1. The parallel between the first seal, which describes a rider on a white horse (Rev 6:1-2), and the birth pains condition concerning false Christs (Matt 24:5, Luke 21:8, Mark 13:5-6) is not strong. Christ described the arrival of multiple individuals instead of the arrival of one person. Also, Antichrist will not proclaim that he is God until later in tribulation.

2. Christ warned there will be pestilence, famines, and earthquakes in many

places when He discussed birth pains (Matt 24:7, Luke 21:11, Mark 13:8). In contrast, Rev 6:7-8 describes how many will die from various causes.

The parallel between the fourth seal and the birth pains conditions Christ described is not strong because the causes of death from the breaking of the fourth seal are markedly different from what Christ described in His discussion of birth pains.

3. The scene in Heaven describes the presence of 24 elders. Many believe that the 24 elders are representatives of the Church that have been taken up in the Rapture. I disagree with this view. I believe the 24 elders are the saints who rose from the dead after Christ's resurrection (Matt 27:52-53). I believe they are part of the firstfruits of the resurrection along with Christ (1Cor 15:20-23). They serve as king-priests in the Order of Melchizedek, which Christ is the chief priest (Heb 5:5-6).

4. Some cite verses like Matt 4:8-9, Luke 4:5-6, John 12:31, John 16:11, and 2Cor 4:4 as evidence that Satan has authority over the world in this age.

5. The kinsman redeemer had to be related to the individual they wanted to help. Heb 2:11-14 tells us that Christ was incarnate as a man when He was on Earth, so He was related to man when He paid our sin debt.

6. Jer 32:6-14 and Ruth 4:1-15 contain two examples of the role the kinsman redeemer plays.

7. It should not take long to erect a new temple once construction starts. Several groups within Israel have already made many of the items that will be part of the temple.

8. Some argue the 2,300 days in Daniel 8 equate to 2,300 years. I disagree. Days are called "the evening and the morning" in Daniel 8. This term refers to:

   ◦ The times of day when the sacrifice would take place.

   ◦ The aspects of a calendar day.

   This leads me to believe the 2,300 days are 2,300 calendar days.

9. War will not exist during the Millennium (Isa 2:4, Mic 4:3). This lack of war will take place as Satan will be imprisoned. Perhaps the title "god of forces" is appropriate for Satan.

CHAPTER 8.

THE ANTICHRIST REVEALED

We return to Revelation 17. Many claim this chapter speaks of a Roman Antichrist who will rule the world from Rome. He will supposedly come from a group of seven Caesars who lived back during the Roman Empire. Some link him to Nero or Caligula, even though the text does not indicate which seven Caesars should be under consideration.

This interpretation is wrong because the wrong group of leaders is under consideration. The seven candidates are, in fact, the seven leaders discussed in chapter six. I will identify which one of these seven men will serve Satan in the role of the Antichrist in this chapter.

WHAT PRECISELY IS THE ANTICHRIST?

The term "antichrist" in Greek (*antichristos*) means "an opponent of the Messiah" and is only used five times in the Bible.[1] The first three instances are in 1 John 2:18-23:

(18) Little children, it is the last time: and as ye have heard that antichrist shall come, even now are there many antichrists; whereby we know that it is the last time.... (22) Who is a liar but he that denieth that Jesus is the Christ? He is antichrist, that denieth the Father and the Son. (23) Whosoever denieth the Son, the same hath not the Father: (but) he that acknowledgeth the Son hath the Father also. (1John 2:18, 22-23)

John called those who deny that Jesus is the Christ an "antichrist". His use of this term in this context was appropriate, since these people's denial made them opponents of Christ. However, John also acknowledged that people in his day expected a coming man known as the "Antichrist".

John used the term "antichrist" again in 1 John 4:1-3. John wrote that every spirit that denies Jesus came in the flesh is the "spirit of the antichrist":

(1) Beloved, believe not every spirit, but try the spirits whether they are of God: because many false prophets are gone out into the world. (2) Hereby know ye the Spirit of God: Every spirit that confesseth that Jesus Christ is come in the flesh is of God: (3) And every spirit that confesseth not that Jesus Christ is come in the flesh is not of God: and this is that spirit of antichrist, whereof ye have heard that it should come; and even now already is it in the world. (1John 4:1-3)

Like in 1 John 2, we learn something critical about the one we call "Antichrist". The spirit of Antichrist was already in the world during John's time, and this spirit relates to the man that is coming.

2 John 1:7 is the last instance where the term "antichrist" appears. This verse is like 1 John 4:3 as John labeled those who deny Jesus Christ came in the flesh an "antichrist":

For many deceivers are entered into the world, who confess not that Jesus Christ is come in the flesh. This is a deceiver and an antichrist. (2John 1:7)

These passages by John reveal that a deceiving spirit, the spirit of Antichrist, has been in the world for at least two millennia. They also confirm that people have expected a man known as the "Antichrist" to come since John's time. Both are (or will be) deceptive entities that deny Jesus is the Christ and that He came in the flesh.

THE FALSE RESURRECTION

We became acquainted with the beast of Revelation 17 in chapter six's discussion of the seven kings Satan has used to persecute and to wage war against the people of Israel.

The beast of Revelation 17 represents the eighth king, the Antichrist, given what Revelation 17:11 says:

And the beast that was, and is not, even he is the eighth, and is of the seven, and goeth into perdition. (Rev 17:11)

Revelation 17:8 describes the beast as the one who "was, and is not, and yet is" when viewed by the inhabitants of the earth:

> The beast that thou sawest was, and is not; and shall ascend out of the bottomless pit, and go into perdition: and they that dwell on the earth shall wonder, whose names were not written in the book of life from the foundation of the world, when they behold the beast that was, and is not, and yet is. (Rev 17:8)

In the vision (which is being viewed from the perspective of those living in the future), the beast once lived (was). However, there is a paradox in phrasing because:

- The beast also "is not", which means the beast is not alive.
- And the beast "yet is", which means the beast is alive.

This description differs from how Revelation describes God, who lives forever: ("which was, and is, and is to come"):

> And the four beasts had each of them six wings about him; and they were full of eyes within: and they rest not day and night, saying, Holy, holy, holy, **Lord God Almighty, which was, and is, and is to come.** (Rev 4:8)

The beast ascends from the bottomless pit, a place described by the Bible where wicked souls go; his soul leaves the bottomless pit. At first glance, we could compare this event to the resurrection of Jesus Christ:

> He seeing this before spake of the resurrection of Christ, that his soul was not left in hell, neither his flesh did see corruption. (Acts 2:31)

Christ vs. Antichrist

To compare the resurrection of Christ to the ascension of the beast, we need to look at Revelation 1:18 where Christ said:

> **I am he that liveth, and was dead; and, behold, I am alive for evermore**, Amen; and have the keys of hell and of death. (Rev 1:18)

The beast and Christ will have both faced temporary death as one already rose from it and another will rise from it. However, the beast's condition when he returns to Earth will differ greatly from when Jesus returned:

- Jesus is One who lives and will live forever.
- The beast "is not" and "yet is".

The paradox of living for the beast suggests he will not perform a real resurrection. Though the beast appears on the earth after rising from the bottomless pit, he cannot do what Jesus did.

A consequence of this false rise is that the beast can only be on Earth for a short time after his return:

- The beast "is", but not always will be; the beast will go to destruction.
- In contrast, Christ taught that those who are truly resurrected will not die again (Luke 20:35-36).

Therefore, we can glean from Revelation 17 that Antichrist will appear as if he's been resurrected from the dead. He will not truly be resurrected, but it will look like he is.

IDENTIFYING THE EIGHTH KING

The eighth king, the Antichrist, is a person who served as one of the seven kings covered in chapter six:

And the beast that was, and is not, even he is the eighth, and is of the seven, and goeth into perdition. (Rev 17:11)

Revelation describes two defining characteristics that enable us to identify the eighth king.

The Fatal Wound

Revelation 13 gives us the first defining characteristic about the Antichrist:

And I saw one of his heads as it were wounded to death; and his deadly wound was healed: and all the world wondered after the beast. (Rev 13:3)

And deceiveth them that dwell on the earth by the means of those miracles which he had power to do in the sight of the beast; saying to them that dwell on the earth, that they should make an image to the beast, **which had the wound by a sword**, and did live. (Rev 13:14)

The eighth king suffered a deadly wound in office when he reigned over his kingdom.

Instant Recognition

Revelation also tells us that people will instantly recognize the eighth king when he reveals his true nature to the world. This detail suggests that Antichrist may have the same physical appearance as he did during his first coming on the earth:

> The beast that thou sawest was, and is not; and shall ascend out of the bottomless pit, and go into perdition: **and they that dwell on the earth shall wonder, whose names were not written in the book of life from the foundation of the world, when they behold the beast that was, and is not, and yet is.** (Rev 17:8)

> And they worshipped the dragon which gave power unto the beast: and they worshipped the beast, saying, **Who is like unto the beast? who is able to make war with him?** (Rev 13:4)

Although the eighth king's return will not be an authentic resurrection, the earth will be amazed because the eighth king will seem resurrected from the dead:

> And I saw one of his heads as it were wounded to death; and his deadly wound was healed: and **all the world wondered after the beast**. (Rev 13:3)

The people of Earth will pay homage to the beast of Revelation 13 through the worship of the eighth king. People will worship the beast since they have never seen an empire led by a man who has returned from the dead. Similarly, people will also ask who can fight him because the eighth king will appear indestructible after seemingly overcoming death:

> And they worshipped the dragon which gave power unto the beast: and they worshipped the beast, saying, **Who is like unto the beast? who is able to make war with him?** (Rev 13:4)

Let's not underestimate what people will see when they behold the Antichrist.

Some people have no problem believing what they hear. Others need to see before they can believe. For instance, some people have no problem believing in Christ's resurrection, while others struggle to believe it or they reject it. Therefore, it is far easier to get a large group of people to believe in something when visible proof exists.

This observation is important because the Antichrist will seek to show visual proof of his "resurrection" when he reappears. This "proof" will likely convince most to believe in his resurrection and compel them to worship him when he demands it:

- The Antichrist will not need to do much to persuade most people to believe in his resurrection if he is a recognizable figure.

- In contrast, it will be much harder for the Antichrist to convince people to believe in his resurrection if he is unrecognizable.

The instant recognition of the Antichrist is the key to identifying him. The first six kings of Revelation 17 died thousands of years ago. We do not know what these kings looked like as photos and videos of them do not exist. However, it is possible for us to know what the seventh king looked like or will look like. Therefore, the seventh king of Revelation 17 is the Antichrist.

In sum, the eighth king of Revelation 17 will likely be a man who proclaims that he is raised from the dead like Christ, even though he will not experience an authentic resurrection. Nevertheless, the people of the earth will worship the eighth king like he truly was resurrected from the dead.

LET'S PAUSE FOR A MOMENT

I appreciate your desire to learn about Bible prophecy and your willingness to consider the teachings found in this book. You may not agree with all that I have to say in this book. But that is perfectly fine because I am not the ultimate authority on Bible prophecy. The Bible is the ultimate authority.

Here is a look at where the unveiling of the Antichrist's true identity fits in our timeline:

Probable Sequence of Events: Ch.8

The Start of the Tribulation: Dan. 9:27 (Ch.5)

1st to 4th Seal: Rev 6:1-8 (Ch.7)

- Start of Temple Sacrifice: Dan 8:13-19 (Ch.7)
- War in Heaven: Rev 12:7-12 (Ch.7)

Midpoint of the Tribulation: Dan 9:27 (Ch.7)

- Abomination of Desolation: Dan 9:27, Matt 24:15 (Ch.7)
- *Antichrist's True Identity Revealed: 2Thess 2:3-4 (Ch.8)*

I will provide insight into the Antichrist's right-hand man, the False Prophet, next.

Notes

1. Strong, James. "antichristos". *Strong's Exhaustive Concordance of the Bible.* New York, Cincinnati, Eaton & Mains; Jennings & Graham, 1890. G500.

CHAPTER 9.

THE FALSE PROPHET REVEALED

The False Prophet is among the most enigmatic individuals in the entire Bible. Some speculate that he could be the Pope or some other prominent religious leader. I will provide you with what we can glean from the Bible about the False Prophet in this chapter.

THE BEAST OF THE EARTH

The False Prophet will begin his ministry after the Antichrist reveals his true identity. The False Prophet is known as the beast of the earth. However, the most striking detail about him is that he will resemble a lamb, but speak like a dragon (more on this shortly):

> And I beheld another beast coming up out of the earth; and he had two horns like a lamb, and he spake as a dragon. (Rev 13:11)

The False Prophet's chief goal will be to make everyone worship the Antichrist (and Satan). He will convince many to worship the Antichrist by performing great miracles and signs:

> (12) And he exerciseth all the power of the first beast before him, and causeth the earth and them which dwell therein to worship the first beast, whose deadly wound was healed. (13) And he doeth great wonders, so that he maketh fire come down from heaven on the earth in the sight of men, (14) And deceiveth them that dwell on the earth by the means of those miracles which he had power to do in the sight of the beast; saying to them that dwell on the earth, that they should make an image to the beast, which had the wound by a sword, and did live. (Rev 13:12-14)

The notion that the False Prophet will resemble a lamb is a detail that may give us valuable insight:

- The Lamb represents Jesus Christ throughout the Book of Revelation, including in verses 5:6, 7:17, 14:10, 15:3, and 19:9.

- Some believe the False Prophet will behave like Jesus. Some suggest this means he will act benevolent.

However, I believe the False Prophet's resemblance to a lamb may be a clue about his physical appearance. Recall that the Apostle Paul warned that fallen angels can masquerade as ministers of righteousness:

> (13) For such are false apostles, deceitful workers, transforming themselves into the apostles of Christ. (14) And no marvel; for Satan himself is transformed into an angel of light. (15) Therefore it is no great thing if his ministers also be transformed as the ministers of righteousness; whose end shall be according to their works. (2Cor 11:13-15)

This ability of fallen angels to change how they look is important in light of the detail that the False Prophet will resemble a lamb. It means we can't rule out this scary possibility:

- Satan could use a fallen angel who physically reminds people of Jesus Christ to serve as the False Prophet.[1]

Why might Satan use a False Prophet who physically reminds people of Jesus? Many would likely believe that the False Prophet is Jesus with the way he looks and with the miracles he performs. He can then use this perception of his identity to persuade people that they should really be worshipping the Antichrist (along with Satan).

Interestingly, Christ warned people to not listen to those who will say that He is at certain places during a period when the False Prophet will be active:

> (23) Then if any man shall say unto you, Lo, here is Christ, or there; believe it not. (24) For there shall arise false Christs, and false prophets, and shall shew great signs and wonders; insomuch that, if it were possible, they shall deceive the very elect. (Matt 24:23-24)

MORE ABOUT THE FALSE PROPHET

The Bible tells us that the False Prophet will also have the power to give life to the images of the Antichrist so that they may speak and cause the deaths of those who do not worship them:

> And he had power to give life unto the image of the beast, that the image of the beast should both speak, and cause that as many as would not worship the image of the beast should be killed. (Rev 13:15)

Finally, the Bible tells us that the False Prophet will require everyone to take the Mark of the Beast (the mark of Antichrist) on their forehead or right hand:

> (16) And he causeth all, both small and great, rich and poor, free and bond, to receive a mark in their right hand, or in their foreheads: (17) And that no man might buy or sell, save he that had the mark, or the name of the beast, or the number of his name. (18) Here is wisdom. Let him that hath understanding count the number of the beast: for it is the number of a man; and his number is Six hundred threescore and six. (Rev 13:16-18)

THE TWO WITNESSES

To counter the False Prophet's spread of the Antichrist's religion across the globe, God will send the Two Witnesses to prophesy near the midpoint of the tribulation. They will prophesy for 1,260 days:[2]

> (3) And I will give power unto my two witnesses, and they shall prophesy a thousand two hundred and threescore days, clothed in sackcloth. (4) These are the two olive trees, and the two candlesticks standing before the God of the earth. (Rev 11:3-4)

The Two Witnesses will be invincible during the 1,260 days they will prophesy. Anyone who tries to harm them will die. Why might people want the Two Witnesses to die? They will have authority to punish the earth with a variety of plagues during their ministry:

> (5) And if any man will hurt them, fire proceedeth out of their mouth, and devoureth their enemies: and if any man will hurt them, he must in this manner be killed. (6) These have power to shut heaven, that it rain not in the days of their prophecy: and have power over waters to turn

them to blood, and to smite the earth with all plagues, as often as they will. (Rev 11:5-6)

The Two Witnesses will likely work with angels to punish the earth during their ministry. We can see this by viewing the parallels between the Two Witnesses and four angels described in Revelation 7.

Revelation 7:1-3 describes four angels who will hold back the winds of the earth. They will receive instructions to not hurt the earth and the sea until a specific condition is met (the subject of chapter thirteen):

(1) And after these things I saw four angels standing on the four corners of the earth, holding the four winds of the earth, that the wind should not blow on the earth, nor on the sea, nor on any tree. (2) And I saw another angel ascending from the east, having the seal of the living God: and he cried with a loud voice to the four angels, to whom it was given to hurt the earth and the sea, (3) Saying, Hurt not the earth, neither the sea, nor the trees, till we have sealed the servants of our God in their foreheads. (Rev 7:1-3)

The power of these angels to harm the earth, harm the sea, and change weather patterns covers the areas that the Two Witnesses have authority. They have the authority to harm the earth, impact the water, and alter weather patterns. Figure 9.1 shows the similarities in the abilities of the four angels and the Two Witnesses:

Figure 9.1: Comparing Abilities

- **Weather**

- *Water*

- <u>The Earth</u>

  Rev 11:6 [The Two Witnesses]: These have **power to shut heaven, that it rain not in the days** of their prophecy: and *have power over waters to turn them to blood*, and <u>to smite the earth with all plagues</u>, as often as they will.

  Rev 7:1-3 [The Four Angels]: (1) And after these things I saw four angels standing on the four corners of the earth, **holding the four winds of the earth, that the wind should not blow on the earth, nor on the sea, nor on any tree.** (2) And I saw another angel ascending from the east, having the seal of the living God: and he cried with a loud voice to the four angels, to whom it was given <u>to hurt the earth</u> and *the sea*, (3) Saying, **Hurt not the earth**, *neither the sea*, <u>nor the trees</u>, till we have sealed the servants of our God in their foreheads.

The abilities of the Two Witnesses and the four angels are so similar that it is probable that the two groups will work together. Revelation 11:6 states that the Two Witnesses will prophesy during their ministry. We could see the Two Witnesses predict events and the four angels help make those events happen.

The Identities of These Individuals

The Bible does not give the identities of the Two Witnesses. However, most believe the Prophet Elijah will be one of the Two Witnesses since God promised He will send Elijah before the coming of the Day of the Lord (see chapter nineteen):

(5) Behold, I will send you Elijah the prophet before the coming of the great and dreadful day of the Lord: (6) And he shall turn the heart of the fathers to the children, and the heart of the children to their fathers, lest I come and smite the earth with a curse. (Mal 4:5-6)

The identity of the second individual is subject to much speculation:

- Some believe the second person will be Enoch because went up to Heaven like Elijah (Gen 5:24).

- Others suggest the second individual will be John, the author of Revelation.

- However, biblical evidence exists for this individual to be Moses!

The following two passages support the notion that Moses will be one of the Two Witnesses. First, Jude mentioned that Satan and the Archangel Michael had a dispute over the body of Moses:

> Yet Michael the archangel, when contending with the devil he disputed about the body of Moses, durst not bring against him a railing accusation, but said, The Lord rebuke thee. (Jude 1:9)

This detail begs the question: "Why would Satan contend with Michael over the physical body of Moses?" Usually, a corpse ought to be of no concern to Satan since it will decompose.

We should not dismiss the notion that Satan tried to prevent Michael from obtaining custody over Moses' physical body because Moses may need it again to testify as one of the Two Witnesses.

Second, Moses and Elijah's appearance with a transfigured Jesus is consistent with imagery of the Two Witnesses standing before God in Revelation 11:4:

> (2) And was transfigured before them: and his face did shine as the sun, and his raiment was white as the light. (3) And, behold, there appeared unto them Moses and Elias [Elijah] talking with him. (Matt 17:2-3)

Some also point out that Moses and Elijah would represent the Law and the Prophets if they serve as the Two Witnesses. No requirement for the Two Witnesses to represent the Law and the Prophets exists. However, the symbolism is worth considering.

Regardless of who the Two Witnesses are, they will serve on Earth during the reign of the Antichrist. In the chapters to come, I will describe what it will be like to live during the reign of the Antichrist.

LET'S PAUSE FOR A MOMENT

The Bible describes some incredible future events, such as the return of Elijah. Remember, the events described in the Bible do not come from man's imagination, but from God for our benefit. Therefore, we ought to seek to learn as much as we can about the future.

Here is a look at where the beginning of the False Prophet's ministry and the Two Witnesses' ministry fit in our timeline:

Probable Sequence of Events: Ch.9

The Start of the Tribulation: Dan. 9:27 (Ch.5)

1st to 4th Seal: Rev 6:1-8 (Ch.7)

- Start of Temple Sacrifice: Dan 8:13-19 (Ch.7)
- War in Heaven: Rev 12:7-12 (Ch.7)
- *The Two Witnesses' Ministry Begins: Rev 11:3-6 (Ch.9)*

Midpoint of the Tribulation: Dan 9:27 (Ch.7)

- Abomination of Desolation: Dan 9:27, Matt 24:15 (Ch.7)
- Antichrist's True Identity Revealed: 2Thess 2:3-4 (Ch.8)
- *The False Prophet's Ministry Begins: Rev 13:11-16 (Ch.9)*

We will look at the empire of the Antichrist next.

Notes

1. Many envision Jesus having long, brown hair and facial hair. In fact, many paintings and images depict Him having these features. I suspect the False Prophet may resemble the Jesus found in these paintings and images.

2. It is highly likely that the bulk of the Two Witnesses' ministry will take place in the second half of the tribulation. The reason is that the Two Witnesses' rise from the dead relates to the second woe (Rev 11:11-14). The first woe is an event that will likely take place in the second half of the tribulation (see chapter eleven).

CHAPTER 10.

THE EMPIRE OF THE ANTICHRIST

The Antichrist will oversee an empire that will dominate the earth, starting at the midpoint of the tribulation. The scope of his empire is up to debate:

- Some believe he will rule the entire world.
- Others believe he will only rule a portion of the world restricted to the ten kingdoms that will work directly with him.

This chapter is an overview of the Antichrist's empire.

THE NATURE OF THE EMPIRE

The Book of Daniel and the Book of Revelation provide us with details about what the empire of the Antichrist will be like:

- The Book of Daniel depicts the empire of the Antichrist as the feet of iron and clay in the statue of Nebuchadnezzar's dream.
- Also, the Book of Daniel and the Book of Revelation depict the empire of the Antichrist as the terrifying beast from the sea.

This section will examine the significance of each depiction.

Theories about Iron & Clay

Recall that Daniel explained to Nebuchadnezzar a statue he saw in his dream. He described a statue made of several components:

(31) Thou, O king, sawest, and behold a great image. This great image, whose brightness was excellent, stood before thee; and the form thereof was terrible. (32) This image's head was of fine gold, his breast and his arms of silver, his belly and his thighs of brass, (33) His legs of iron, his feet part of iron and part of clay. (Dan 2:31-33)

The feet of iron mixed with clay represent the Antichrist's empire. Each toe represents a kingdom that will be part of his empire:

(41) And whereas thou sawest the feet and toes, part of potters' clay, and part of iron, the kingdom shall be divided; but there shall be in it of the strength of the iron, forasmuch as thou sawest the iron mixed with miry clay. (42) And as the toes of the feet were part of iron, and part of clay, so the kingdom shall be partly strong, and partly broken. (43) And whereas thou sawest iron mixed with miry clay, they shall mingle themselves with the seed of men: but they shall not cleave one to another, even as iron is not mixed with clay. (Dan 2:41-43)

The iron portion of the toes signifies strength, while the clay portion of the toes signifies brittleness. The ten kingdoms will unite in some way, even if they are not compatible with one another.

Here are a few theories about the significance of the contrasting elements.

Roots of the Roman Empire & Elsewhere

Recall that the legs of iron represent the Roman Empire. The iron in the toes means the Antichrist's empire could have links to the Roman Empire. The clay in the toes means the Antichrist's empire could also have links to areas outside of the Roman Empire.

Commitment & Infighting

The ten kings will be loyal to the Antichrist, but they may not get along with each other:

- The strong elements of the empire could reflect the loyalty that each king has to the Antichrist. The ten kings will give their power and authority to the Antichrist (Rev 17:12-13).
- The clay elements could reflect the fragile relationship between the different kings of the empire.

The ten kings may not fully get along with each other since different kingdoms with contrasting cultures and conflicting national interests will be expected to cooperate with one another to maintain the integrity of the Antichrist's empire.

Fallen Angels & Man

The most speculative theory posits that the contrast between iron and clay depicts the interaction between fallen angels and man. The theory is possible since fallen angels will be on Earth when the Antichrist rules the world (Rev 12:9, 12):[1]

Proponents of the theory argue that iron represents non-human entities while clay represents humankind, since Isaiah 64:8 depicts humankind as clay:

> But now, O LORD, thou art our father; we are the clay, and thou our potter; and we all are the work of thy hand. (Isa 64:8)

Also, recall that Daniel 2:43 states "they shall mingle themselves with the seed of men: but they shall not cleave one to another, even as iron is not mixed with clay." Proponents of the theory argue "they" represent non-human entities since Daniel differentiates "they" from the seed of men.

Fallen angels will likely interact with humans during the reign of Antichrist no matter which view of the iron and clay is correct. However, the interaction will not last long. Proponents of this theory would argue that this is fitting since iron does not mix with clay.

The Beast from the Sea

The Antichrist's empire is characterized as a ferocious beast from the sea. The beast from the sea is the focus of Revelation 13 and Daniel 7.

Revelation 13 introduces the beast from the sea in verses 1-3. The beast is an evil entity since the dragon (Satan) will empower it:

> (1) And I stood upon the sand of the sea, and saw a beast rise up out of the sea, having seven heads and ten horns, and upon his horns ten crowns, and upon his heads the name of blasphemy. (2) And the beast which I saw was like unto a leopard, and his feet were as the feet of a bear, and his mouth as the mouth of a lion: and the dragon gave him his

power, and his seat, and great authority. (3) And I saw one of his heads as it were wounded to death; and his deadly wound was healed: and all the world wondered after the beast. (Rev 13:1-3)

The beast of Revelation 13 is likely the same entity as the fourth beast of Daniel 7 for a couple of reasons:

- The beast of Revelation 13 originates from the sea like the four beasts of Daniel 7, including the fourth beast (Rev 13:1, Dan 7:3).

- The beast of Revelation 13 and the fourth beast of Daniel 7 both have ten horns (Rev 13:1, Dan 7:7).

The ten horns are distinct because they are a feature that the other three beasts in Daniel 7 lack.[2] Although the fourth beast of Daniel 7 differs from its predecessors, Revelation 13 indicates that the beast has qualities of the first three beasts in Daniel 7:

- Its feet will crush like a bear (Dan 7:5, Rev 13:2)

- Its speed is like a leopard (Dan 7:6, Rev 13:2)

- Its sound is ferocious as a lion (Dan 7:4, Rev 13:2)

The qualities the beast of Revelation 13 share with the first three beasts of Daniel 7 share suggest that the empire of the Antichrist will:

- Emerge quickly (speed like a leopard).

- Beat down its victims (crushing feet like a bear).

- Instill fear in people (sound like a ferocious lion).

The Healed Head Wound

Revelation 13:3 contains the most interesting detail about the beast from the sea. The fatal wound to one of the beast's heads will heal, and that will amaze the world:

And I saw one of his heads as it were wounded to death; and his deadly wound was healed: and all the world wondered after the beast. (Rev 13:3)

Given that "head" can signify a king or kingdom (see chapter six), debate exists about what it means for the fatal head wound to heal. Some believe the healed wound means that a former empire will return. Others believe a dead leader will have his life restored in perhaps a false resurrection as discussed in chapter eight.

We can glean which possibility is likely the case. Revelation 13:4 onward continues to depict the beast from the sea and describes the actions of the Antichrist in terms of the beast's actions:

- Revelation 13:4 states that people will worship the beast.

- Revelation 13:14-15 states that people will make and worship images of the beast with the healed wound.

The fact that people will worship an entity that had a fatal wound healed suggests that a dead leader will have their life restored. It is hard to imagine people worshipping an empire. Also, people would not be awed by the return of an empire like they would if a dead leader had their life restored.

The Ten Horns

The Antichrist will have control of ten kingdoms (or districts) and will influence their leaders at the midpoint of the tribulation. The ten kings will reign with him for a short time:

> (12) And the ten horns which thou sawest are ten kings, which have received no kingdom as yet; but receive power as kings one hour with the beast. (13) These have one mind, and shall give their power and strength unto the beast. (Rev 17:12-13)

The empire of Antichrist will dominate the entire world (Dan 7:23-24, Rev 13:7, 17:12-13). His empire will draw its power from the dragon (Satan) and the ten kings who will give their power and strength to him.

THE GEOGRAPHIC EXTENT OF THE EMPIRE

Some believe the borders of the Antichrist's empire will span the whole world. According to this theory, the ten kingdoms will be ten jurisdictions that cover the whole globe. However, the Bible indicates that the borders of the Antichrist's empire will not span the whole globe.

I provide three examples that show why the Antichrist's empire will not cover the entire world next.

Example 1: The Need to Persuade the Kings of the Earth

Satan, the Antichrist, and the False Prophet will try to persuade the kings of the earth to gather for battle by sending spirits capable of performing miracles to them (see chapter fourteen):

> (13) And I saw three unclean spirits like frogs come out of the mouth of the dragon, and out of the mouth of the beast, and out of the mouth of the false prophet. (14) For they are the spirits of devils, working miracles, which go forth unto the kings of the earth and of the whole world, to gather them to the battle of that great day of God Almighty. (Rev 16:13-14)

There would be no need to send miracle-working spirits to persuade the kings of the earth to join the fight if the ten kings governed all parts of the world since they will have already provided their power and strength to the Antichrist (Rev 17:12-14).

Therefore, it is likely that the Antichrist's empire will only cover the areas that the ten kings oversee. He will need to compel the other kings of the earth to go along with his agenda.

Example 2: The Stone Grows After It Destroys

Daniel told Nebuchadnezzar that a stone (representing the kingdom of God) will destroy the kingdoms of the statue in his dream (including the kingdom of the Antichrist) *before it grows* to become a mountain that fills the whole planet:

> (34) Thou sawest till that a stone was cut out without hands, which smote the image upon his feet that were of iron and clay, and brake them to pieces. (35) Then was the iron, the clay, the brass, the silver, and the gold, broken to pieces together, and became like the chaff of the summer threshingfloors; and the wind carried them away, that no place was found for them: and the stone that smote the image became a great mountain, and filled the whole earth.(Dan 2:34-35)

The fact that the stone will destroy the kingdoms of the statue before it grows to cover the whole planet suggests that the geographic area of the Antichrist's kingdom will not cover the entire world.

Example 3: The Reaction to Babylon the Great's Destruction

The differing reactions to the destruction of Babylon the Great (see chapter seventeen) suggest that the ten kings are independent of the other kings of the earth, and thereby, do not oversee all parts of the world. Revelation 17 states that the ten kings will grow to hate Babylon the Great to the point they will destroy her with fire:

> (16) And the ten horns which thou sawest upon the beast, these shall hate the whore [Babylon the Great], and shall make her desolate and naked, and shall eat her flesh, and burn her with fire. (17) For God hath put in their hearts to fulfil his will, and to agree, and give their kingdom unto the beast, until the words of God shall be fulfilled. (Rev 17:16-17)

In contrast, the kings of the earth will mourn her annihilation:

> (9) And the kings of the earth, who have committed fornication and lived deliciously with her, shall bewail her, and lament for her, when they shall see the smoke of her burning, (10) Standing afar off for the fear of her torment, saying, Alas, alas, that great city Babylon, that mighty city! for in one hour is thy judgment come. (Rev 18:9-10)

Given the ten kings' hatred for Babylon the Great, it would not make much sense for the ten kings to mourn the loss of something they hate. However, it would be easy to envision a scenario where the ten kings are satisfied with Babylon the Great's demise, while other kings are upset with her demise.

The Kingdoms of the Empire

This chapter will not cover which places may or may not be part of the empire of the Antichrist in detail for the sake of brevity. A more detailed overview of which places may or may not be a part of his empire is available in the appendix of this book. However, for now, know that I do not dismiss the possibility that many European countries and Russia may be part of the Antichrist's empire.

GLOBAL INFLUENCE

Although the borders of the Antichrist's empire are unlikely to span the globe, its impact will be felt across the world. Revelation and Daniel describe how the empire will influence the whole world:

> And it was given unto him to make war with the saints, and to overcome them: and power was given him over all kindreds, and tongues, and nations. (Rev 13:7)

> Thus he said, The fourth beast shall be the fourth kingdom upon earth, which shall be diverse from all kingdoms, and shall devour the whole earth, and shall tread it down, and break it in pieces. (Dan 7:23)

The beast's actions suggest that the empire of the Antichrist will make the whole world its prey; meaning that the empire will subjugate the world under its sphere of influence.

The Oppression of the Antichrist

The Bible tells us the Antichrist will oppress people during his reign. For instance:

- Isaiah 14:6 suggests that the Antichrist will treat the nations of the earth with brutality:

- Habakkuk 2:2-10 suggests that the Antichrist, who represents the end time king of Babylon, will eventually be spoiled by "the remnant of the people" because he will have spoiled many nations and caused a lot of violence:[3]

Examples of the Antichrist's Influence

Limits on Transactions & the Mark of the Beast

The Antichrist will limit transactions so that only those who meet certain conditions may conduct them. Revelation states that no one may buy or sell unless the participants have: the Mark of the Beast, the name of the beast, or the number of the beast's name:

> (16) And he causeth all, both small and great, rich and poor, free and bond, to receive a mark in their right hand, or in their foreheads: (17) And that no man might buy or sell, save he that had the mark, or the

name of the beast, or the number of his name. (18) Here is wisdom. Let him that hath understanding count the number of the beast: for it is the number of a man; and his number is Six hundred threescore and six. (Rev 13:16-18)

The Mark of the Beast's main purpose is to serve as a way for people to prove that their allegiances are with the Antichrist. In other words, accepting the Mark of the Beast means that you have declared yourself a follower of the Antichrist and thereby an opponent of God. There will be grave consequences for those who do not pledge allegiance, and I will cover them in the next chapter.

Changing Laws and Times

The Antichrist will change laws that existed before his rise to power and will alter the calendar system:

> And he shall speak great words against the most High, and shall wear out the saints of the most High, and think to change times and laws: and they shall be given into his hand until a time and times and the dividing of time. (Dan 7:25)

BABYLON THE GREAT: CAPITAL CITY OF THE WORLD

The Book of Revelation discusses a great city called Babylon the Great in-depth and depicts her as a harlot:[4]

> (4) And the woman was arrayed in purple and scarlet colour, and decked with gold and precious stones and pearls, having a golden cup in her hand full of abominations and filthiness of her fornication: (5) And upon her forehead was a name written, MYSTERY, BABYLON THE GREAT, THE MOTHER OF HARLOTS AND ABOMINATIONS OF THE EARTH.... (18) And the woman which thou sawest is that great city, which reigneth over the kings of the earth. (Rev 17:4-5, 18)

Babylon the Great City will be the most crucial city in the world during the reign of Antichrist. The city will serve as the center of global economic activity (Rev 18:12-17). The city will be so vital to the world economy that world leaders and business leaders will lament her destruction (Rev 18:9-11, 15-18).

Also, Babylon the Great City may also be the center of political power. She will rule over every population group and over the kings of the earth (Rev 17:1, 15, 18)

The Harlot's Interactions

We have just seen that Babylon the Great will be the center of world economic and political power during the end times. This section details the interaction between:

- Babylon the Great and the Antichrist.
- Babylon the Great and the kings of the earth.

The Antichrist and the Harlot

Revelation 17 reveals the relationship between the Antichrist and the harlot Babylon the Great. Verse 3 and 7 depict the harlot riding on the beast (which recall from chapter eight is the Antichrist) while verse 7 mentions that the beast carries the harlot:

> (3) So he carried me away in the spirit into the wilderness: and I saw a woman sit upon a scarlet coloured beast, full of names of blasphemy, having seven heads and ten horns.... (7) And the angel said unto me, Wherefore didst thou marvel? I will tell thee the mystery of the woman, and of the beast that carrieth her, which hath the seven heads and ten horns. (Rev 17:3, 7)

The imagery of the harlot riding the beast suggests they will cooperate, at least at the start. The accord between the beast and the harlot suggests:

- The harlot may work on behalf of the beast.
- The beast may help to sustain the harlot's powerful position.

The Harlot Working for the Beast

The harlot will likely tempt people to worship the beast and to encourage people to persecute the beast's enemies. Revelation 17:6 tells us that the harlot will be drunk with blood:

> And I saw the woman drunken with the blood of the saints, and with the blood of the martyrs of Jesus: and when I saw her, I wondered with great admiration. (Rev 17:6)

This example suggests that the harlot is at least willing to go along with the beast's desire to crush his enemies. The enemies of the Antichrist will include the saints whose blood the harlot will drink:

> And it was given unto him to make war with the saints, and to overcome them: and power was given him over all kindreds, and tongues, and nations. (Rev 13:7)

The Beast Supporting the Harlot

The Antichrist will have a far-reaching influence over the world (Rev 13:7) while the harlot will preside over practically every population group on Earth (Rev 17:15):

> And he saith unto me, The waters which thou sawest, where the whore sitteth, **are peoples, and multitudes, and nations, and tongues.** (Rev 17:15)

Given the far-reaching influence of the Antichrist and his support for her, the harlot's influential position over the world will likely be due to the Antichrist empowering her.

The Kings of the Earth and the Harlot

Recall that Revelation 17:18 states that the harlot will reign over the kings of the earth. The kings of the earth may follow her because she will pay them for their obedience. Revelation 18:9 suggests that they will indeed be well-compensated for following her:

> And **the kings of the earth**, who have committed fornication and **lived deliciously with her**, shall bewail her, and lament for her, when they shall see the smoke of her burning. (Rev 18:9)

The harlot will likely entice the kings of the earth to follow the Antichrist's orders. This probably will involve the worship of the Antichrist and the persecution of his enemies. The kings of the earth will pass along these orders to their people. Most will comply lest they risk the penalties for disobedience.

In the end, God will hold Babylon the Great accountable for corrupting the world and for the bloodshed of His people:

> For true and righteous are his judgments: for he hath judged the great

whore, which did corrupt the earth with her fornication, and hath avenged the blood of his servants at her hand. (Rev 19:2)

The bloodshed of the Antichrist's opponents will occur in earnest during the great tribulation, the subject of the next chapter.

LET'S PAUSE FOR A MOMENT

We examined the empire of the Antichrist in this chapter. The Bible tells us he will have an empire that will dominate the world during his reign. He will control the areas of economics, governance, and religion.

I encourage you to reflect on what you have read and to reread any parts that might have been difficult to understand before you go to the next chapter. As you reflect, remember that God's power is greater than the Antichrist's power. This will be true even when Antichrist reigns over the whole earth.

Notes

1. Christ compared the time leading up to His coming to the days of Noah (Matt 24:37-38). Some think this only means that people will live life unaware of what will soon take place. Others think this means that fallen angels will interact with humans like in the days of Noah.

2. Dan 7:7, 19 acknowledges that the fourth beast is different than the first three beasts.

3. The idea that the end time king of Babylon will inflict a lot of violence on the earth may explain why Babylon has the reputation as "the hammer of the whole earth" (Jer 50:23).

4. A detailed discussion about the identity of Babylon the Great is available in the appendix section titled "Babylon the Great's Identity".

CHAPTER 11.

THE GREAT TRIBULATION & END TIME HOLOCAUST

The world will marvel at the Antichrist for being a man raised from the dead. However, a few will heed Christ's call to flee as soon as they see the Antichrist set up the abomination of desolation:

(15) When ye therefore shall see the abomination of desolation, spoken of by Daniel the prophet, stand in the holy place, (whoso readeth, let him understand:) (16) Then let them which be in Judaea flee into the mountains: (Matt 24:15-16)

Also, a group who may be unaware of Christ's call to flee will instinctively flee to a wilderness area where they will remain protected for the rest of the tribulation:

And the woman fled into the wilderness, where she hath a place prepared of God, that they should feed her there a thousand two hundred and threescore days. (Rev 12:6)

Christ warned people to flee after the defiling of the Jerusalem temple by the Antichrist because an unprecedented period of great tribulation will begin next:

For then shall be great tribulation, such as was not since the beginning of the world to this time, no, nor ever shall be. (Matt 24:21)

The persecution will start when Satan (via the Antichrist) tries to attack those that will flee to the wilderness. Revelation 12:15-16 depicts this attack as a flood that chases after a woman. However, the attack will fail with the help of divine intervention:

(15) And the serpent cast out of his mouth water as a flood after the woman, that he might cause her to be carried away of the flood. (16) And the earth helped the woman, and the earth opened her mouth, and swallowed up the flood which the dragon cast out of his mouth. (Rev 12:15-16)

Satan will be enraged that he missed his opportunity to wipe out those who flee to the wilderness. He will then seek to annihilate anyone related to the woman, those who "keep the commandments of God, and have the testimony of Jesus Christ":

And the dragon was wroth with the woman, and went to make war with the remnant of her seed, which keep the commandments of God, and have the testimony of Jesus Christ. (Rev 12:17)

This chapter focuses on the persecution of the enemies of the Antichrist, particularly those without the Mark of the Beast, will endure during this time of great tribulation.

THE FORTY-TWO MONTH WAR WITH THE SAINTS

It is important to understand that the great tribulation Christ warned about ought to be characterized as the wrath of Satan. *It is not the wrath of God.* Recall that Revelation 12:17 states that Satan will be angry when he goes to make war with the woman's seed:

And the dragon was wroth with the woman, and went to make war with the remnant of her seed, which keep the commandments of God, and have the testimony of Jesus Christ. (Rev 12:17)

Satan will use the Antichrist to make war with the woman's seed: the saints. Daniel 7:21, 25 states that the Antichrist will make war with the saints and that the war will last for 3.5 years:

(21) I beheld, and the same horn made war with the saints, and prevailed against them;... (25) And he shall speak great words against the most High, and shall wear out the saints of the most High, and think to change times and laws: and they shall be given into his hand until a time and times and the dividing of time. (Dan 7:21, 25)

Similarly, Revelation 13:5-7 states that the Antichrist will blasphemy God and will make war with the saints for a forty-two month or a 3.5-year period:

(5) And there was given unto him a mouth speaking great things and blasphemies; and power was given unto him to continue forty and two months.... (7) And it was given unto him to make war with the saints, and to overcome them: and power was given him over all kindreds, and tongues, and nations. (Rev 13:5, 7)

Recall that Daniel 9:27 tells us that the abomination of desolation will be set up at the midpoint of the tribulation, and the Antichrist will sit in the temple of Jerusalem and proclaim that he is God (2Thess 2:4). This event will mark the start of the forty-two month (or 3.5 year) period that he will blasphemy God and wage war with the saints. Thus, the war against the saints will encompass the whole second half of the tribulation.

The Ultimate Total War

Many ways to categorize a conflict exist. The most extreme type of conflict is total war. Total war occurs when at least one side mobilizes all its resources and population to wage war.

Total war can be very deadly. Those who wage total war are often willing to sacrifice everything to win. The conflict between the Soviet Union and Nazi Germany in World War 2 is a prime example of total war. Both sides waged a brutal war of annihilation that resulted in millions of deaths on both sides.

The Antichrist will wage the ultimate total war during the end times: he will rally the world's economic, political, societal, and even spiritual resources to wage war against his enemies.

Economic Resources

The Antichrist will structure the global economy to make it very tough for his enemies to survive long-term. People may not buy or sell if they do not have the name of the beast, the number of the beast's name, or the Mark of the Beast:

(16) And he causeth all, both small and great, rich and poor, free and bond, to receive a mark in their right hand, or in their foreheads: (17) And that no man might buy or sell, save he that had the mark, or the name of the beast, or the number of his name. (Rev 13:16-17)

This harsh restriction will make it very hard for the enemies of the Antichrist to get food, water, and other essentials of life. Many will die from just this restriction.

The Antichrist may even use his control over the world economy to reward those who turn in or kill his enemies. Recall that Babylon the Great City will be responsible for the deaths of many. This could be due to the Antichrist using her riches to entice world leaders and their people to go after his enemies.

Political Resources

Many leaders will aid the Antichrist in his war against his enemies. Recall that the ten kings will submit to the Antichrist:

> (12) And the ten horns which thou sawest are ten kings, which have received no kingdom as yet; but receive power as kings one hour with the beast. (13) These have one mind, and shall give their power and strength unto the beast. (Rev 17:12-13)

Meanwhile, other leaders will at least agree to support the severe economic restrictions that will exist during the Antichrist's reign.

Societal Resources

Severe social pressure will be placed on the Antichrist's enemies. Many will be encouraged and perhaps coerced into turning over the enemies of the Antichrist to the authorities. The pressure will be so severe that people will betray one another. Some won't be able to trust their own family:

> (9) Then shall they deliver you up to be afflicted, and shall kill you: and ye shall be hated of all nations for my name's sake. (10) And then shall many be offended, and shall betray one another, and shall hate one another.... (12) And because iniquity shall abound, the love of many shall wax cold. (Matt 24:9-10, 12)

> (12) Now the brother shall betray the brother to death, and the father the son; and children shall rise up against their parents, and shall cause them to be put to death. (13) And ye shall be hated of all men for my name's sake:... (Mark 13:12-13)

Spiritual Resources

The Antichrist will also rally spiritual resources to persecute his enemies. This will come at a time when Satan will use all his power to deceive those who do not believe in the truth:

(9) him, whose coming is after the working of Satan with all power and signs and lying wonders,... (11) And for this cause God shall send them strong delusion, that they should believe a lie: (12) That they all might be damned who believed not the truth, but had pleasure in unrighteousness. (2Thess 2:9, 11-12)

False prophets and false Christs will arise and pose a serious hazard to the enemies of the Antichrist as they try to tempt some of them out of hiding:[1]

(23) Then if any man shall say unto you, Lo, here is Christ, or there; believe it not. (24) For there shall arise false Christs, and false prophets, and shall shew great signs and wonders; insomuch that, if it were possible, they shall deceive the very elect. (Matt 24:23-24)

Satan's fallen angels will also pose a hazard to the enemies of the Antichrist. The danger they will pose during the time of Satan's wrath is hard to describe fully, but they could pose a serious threat.

Recall that fallen angels can transform or masquerade as ministers of righteousness (2Cor 11:13-15) and that angels can resemble people (Heb 13:2). The ability of fallen angels to conceal their true identity will make them a hazard for many who will oppose the Antichrist. Some angels could try to pretend to be an ally of theirs. Many could unknowingly befriend those who will later betray them.

The testing of spirits will be paramount during this time. A person may not be able to visually tell the difference between friend or foe, but they may be able to identify friend or foe by asking questions like "Did Christ come in the flesh?"[2]

The images of the beast (the Antichrist) will be a third hazard that the enemies of the Antichrist shall face. Millions, if not billions, of these images will be prevalent around the world at that time.

The images of the Antichrist will cause the death of those who do not worship them (Rev 13:15). Regardless of how the images will do that, it is apparent that they will serve as another major obstacle for the enemies of the Antichrist.[3] The enemies of the Antichrist will need to avoid the images of the Antichrist lest they risk death for not worshiping them. This challenge could be very difficult given how widespread the images of the Antichrist will be at that time.

THE SEVERITY OF THE CONFLICT

The war the Antichrist will wage against his enemies will be a massacre far worse than the war of annihilation waged by Nazi Germany and the Soviet Union. He will wage total war against those who will not be able to put up much (if any) resistance. Therefore, it should not be a surprise that Christ warned that there would be no one left to save if the persecution were to continue indefinitely:

> And except those days should be shortened, there should no flesh be saved: but for the elect's sake those days shall be shortened. (Matt 24:22)

THE FIFTH SEAL

The fifth seal encapsulates the great tribulation. After the breaking of the fifth seal, a group of martyred souls underneath the altar in Heaven will ask the Lord when He will avenge them:

> (9) And when he had opened the fifth seal, I saw under the altar the souls of them that were slain for the word of God, and for the testimony which they held: (10) And they cried with a loud voice, saying, How long, O Lord, holy and true, dost thou not judge and avenge our blood on them that dwell on the earth? (Rev 6:9-10)

Revelation 20:4 states that they are followers of Jesus who will die for not worshiping the Antichrist or pledging loyalty to him. This confirms they will die in the great tribulation.

These martyrs will have to wait until more of their brethren and fellow-servants are killed before they are avenged:

> And white robes were given unto every one of them; and it was said unto them, that they should rest yet for a little season, until their fellowservants also and their brethren, that should be killed as they were, should be fulfilled. (Rev 6:11)

THE END TIME HOLOCAUST

The people of Israel will also face severe persecution. They will face an end time holocaust. This period is known as the time of Jacob's trouble. It will be the most trying time in Israel's history:

> And at that time shall Michael stand up, the great prince which standeth for the children of thy people: **and there shall be a time of trouble, such as never was since there was a nation even to that same time: and at that time** thy people shall be delivered, every one that shall be found written in the book. (Dan 12:1)

> Alas! for that day is great, so that none is like it: it is even **the time of Jacob's trouble;** but he shall be saved out of it. (Jer 30:7, also see Luke 21:23, Obad 1:10-14)

The fact that Israel will face its most troubling period in its history means that the end time holocaust will be more severe than the Holocaust of World War 2. It will be unmatched in the distress that it will cause for Israel.

The End Time Wilderness Experience

The Bible describes how the people of Israel will go through an end time wilderness experience at this time. We see this experience alluded to in: Revelation 12:6, 14-16, Hosea 2:14-15, Jeremiah 31:2, and Ezekiel 20:33-38.[4]

Some will actually live in wilderness areas. I believe Edom, Moab, and Ammon, located in the country of Jordan, are the main sites where people will stay. Daniel 11:41 suggests that each place will escape an attack by the Antichrist:[5]

> He shall enter also into the glorious land, and many countries shall be overthrown: but these shall escape out of his hand, even Edom, and Moab, and the chief of the children of Ammon. (Dan 11:41)

Although Edom, Moab, and Ammon are the primary areas of the wilderness where the people of Israel will seek refuge, it does not mean that people won't seek refuge in other nearby locations as wilderness is prevalent in that part of the Mideast.

Taken into Captivity

Many Jews in Europe were sent to places to die during World War 2. History is likely to repeat itself during the end time holocaust. For instance, recall that Christ warned people, notably those near Jerusalem, to flee when they see the abomination of desolation (Matt 24:15-20, Luke 21:20-24, Mark 13:14-19).

One reason Christ urged people to flee is that many will be taken captive when the great tribulation starts. These verses show that the people of Israel will face captivity:[6]

> **And they shall fall by the edge of the sword, and shall be led away captive into all nations**: and Jerusalem shall be trodden down of the Gentiles, until the times of the Gentiles be fulfilled. (Luke 21:24)

> Thus saith the LORD of hosts; **The children of Israel and the children of Judah were oppressed together: and all that took them captives held them fast; they refused to let them go.** (Jer 50:33)

Many will suffer greatly during their captivity. Psalm 107 tells us that many captives will become so weak that they will be on the brink of death:[7]

> (10) Such as sit in darkness and in the shadow of death, being bound in affliction and iron;... (18) Their soul abhorreth all manner of meat; and they draw near unto the gates of death. (Ps 107:10, 18)

Collaborating with Antichrist

Although the people of Israel will endure severe persecution, some will be allowed to remain in Israel and Jerusalem (Isa 3:2-4, 16, Jer 4:9). Many of those who will stay are likely those who will collaborate with the Antichrist. However, this will not bring them long-term security. I will describe future military efforts to destroy the people of Israel in chapter fifteen.

THE FIRST FIVE TRUMPETS

Revelation 8:2-5 describes a heavenly scene where seven angels will be given seven trumpets to sound. An angel at that time will offer a censer consisting of incense and the prayers of the saints to God. After God receives the offering, the angel will take the censer, fill it with fire, and cast it to the earth:

> (2) And I saw the seven angels which stood before God; and to them were given seven trumpets. (3) And another angel came and stood at

the altar, having a golden censer; and there was given unto him much incense, that he should offer it with the prayers of all saints upon the golden altar which was before the throne. (4) And the smoke of the incense, which came with the prayers of the saints, ascended up before God out of the angel's hand. (5) And the angel took the censer, and filled it with fire of the altar, and cast it into the earth: and there were voices, and thunderings, and lightnings, and an earthquake. (Rev 8:2-5)

Recall that the martyrs of the fifth seal will plead to God to avenge them and that they will be told to wait (Rev 6:9-11). The casting of the censer filled with fire to Earth means that the pleads of the martyrs will soon be avenged with the sounding of the trumpets.

Revelation 8:7 to 9:12 covers the sounding of five out of seven trumpets. Each angel will sound their trumpet, and an event or series of events will follow each sounding. The events related to the sounding of the first five trumpets will bring hardship to the inhabitants of the world (see Figure 11.1).

Figure 11.1: The Impacts of the First Five Trumpets

First (Rev 8:7): 1/3 of trees and all green grass burn with fire after hail and fire mixed with blood falls on the earth.

Second (Rev 8:8-9): The destruction of 1/3 of the ships at sea and the death of 1/3 of the creatures in the sea after a burning mountain falls into the sea. 1/3 of the sea becomes blood.

Third (Rev 8:10-11): Many people die after drinking water made bitter by a celestial object called "Wormwood".

Fourth (Rev 8:12-13): 1/3 of the sun, the moon, and the stars become dark.

Fifth (Rev 9:1-12): Locusts from the abyss arise to torment people that do not have the seal of God on their foreheads for five months. Represents the first of three woes.

THE ARRIVAL OF MANY

John records a large gathering of people in Heaven in Revelation 7:9-17. Verse 14 reveals that the people John saw came out of the great tribulation:

(9) After this I beheld, and, lo, a great multitude, which no man could number, of all nations, and kindreds, and people, and tongues, stood before the throne, and before the Lamb, clothed with white robes, and palms in their hands;... (13) And one of the elders answered, saying unto me, What are these which are arrayed in white robes? and whence came they? (14) And I said unto him, Sir, thou knowest. And he said to me, These are they which came out of great tribulation, and have washed their robes, and made them white in the blood of the Lamb. (Rev 7:9, 13-14)

These individuals (Rev 7:14) will wear white robes just like the martyrs under the altar (Rev 6:11):

And white robes were given unto every one of them; and it was said unto them, that they should rest yet for a little season, until their fellowservants also and their brethren, that should be killed as they were, should be fulfilled. (Rev 6:11)

And I said unto him, Sir, thou knowest. And he said to me, These are they which came out of great tribulation, **and have washed their robes, and made them white in the blood of the Lamb**. (Rev 7:14)

Given that this group will wear white robes like the martyrs under the altar will wear, it is reasonable to assume that this group will consist of many who will die during the great tribulation.

I believe the gathering of these individuals will take place in the latter stages of the great tribulation, given the size of the group. The fact that no one could count the size of the group gives us a sense of how severe the great tribulation will be. Many people will die for refusing to submit to the Antichrist.

The struggle to survive for the Antichrist's enemies will continue even as the world falls apart. The next chapter will focus on the chaos brought to the world by the sounding of the sixth trumpet.

LET'S PAUSE FOR A MOMENT

Life will be very tough for the opponents of the Antichrist, especially for those who follow Christ. Many will be martyred for their beliefs. Others will be denied the basic essentials of life.

Remember, this persecution is the wrath of Satan and not the wrath of God. Here is a look at where the key events discussed in this chapter fit in our timeline:

Probable Sequence of Events: Ch.11

Midpoint of the Tribulation: Dan 9:27 (Ch.7)

- Abomination of Desolation: Dan 9:27, Matt 24:15 (Ch.7)
- Antichrist's True Identity Revealed: 2Thess 2:3-4 (Ch.8)
- The False Prophet's Ministry Begins: Rev 13:11-16 (Ch.9)
- *Great Tribulation Begins: Matt 24:21 (Ch.11)*

5th Seal: Rev 6:9-11 (Ch.11)

Trumpets 1-5: Rev 8:7-13, 9:1-12 (Ch.11)

Once again, ask God to remove your fear if you are afraid. He will remove your fear as He removed my fear. I know it is hard to read about so many people dying for their beliefs, but take comfort that God is just and will not let these deaths to go unavenged.

Notes

1. I would not be surprised if the coming false prophets and false Christs will be fallen angels masquerading as prophets and messianic figures to deceive undecided people of all religions about whom to follow.

2. 1John 4:1-3 provides a guide to determining if a spirit is from God.

3. Interestingly, Rev 9:20 tells us that people "repented not of the works of their hands, that they should not worship devils, and idols of gold, and silver, and brass, and stone, and of wood: which neither can see, nor hear, nor walk:" even after being punished by plagues. Some may ask: "Why will people be worshiping devils?" The theory that may best address this issue is that demons may inhabit the idols and images of Antichrist. Notably, Rev 13:15 suggests the images of the beast will have some type of "life".

People may be also worshiping a devil when they worship an image or idol of the Antichrist. If this is the case, a global monitoring network with billions of images or idols could exist. The spirit or demon in each image or idol could help track the whereabouts of most people.

4. The wilderness referred to in Ezek 20:33-38 refers to the many nations the people of Israel will be scattered. Isa 11:11-12 gives a sense of how far the people of Israel will be scattered before their recovery.

5. Obad 1:12-14 is more evidence that some people will seek refuge in Edom. The passage criticizes Edom's treatment of the Lord's people during the time of their distress. The fact that Edom is able to treat the Lord's people harshly means that the Lord's people will be there.

6. Isa 14:2 and Joel 3:6 also show that the people of Israel will face captivity during the end times. Joel 3:1, Jer 30:2-3, Amos 9:14, and Ezek 39:25-26 speak of the Lord bringing His people back from their end time captivity.

7. Ps 79:11 and 102:19-20 also indicate that many captives will be on the brink of death.

CHAPTER 12.

THE SIXTH TRUMPET WARS

The sounding of the sixth trumpet will lead to a time of wide-spread conflict in the latter part of the tribulation. This time of conflict will involve 200 million participants and will bring the death of a third of the world's population. I will summarize this period of conflict in this chapter.

THE FOUR ANGELS UNLEASHED

Revelation 9:14-15 states that four angels will be released from the Euphrates River after the sounding of the sixth trumpet:

> (14) Saying to the sixth angel which had the trumpet, Loose the four angels which are bound in the great river Euphrates. (15) And the four angels were loosed, which were prepared for an hour, and a day, and a month, and a year, for to slay the third part of men. (Rev 9:14-15)

These four angels will stir up trouble on the earth when they are set free. Revelation 9:15 tells us that these angels will be primarily responsible for the severe casualties of the sixth trumpet:

- They will be responsible for the deaths of many when they instigate the widespread conflict and chaos described by various Bible prophecy passages.

- They will probably rally troops to fight like the unclean spirits mentioned in Revelation 16:13-14 will rally the kings of the earth to battle. They may perform miracles if they work like those spirits.

Possible Causes of War

As just stated, the four angels will be the chief catalyst for widespread conflict. Beyond that, leaders may lead their countries into battle in response to the hardships that will exist.

One long-lasting hardship that the world may endure at that time is a lack of rainwater. Revelation 11 indicates that the world could be without rain for up to 1,260 days. The Two Witnesses will have the authority to prevent rain from falling during their 1,260-day ministry (Rev 11:3, 6).

The world could face severe shortages due to a lack of rain, including food and water shortages. These shortages could lead to unrest in many countries that have submitted to the Antichrist's authority. The unrest could lead some leaders to revolt against the Antichrist. Other leaders may wage war to secure scarce resources for their people.

THE POWERFUL COMBATANTS

Revelation 9:16-19 describes the slaying of a third of humankind in conflict that involves 200 million soldiers. I believe the 200 million will represent the total sum of all the soldiers that will fight on the opposing sides in this time of conflict.

(16) And the number of the army of the horsemen were two hundred thousand thousand: and I heard the number of them. (17) And thus I saw the horses in the vision, and them that sat on them, having breastplates of fire, and of jacinth, and brimstone: and the heads of the horses were as the heads of lions; and out of their mouths issued fire and smoke and brimstone. (18) By these three was the third part of men killed, by the fire, and by the smoke, and by the brimstone, which issued out of their mouths. (19) For their power is in their mouth, and in their tails: for their tails were like unto serpents, and had heads, and with them they do hurt. (Rev 9:16-19)

I believe that Daniel 11:40 provides us with information about some of the principal combatants of the conflicts that will arise after the sounding of the sixth trumpet. Daniel 11:40 tells us that the king described in Daniel 11:36-11:39 (the Antichrist) will face an attack from the king of the south *and* the king of the north:

And at the time of the end shall the king of the south push at him: and the king of the north shall come against him like a whirlwind, with chariots, and with horsemen, and with many ships; and he shall enter into the countries, and shall overflow and pass over. (Dan 11:40)

The King of the South

Daniel 11:40 suggests that the king of the south, the king of Egypt, will initiate the war with an attack against the Antichrist. The Antichrist will then repel the coalition forces led by Egypt and destroy the places where they will come from. Ezekiel 30:1-9 and Daniel 11:42-43 describe the destruction of these armies and lands.

Daniel 11:42-43 tells us that the Antichrist will plunder the land of Egypt while Libya and Ethiopia will also be in big trouble:[1]

(42) He shall stretch forth his hand also upon the countries: and the land of Egypt shall not escape. (43) But he shall have power over the treasures of gold and of silver, and over all the precious things of Egypt: and the Libyans and the Ethiopians shall be at his steps. (Dan 11:42-43)

Ezekiel 30 states that other places will fall for supporting Egypt:

(3) For the day is near, even the day of the LORD is near, a cloudy day; it shall be the time of the heathen. (4) And the sword shall come upon Egypt, and great pain shall be in Ethiopia, when the slain shall fall in Egypt, and they shall take away her multitude [wealth], and her foundations shall be broken down. (5) Ethiopia, and Libya, and Lydia, and all the mingled people, and Chub, and the men of the land that is in league, shall fall with them by the sword. (Ezek 30:3-5)

Notice how verse 4 states that Egypt's wealth will be taken away. This is consistent with Daniel 11:43 where it says that the Antichrist will have power over the treasures of Egypt.

Edom, Moab, and Ammon

The Bible notes that the Antichrist will spare Edom, Moab, and Ammon during his counterattack:

He shall enter also into the glorious land, and many countries shall be overthrown: but these shall escape out of his hand, even Edom, and Moab, and the chief of the children of Ammon. (Dan 11:41)

However, the inhabitants of these lands probably won't be on the sidelines during this time of conflict. Psalm 83 indicates they will be part of a coalition whose goal is to wipe out the remnant of Israel:

(4) They have said, Come, and let us cut them off from being a nation; that the name of Israel may be no more in remembrance. (5) For they have consulted together with one consent: they are confederate against thee: (6) The tabernacles of Edom, and the Ishmaelites; of Moab, and the Hagarenes; (7) Gebal, and Ammon, and Amalek; the Philistines with the inhabitants of Tyre; (8) Assur also is joined with them: they have holpen the children of Lot. Selah. (Ps 83:4-8)

I'll have more to say about this coalition and this campaign against the people of Israel in chapter fifteen.

The King of the North

Daniel 11:40 tells us the king of the north will lead a formidable force as he comes against Antichrist. Who is the king of the north?

Ezekiel 38 and Ezekiel 39 mention a leader named Gog. Many identify Gog as the Antichrist, but I believe Gog and the Antichrist are not the same individuals.[2] More specifically, I believe Gog is the king of the north. Here's why:

1. Ezekiel 39:1-2 tells us that Gog, the leader of an invasion force, will come from the north. The northern origin of Gog's military force makes Gog a strong candidate to represent the king of the north in Daniel 11:40. Gog shares the same origin as the king of the north.

2. Ezekiel 38:3-6 indicates that Gog will oversee a vast military force, fitting the detail that the king of the north will have a formidable military force.

3. Ezekiel 38:5 suggests that Ethiopia and Libya will be allies of Gog, which recall will be allies of the king of Egypt, the king of the south. The mention of these countries in the verses about Gog and in the verses about Egypt suggests that Gog and the king of Egypt will fight for a common cause. This cooperation parallels the king of the south and the king of the north fighting a common foe: the Antichrist.

4. Given the parallels, Gog must be the king of the north as the king of Egypt must be the king of the south. The two will wage war against the Antichrist in a joint effort.

I will describe the exploits of the king of the north in chapter fourteen. Remember, the war between the Antichrist and his foes will unlikely be the only conflict ongoing at that time.

LET'S PAUSE FOR A MOMENT

This chapter covered the chaos that will ensue after the sixth trumpet sounds. The conflicts at that time will involve 200 million participants, and one-third of the world's population will die. The Antichrist will likely face challenges to his authority at this time. Here is a look at where the sixth trumpet fits in our timeline:

———

Probable Sequence of Events: Ch.12

Midpoint of the Tribulation: Dan 9:27 (Ch.7)

- Abomination of Desolation: Dan 9:27, Matt 24:15 (Ch.7)
- Antichrist's True Identity Revealed: 2Thess 2:3-4 (Ch.8)
- The False Prophet's Ministry Begins: Rev 13:11-16 (Ch.9)
- Great Tribulation Begins: Matt 24:21 (Ch.11)

5th Seal: Rev 6:9-11 (Ch.11)

Trumpets 1-5: Rev 8:7-13, 9:1-12 (Ch.11)

6th Trumpet: Rev 9:13-21 (Ch.12)

———

Thanks again for taking the time to read this book. I hope you have learned a lot so far. There is much more to learn in this book!

Notes

1. Isaiah 19 may describe a devastated Egypt after Antichrist attacks them.
2. I explain why Antichrist and Gog are not the same individuals in the appendix section titled "Is Gog the Antichrist?".

CHAPTER 13.

THE MYSTERIOUS 144,000

The 144,000 of the Book of Revelation are amongst the most mysterious Bible prophecy topics. We know little about them. Revelation 7 and Revelation 14 contain the few details that we have about them. The lack of information we have about the 144,000 means that much speculation about their identity and their significance exists.

My intention in this chapter is to tell you what I believe to be true about the 144,000 based on what the Bible says about them.

REVELATION 7: INTRODUCING THE 144,000

Revelation 7 introduces us to the 144,000 who will have the seal of God on their foreheads:

(2) And I saw another angel ascending from the east, having the seal of the living God: and he cried with a loud voice to the four angels, to whom it was given to hurt the earth and the sea, (3) Saying, Hurt not the earth, neither the sea, nor the trees, till we have sealed the servants of our God in their foreheads. (Rev 7:2-3)

The Identity of the 144,000

Some believe that the 144,000 represent the Church, but Revelation 7 states they relate to the descendants of Israel:

And I heard the number of them which were sealed: and there were sealed an hundred and forty and four thousand of all the tribes of the children of Israel. (Rev 7:4)

Furthermore, Revelation 7 lists the tribes of the children of Israel that the 144,000 will come from, and the tribes mentioned in this passage are physical descendants of Jacob (Israel):

(5) Of the tribe of Juda were sealed twelve thousand. Of the tribe of Reuben were sealed twelve thousand. Of the tribe of Gad were sealed twelve thousand. (6) Of the tribe of Aser were sealed twelve thousand. Of the tribe of Nepthalim were sealed twelve thousand. Of the tribe of Manasses were sealed twelve thousand. (7) Of the tribe of Simeon were sealed twelve thousand. Of the tribe of Levi were sealed twelve thousand. Of the tribe of Issachar were sealed twelve thousand. (8) Of the tribe of Zabulon were sealed twelve thousand. Of the tribe of Joseph were sealed twelve thousand. Of the tribe of Benjamin were sealed twelve thousand. (Rev 7:5-8)

Some claim there will not actually be 144,000 people in the group. I believe there will be precisely 144,000 people in the group, since the Bible meticulously describes how 12,000 people will come from each of the twelve tribes it lists.

Some believe that the 144,000 mentioned in Revelation 7 are a different group than the 144,000 referred to Revelation 14. I do not believe they are separate groups as Revelation 7 and Revelation 14 each indicate that the 144,000 have the seal of God on their foreheads (Rev 7:2-3, 14:1).

I also believe that the 144,000 will only consist of males, as Revelation 14:4 indicates that the 144,000 are virgin males:

These are they which were not defiled with women; for they are virgins. These are they which follow the Lamb whithersoever he goeth. These were redeemed from among men, being the firstfruits unto God and to the Lamb. (Rev 14:4)

Servants of God

Revelation 7:3 refers to the 144,000 as God's servants. This title has led some to speculate about what role they will have:

- Some theorize that the 144,000 will evangelize to the world or the people of Israel specifically.

- Some even have suggested that the 144,000 will serve as warriors against the Antichrist and his forces.

The key thing to remember is that *this is all speculation*. We lack scriptural information to say definitively what role the 144,000 will play as servants of God.

The Significance of the Seal

Recall that the 144,000 will have the seal of God, which will consist of the name of the God written on their forehead (Rev 14:1). What might be the significance of the seal?

- The Lord could use the seal of the 144,000 to distinguish them as His property (contrast this to the wicked who have accepted the Mark of the Beast on their forehead).

- Another possibility is that the seal could serve as a marking that will bring divine protection to the 144,000. It is not unprecedented for the Lord to spare the people He marked (Ezek 9:4-6).

Interestingly, Revelation 9 tells us that the locusts that arise after the sounding of the fifth trumpet will not harm those who have the seal of God on their foreheads:

> And it was commanded them that they should not hurt the grass of the earth, neither any green thing, neither any tree; but only those men which have not the seal of God in their foreheads. (Rev 9:4)

Given this, it is reasonable to assume that the 144,000 will at least have some divine protection from the chaos of the end times.

When They're Sealed

Many believe the sealing of the 144,000 will take place between the breaking of the sixth seal and the breaking of the seventh seal. The reason for this belief is that the introduction of the 144,000 is in Revelation 7. This places the sealing of 144,000:

- After the description of the sixth seal's breaking in Revelation 6.
- Before the description of the seventh seal's breaking in Revelation 8.

However, I argue that the sealing of the 144,000 will probably take place just before the start of the great tribulation.

First, the great tribulation will be a time of unprecedented persecution. Recall that those with the seal of God will have some level of divine protection from the chaos that will take place around them. The sealing of the 144,000 just before the start of the great tribulation means that they will have divine protection through the worst persecution in history.

Second, recall that the Two Witnesses will likely work with angels to harm the earth during the days of their ministry, which will begin near the midpoint of the tribulation. Revelation 7:3 gives another revealing detail about when the angels (and the Two Witnesses) can begin to harm the earth. The verse reveals that they must wait until the 144,000 are sealed before they can begin to harm the earth:

> Saying, Hurt not the earth, neither the sea, nor the trees, till we have sealed the servants of our God in their foreheads. (Rev 7:3)

The Two Witnesses (and angels) will start to harm the world when their ministry begins with the start of a long drought (Rev 11:6). Therefore, the sealing of the 144,000 must take place near the midpoint of the tribulation (before the start of the great tribulation).[1]

The Location of the 144,000

The 144,000 will likely be scattered across the world when they are sealed. The fact that the earth, the sea, and the trees could harm them if they are not sealed implies that they will not be in one place when they are sealed. However, they will come together later on.

REVELATION 14: THE 144,000 TOGETHER

Revelation 14 provides another look at the 144,000. The chapter describes Christ with the 144,000 together on Mount Zion:[2]

> And I looked, and, lo, a Lamb stood on the mount Sion, and with him an hundred forty and four thousand, having his Father's name written in their foreheads. (Rev 14:1)

Where is Mount Zion?

Debate exists about whether Mount Zion mentioned in Revelation 14:1 is in Jerusalem or in Heaven.

- Some believe this Mount Zion is in Heaven. Hebrews 12:22 refers to Mount Zion as the heavenly Jerusalem.

- Others believe this Mount Zion refers to its location on Earth. Obadiah 1:21, an end time verse, mentions how deliverers will come up to Mount Zion to judge Edom.

I believe the Mount Zion of Revelation 14 is on Earth, and I will clarify why soon.

Learning a New Song

John wrote that he heard a powerful voice coming from Heaven and the voice of harpers as they play. John also noted that a new song will be sung that no man except for the 144,000 can learn:

(2) And I heard a voice from heaven, as the voice of many waters, and as the voice of a great thunder: and I heard the voice of harpers harping with their harps: (3) And they sung as it were a new song before the throne, and before the four beasts, and the elders: and no man could learn that song but the hundred and forty and four thousand, which were redeemed from the earth. (Rev 14:2-3)

Some argue that the 144,000 are the singing the new song. I believe the harpers are singing the new song because John heard their voice and the 144,000 need to learn the new song. Why is there singing?

The 144,000 have been redeemed or purchased from the earth. This indicates that they are saved. The Bible tells us that there is joy in Heaven when one person gets saved (Luke 15:7). How much more would Heaven rejoice if 144,000 people got saved at the same time?

The Firstfruits of the Harvest

Revelation 14:4-5 describes the 144,000 redeemed or purchased from the earth and man as firstfruits to God and the Lamb (Christ):[3]

(4) These are they which were not defiled with women; for they are virgins. These are they which follow the Lamb whithersoever he goeth. These were redeemed from among men, being the firstfruits unto God and to the Lamb. (5) And in their mouth was found no guile: for they are without fault before the throne of God. (Rev 14:4-5)

The depiction of the 144,000 as firstfruits to God and Christ again suggests that the 144,000 are saved.

What is the significance of labeling the 144,000 as "firstfruits"? The firstfruits represent the initial portion of the harvest that had to be offered to God before the rest of the harvest could be gathered. God required the best of a harvest serve as the firstfruits offering (Num 18:12).

Therefore, the term "firstfruits" implies that the 144,000 are the first and the best of an upcoming harvest. But what harvest will the 144,000 serve as firstfruits?:

- Some argue that they represent the firstfruits of the figurative wheat harvest at the end of the age. I previously thought that this is what they represent, but I no longer believe this is the case.[4]

- Others argue that they represent the firstfruits of a saved Israel.

I believe the 144,000 represent the firstfruits of a saved Israel. In fact, Revelation 14 may depict the 144,000 just after they got saved. More will get saved soon:

- We will look at the salvation of the remnant of Israel later in this book, but for now, know that I believe Revelation 14:1-5 takes place between the end of the war of Armageddon and the start of the Millennium.

The depiction of the 144,000 in verse 5 as blameless may describe the high-quality nature of the firstfruits. The rest of the remnant of Israel will eventually resemble the 144,000 firstfruits:

> (12) I will also leave in the midst of thee an afflicted and poor people, and they shall trust in the name of the Lord. (13) The remnant of Israel shall not do iniquity, nor speak lies; neither shall a deceitful tongue be found in their mouth: for they shall feed and lie down, and none shall make them afraid. (Zep 3:12-13)

LET'S PAUSE FOR A MOMENT

We looked at the mysterious 144,000 in this chapter. We saw that the 144,000 will consist of virgin males from the tribes of Israel and may represent the firstfruits of the saved remnant of Israel. Here is a look at where the sealing of the 144,000 fits in our timeline:

Probable Sequence of Events: Ch.13

The Start of the Tribulation: Dan. 9:27 (Ch.5)

1st to 4th Seal: Rev 6:1-8 (Ch.7)

- Start of Temple Sacrifice: Dan 8:13-19 (Ch.7)
- War in Heaven: Rev 12:7-12 (Ch.7)
- *144,000 Sealed: Rev 7:1-8 (Ch.13)*
- The Two Witnesses' Ministry Begins: Rev 11:3-6 (Ch.9)

Midpoint of the Tribulation: Dan 9:27 (Ch.7)

- Abomination of Desolation: Dan 9:27, Matt 24:15 (Ch.7)
- Antichrist's True Identity Revealed: 2Thess 2:3-4 (Ch.8)
- The False Prophet's Ministry Begins: Rev 13:11-16 (Ch.9)
- Great Tribulation Begins: Matt 24:21 (Ch.11)

I encourage you to reflect on what you have read and to reread any parts that might have been difficult to understand before continuing to the next chapter.

Notes

1. We can also conclude that the sealing of the 144,000 will occur before the start of the seven trumpets because the first trumpet will harm the earth.

2. Why does this scene of the 144,000 appear at this point in the Book of Revelation? It likely appears to contrast between those who belong to the Antichrist (as seen in Rev 13) and those who belong to Christ.

3. The phrase "before the throne of God" does not appear in most Bible ver-

sions of Rev 14:5. The phrase appears in Rev 14:5 in the King James Bible. This discrepancy is due to a difference in the Greek manuscripts used by these translations

4. I previously thought that the 144,000 were pictured in Heaven and were the firstfruits of the upcoming wheat harvest. In other words, I thought the 144,000 may take part in an early Rapture. After further study, I no longer believe that is the case.

The main reason is that 1 Thessalonians 4:15-17 gives us the order of events for the Rapture. The dead in Christ will rise before the living are transformed and join Christ. The 144,000 will unlikely die since they have a seal of God that gives them divine protection. Therefore, they would likely wait until the dead rise first before they join Christ if they take part in the Rapture (which I do not believe they will, since they will be part of the remnant of Israel).

Also, I also realized that being before the throne of God does not mean you need to be in the physical presence of God. Being before the throne of God means that you have God's attention. He is looking at you from His throne.

To better grasp this, think of David when he committed adultery with Bathsheba and had Uriah killed. David wrote he sinned in God's sight (Ps 51:4). He was on Earth while God was in Heaven when he sinned. David did not need to be in the throne room of Heaven to sin in God's sight.

Likewise, the 144,000 do not need to be in Heaven to be in God's sight. They can be before the throne of God when He focuses on them.

CHAPTER 14.

THE GOSPEL OF THE KINGDOM & THE END OF THE AGE

Revelation 14:6-13 records three announcements that angels will give to the world. The first angel will preach an "everlasting gospel" to the entire world:

> And I saw another angel fly in the midst of heaven, having the everlasting gospel to preach unto them that dwell on the earth, and to every nation, and kindred, and tongue, and people, (Rev 14:6)

Many assume this angel will preach the gospel of Christ. However, many scholars who analyze the Greek of this verse note that an article is missing from the term "everlasting gospel".

In other words, the angel is not preaching *"the gospel"* but a "gospel". This missing article implies that the gospel this angel will preach is a message of good news, but not the gospel of Christ.

Verse 7 presents the message of the everlasting gospel. The nature of the message supports the view that the everlasting gospel is *not* the gospel of Christ. The angel will tell the world to fear God and worship Him because the time of judgment is near:

> Saying with a loud voice, Fear God, and give glory to him; for the hour of his judgment is come: and worship him that made heaven, and earth, and the sea, and the fountains of waters. (Rev 14:7)

This chapter sheds light on what the everlasting gospel message represents and the significance of its preaching to the world.

THE PREACHING OF AN END TIME GOSPEL

We can learn when the everlasting gospel will be preached by examining other verses and passages.

The Circumstances of Its Preaching

Matthew 24 provides the context of the preaching of a gospel to the world during the end times. The disciples that accompanied Christ on the Mount of Olives asked Him to tell them about the sign of His coming and the end of the age (Matt 24:3).

The request to reveal "the sign" about two events indicates that these events are connected: the coming of Christ relates to the end of the age.

Christ gave insight about what events will take place before His coming and the end of the age to His disciples. Recall that Christ taught that many unnerving events will occur, including:

- Wars and rumors of wars (Matt 24:6-7, Luke 21:9-10, Mark 13:7-8).

- Earthquakes, famines, and pestilences in many parts of the world (Matt 24:7, Luke 21:11, Mark 13:8).

- Ethnic conflict and political instability (Matt 24:7, Luke 21:9-10, Mark 13:8)

- False Christs and false prophets arising who shall deceive many (Matt 24:5, 23-24, Luke 21:8, Mark 13:6, 21-22).

Christ added that people will be hated worldwide for following Him (Matt 24:9), and the most challenging time for them will be during the great tribulation. Christ mentioned twice that some people (the elect) will eventually be saved or delivered. He indicated:

- People who faithfully endure to the end (of the age) will be saved (Matt 24:13).

- The great tribulation will be cut short so there will be faithful people left to save when the end of the age arrives (Matt 24:22).

(13) But he that shall endure unto the end, the same shall be saved.... (22) And except those days should be shortened, there should no flesh

be saved: but for the elect's sake those days shall be shortened. (Matt 24:13, 22)

The period when the elect will be saved shall mark the beginning of the end of the age because the elect will have endured to the end. Matthew 24:29-31 indicates that the elect will be saved after the great tribulation and after the appearance of heavenly signs, which will be discussed in future chapters:

(29) Immediately after the tribulation of those days shall the sun be darkened, and the moon shall not give her light, and the stars shall fall from heaven, and the powers of the heavens shall be shaken:... (31) And he shall send his angels with a great sound of a trumpet, and they shall gather together his elect from the four winds, from one end of heaven to the other. (Matt 24:29, 31)

Thus, the end of the age will begin after the great tribulation and after the appearance of heavenly signs.

Christ provided another landmark to help us identify when the end of the age will come. Christ said that the end (of the age) will come after the "gospel of the kingdom" is preached to all the nations:

And this gospel of the kingdom shall be preached in all the world for a witness unto all nations; and then shall the end come. (Matt 24:14)

The gospel of the kingdom is a message centered on urging people to repent because God's reign is approaching (Mark 1:14-15), and the preaching of this message to all nations at that time suggests that God's reign will begin soon:

(14) Now after that John was put in prison, Jesus came into Galilee, preaching the gospel of the kingdom of God, (15) And saying, The time is fulfilled, and the kingdom of God is at hand: repent ye, and believe the gospel. (Mark 1:14-15)

Overall, the preaching of the gospel of the kingdom will precede the end of the age and the coming of Christ. Also, the preaching of the gospel of the kingdom will occur near the end of the great tribulation, the appearance of heavenly signs, and the onset of God's reign. The elect will be saved at the end of the age (Matt 24:29-31) while the wicked will be punished (Matt 13:40-42):

(40) As therefore the tares are gathered and burned in the fire; so shall it be in the end of this world. (41) The Son of man shall send forth his angels, and they shall gather out of his kingdom all things that offend, and them which do iniquity; (42) And shall cast them into a furnace of fire: there shall be wailing and gnashing of teeth. (Matt 13:40-42, also see Matt 13:49-50)

The fact that Matthew 24 and Revelation 14 each mention the preaching of an end time gospel to the world leads to the theory that the angel of Revelation 14:6-7 will preach the gospel of the kingdom to the world.

I'll examine this theory by comparing the time of the everlasting gospel's preaching with the time of the gospel of the kingdom's preaching.

The Time of Its Preaching

We know that the time of judgment will be near when an angel preaches the everlasting gospel to the world. We can glean more insight about the period when the angel preaches the everlasting gospel by looking at what will happen after its preaching to the world.

A second angel will follow the first angel with another message:

And there followed another angel, saying, Babylon is fallen, is fallen, that great city, because she made all nations drink of the wine of the wrath of her fornication. (Rev 14:8)

Despite the announcement, I do not believe Babylon the Great's fall will take place at that time. I will discuss her demise later in this book, but for now know that this is a case where the certainty of a future event is emphasized by speaking of it in past tense.[1]

A third angel will warn the people of the earth that those who pledge loyalty to the beast, the Antichrist, will experience the full brunt of the wrath of God. The third angel will also recognize the patience of the saints and the dead who die in the Lord and rest:

(9) And the third angel followed them, saying with a loud voice, If any man worship the beast and his image, and receive his mark in his forehead, or in his hand, (10) The same shall drink of the wine of the wrath of God, which is poured out without mixture into the cup of his indig-

nation; and he shall be tormented with fire and brimstone in the presence of the holy angels, and in the presence of the Lamb: (11) And the smoke of their torment ascendeth up for ever and ever: and they have no rest day nor night, who worship the beast and his image, and whosoever receiveth the mark of his name. (12) **Here is the patience of the saints: here are they that keep the commandments of God, and the faith of Jesus.** (13) And I heard a voice from heaven saying unto me, Write, **Blessed are the dead which die in the Lord from henceforth: Yea, saith the Spirit, that they may rest from their labours; and their works do follow them.** (Rev 14:9-13)

The acknowledgment of the saints' patience suggests that they have endured much adversity on Earth and remain on Earth. The recognition of the dead who die in the Lord and rest further suggests that the resurrection of the righteous dead and the coming of Christ have not yet taken place. The dead will rise at the coming of Christ (1Thess 4:15-17).[2]

Revelation 14:14-20 describes the harvest of the earth that will occur at the end of the age in two ways. Each description depicts the same harvest but emphasizes a different aspect of it.

Revelation 14:14-16 provides the first description and emphasizes the coming of Christ to gather His elect, given that it strongly parallels the coming of Christ scene detailed in Matthew 24:30-31:

(14) And I looked, and behold a white cloud, and **upon the cloud one sat like unto the Son of man**, having on his head a golden crown, and in his hand a sharp sickle. (15) And another angel came out of the temple, crying with a loud voice to him that sat on the cloud, Thrust in thy sickle, and reap: for the time is come for thee to reap; for the harvest of the earth is ripe. (16) And he that sat on the cloud thrust in his sickle on the earth; and the earth was reaped. (Rev 14:14-16)

(30) And then shall appear the sign of the Son of man in heaven: and then shall all the tribes of the earth mourn, and **they shall see the Son of man coming in the clouds of heaven with power and great glory.** (31) And he shall send his angels with a great sound of a trumpet, and they shall gather together his elect from the four winds, from one end of heaven to the other. (Matt 24:30-31)

Revelation 14:17-20 provides the second description and emphasizes the reaping and destruction of the wicked, events that I will cover further in-depth in future chapters:

(17) And another angel came out of the temple which is in heaven, he also having a sharp sickle. (18) And another angel came out from the altar, which had power over fire; and cried with a loud cry to him that had the sharp sickle, saying, Thrust in thy sharp sickle, and gather the clusters of the vine of the earth; for her grapes are fully ripe. (19) And the angel thrust in his sickle into the earth, and gathered the vine of the earth, and cast it into the great winepress of the wrath of God. (20) And the winepress was trodden without the city, and blood came out of the winepress, even unto the horse bridles, by the space of a thousand and six hundred furlongs. (Rev 14:17-20)

Comparing Circumstances

The preaching of the everlasting gospel and the preaching of the gospel of the kingdom will take place under similar circumstances:

- The saints/the elect have already endured much adversity by the time of each announcement (Rev 14:12, Matt 24:9-13).
- People worldwide will hear each announcement.
- Each announcement will occur before the harvesting of the earth, (Matt 24:14, Rev 14:6-7), which will include the harvest of the good (Matt 24:29-31, Rev 14:14-16).
- Each announcement will come before the punishment of the wicked begins (Matt 13:40-42, Rev 14:9-11, 17-20).

Given these parallels, it is likely that the everlasting gospel that the angel will preach is the gospel of the kingdom that Christ referred to in Matthew 24:14.

The preaching of the gospel of the kingdom to the world at this point in the end times is significant. It represents a final warning to the people of the earth that they need to repent and worship God.

THE FIRST FIVE BOWL JUDGMENTS

The bowl (or vial) judgments will begin shortly after the three angel announcements.[3] The primary target of the bowl judgments will be the kingdom of the Antichrist (Rev 16:10) and those with the Mark of the Beast (Rev 16:2). Figure 14.1 summarizes the effects of the first five bowl judgments:

Figure 14.1: The First Five Bowl Judgments

First (Rev 16:2): Sores shall appear on those who have the Mark of the Beast & worship his image.

Second (Rev 16:3): Every living soul in the sea will die & the sea will become like blood.

Third (Rev 16:4-7): Rivers and fountains of water will turn into blood.

Fourth (Rev 16:8-9): The sun will scorch men with extreme heat.

Fifth (Rev 16:10-11): The kingdom of the Antichrist will be full of darkness, and people will experience severe pain.

The fact that the fifth bowl affects the Antichrist's kingdom suggests that the end of the 42 months of the Antichrist's reign has not arrived yet given that the Antichrist is still a ruler of his empire.

Revelation 16 mentions that the wicked blasphemed God instead of repenting their deeds and giving glory to God:

> (8) And the fourth angel poured out his vial upon the sun; and power was given unto him to scorch men with fire. (9) And men were scorched with great heat, and blasphemed the name of God, which hath power over these plagues: and **they repented not to give him glory**. (10) And the fifth angel poured out his vial upon the seat of the beast; and his kingdom was full of darkness; and they gnawed their tongues for pain, (11) And blasphemed the God of heaven because of their pains and their sores, and **repented not of their deeds**. (Rev 16:8-11)

This detail is noteworthy because the gospel of the kingdom centers on repentance. Revelation 16's mention of the unrepentant recipients of the bowl judgments suggests many have rejected the gospel of the kingdom.[4][5]

ANTICHRIST RECEIVES TROUBLING NEWS

Recall that the Antichrist will be at war with the king of the south (Dan 11:40). The Antichrist will repel the initial attack by the king of the south and destroy much of his southern foes. However, Antichrist won't be done fighting. Daniel 11:44 states that he will be so upset by developments out of the north and out of the east that he will seek to kill and to destroy:

> But tidings out of the east and out of the north shall trouble him: therefore he shall go forth with great fury to destroy, and utterly to make away many. (Dan 11:44)

I've wondered for years about what could upset the Antichrist to the level that verse 44 describes. Here is a likely possibility:

The King of the North's Advance

The advance of the king of the north's forces could upset the Antichrist. Interestingly, Antiochus Epiphanes IV and the Antichrist seem to respond to unsettling news similarly.

Daniel 11:29-30 indicates that Antiochus was unhappy when he learned about the resistance from his northern adversary (the ships of Chittim). Likewise, the Antichrist will be upset when he learns about the advance of the king of the north. Figure 14.2 shows this parallel in the careers of these men:

Figure 14.2: Facing Northern Challenges

- **War Against the South**

- *Disturbed*

Dan 11:29-30 [Antiochus]: (29) At the time appointed he shall return, **and come toward the south; but it shall not be as the former, or as the latter.** (30) For the ships of Chittim shall come against him: *therefore he shall be grieved, and return, and have indignation against the holy covenant*: so shall he do; he shall even return, and have intelligence with them that forsake the holy covenant.

Dan 11:40, 44 [Antichrist]: (40) **And at the time of the end shall the king of the south push at him:** and the king of the north shall come against him like a whirlwind, with chariots, and with horsemen, and with many ships; and he shall enter into the countries, and shall overflow and pass over.... (44) But tidings out of the east and out *of the north shall trouble him: therefore he shall go forth with great fury to destroy, and utterly to make away many.*

Damascus's Annihilation

Isaiah 17 is a prophecy about the destruction of Damascus and other Mideast locations. I believe this event will take place when the king of the north's forces advance from the north. This is an event could draw the Antichrist's ire:[6]

> (1) The burden of Damascus. Behold, Damascus is taken away from being a city, and it shall be a ruinous heap. (2) The cities of Aroer are forsaken: they shall be for flocks, which shall lie down, and none shall make them afraid. (3) The fortress also shall cease from Ephraim, and the kingdom from Damascus, and the remnant of Syria: they shall be as the glory of the children of Israel, saith the LORD of hosts. (4) And in that day it shall come to pass, that the glory of Jacob shall be made thin, and the fatness of his flesh shall wax lean. (Isa 17:1-4)

The attackers will travel through Syria and northern Israel and leave a wake of destruction as they advance to besiege Jerusalem (Isa 17:12-13), an event that I will discuss in detail in coming chapters.

THE SIXTH BOWL JUDGMENT

The Euphrates River will dry up after the pouring of the sixth bowl. This will allow the kings of the east to travel westward:

> And the sixth angel poured out his vial upon the great river Euphrates; and the water thereof was dried up, that the way of the kings of the east might be prepared. (Rev 16:12)

The loyalties of the kings of the east are unknown, but it is entirely possible that they will oppose the Antichrist like the king of the north and the king of the south. Therefore, the movement of the kings of the east may also draw the ire of the Antichrist.

Meanwhile, Satan, the Antichrist, the False Prophet, and their spiritual subordinates will work together to convince the kings of the earth and their armies to gather to battle:

> (13) And I saw three unclean spirits like frogs come out of the mouth of the dragon, and out of the mouth of the beast, and out of the mouth of the false prophet. (14) For they are the spirits of devils, working miracles, which go forth unto the kings of the earth and of the whole world, to gather them to the battle of that great day of God Almighty.…

(16) And he gathered them together into a place called in the Hebrew tongue Armageddon. (Rev 16:13-14, 16)

They will assemble a massive force to wage war against God and His people. They will fight in the war of Armageddon.

LET'S PAUSE FOR A MOMENT

This chapter covered the preaching of the everlasting gospel (the gospel of the kingdom) and the pouring of the first six bowl judgments. We saw that the gospel of the kingdom is a message urging people to repent and worship God before the coming of God's reign.

The followers of the Antichrist will reject the gospel of the kingdom and suffer the plagues of the bowl judgments. Here is a look at where the key events detailed in this chapter fit in our timeline:

Probable Sequence of Events: Ch.14

Midpoint of the Tribulation: Dan 9:27 (Ch.7)

- Abomination of Desolation: Dan 9:27, Matt 24:15 (Ch.7)
- Antichrist's True Identity Revealed: 2Thess 2:3-4 (Ch.8)
- The False Prophet's Ministry Begins: Rev 13:11-16 (Ch.9)
- Great Tribulation Begins: Matt 24:21 (Ch.11)

5th Seal: Rev 6:9-11 (Ch.11)

Trumpets 1-5: Rev 8:7-13, 9:1-12 (Ch.11)

6th Trumpet: Rev 9:13-21 (Ch.12)

Three Angel Announcements: Rev 14:6-13 (Ch.14)

- *Gospel of the Kingdom Preached: Rev 14:6-7, Matt 24:14 (Ch.14)*

Bowls 1-6: *Rev 16:1-16 (Ch.14)*

Once again, I encourage you to reflect on what you have read and to reread any parts that might have been difficult to understand before continuing to the next chapter.

Notes

1. Some believe that Rev 14:8 and Rev 18:2 are verses where a literary technique called "prophetic perfect" tense is used. This technique conveys that a future event is so sure to happen that we can speak of it in past tense. In other words, the writer seeks to emphasize the certainty of a future event by speaking of it in past tense, like we would use italics to emphasize a major point we are trying to make.

   If Rev 14:8 is indeed a case of prophetic perfect tense, John's audience would have seen the announcement as a firm promise that Babylon the Great will fall. This look towards the future contextually makes sense when you consider that the third angel will ensure that anyone who takes the Mark of the Beast will face severe punishment.

2. Dan 12:13 indicates that the righteous rest until their resurrection.

3. We can conclude that the bowl judgments will come after the announcements by the three angels since two angels link the bowl judgments with God's judgments as the contents of the bowls are poured out (Rev 16:5 & 16:7). Despite the association with God's judgments, the first six bowl judgments do not represent the punishment of the wicked at the end of the age. I will explain why in chapter sixteen.

4. Rev 9:20-21 says the wicked survivors of the sixth trumpet events will not repent. This detail suggests that the preaching of the gospel of the kingdom may take place before the end of the sixth trumpet events.

5. Some compare the bowl judgments to the plagues of Egypt. Pharaoh had an opportunity to repent and release the Israelites after each plague, but he refused, and more plagues came. The wicked will have opportunities to repent during the bowl judgments, but they will not repent.

6. See the article on my website titled "Isaiah 17: Pinpointing the Timing of Damascus's Destruction" for an in-depth look at the fall of Damascus.

CHAPTER 15.

THE CAMPAIGNS TO DESTROY THE PEOPLE OF ISRAEL

The great tribulation will take a huge toll on the people of Israel. Many will die from the persecution. But the nations will seek to finish them off near the end of the tribulation. We will look at this effort to destroy the people of Israel in this chapter.

THE WAR OF ARMAGEDDON

Recall that the Antichrist, the False Prophet, and Satan will gather the kings of the earth to battle. The kings of the earth (and their armies) will gather at a place called Armageddon:

> And he gathered them together into a place called in the Hebrew tongue Armageddon. (Rev 16:16)

The name "Armageddon" means "Mount Megiddo". Many believe it refers to the city of Megiddo, located in the Jezreel Valley in the northern part of Israel. Megiddo was the site of major Old Testament battles (2Kgs 23:29-30, Judg 5:19). The nations that will gather there in the future will be ready for war (Rev 16:14).

Enemies Join Forces

The gathering of the kings of the earth to Armageddon may include kings that have opposed the Antichrist. As we will see soon, all the nations of the earth will gather against Jerusalem and the people of Israel. This development suggests that the nations of the earth will unite against a common foe: the people of Israel.

I suspect the evil spirits that Satan, the False Prophet, and the Antichrist will send will stir up hatred against the people of Israel. They may deceive the kings of the earth into believing that destroying them will solve the world's problems. They may even convince the kings that have opposed the Antichrist to join the effort to destroy the people of Israel.

THE ATTACK AGAINST THOSE IN HIDING

Psalm 83 describes one of the key military campaigns against the people of Israel. This attack will involve many nearby nations. These nations will attack those who are in hiding:

(3) They have taken crafty counsel against thy people, and consulted against thy hidden ones. (4) They have said, Come, and let us cut them off from being a nation; that the name of Israel may be no more in remembrance. (5) For they have consulted together with one consent: they are confederate against thee: (Ps 83:3-5)

Psalm 83:6-8 names the nations involved in the attack. Figure 15.1 outlines the modern day locations of these nations:

Figure 15.1: Psalm 83 Participants

- **Amalek:** Sinai

- **Edom, Ammon, Moab:** Jordan

- **Hagarenes:** Jordan (1Chr 5:10)

- **Gebal & Tyre:** Lebanon

- **Assur:** N. Iraq, parts of Syria & Turkey

- **Philistines:** Gaza Strip

- **Ishmaelites:** Saudi Arabia

I believe Psalm 83:3 refers to a remnant of Israel that will hide in the wilderness to avoid the Antichrist's attacks (Rev 12:6, 14-16).

Verse 4 indicates that the aim of the attack is to eliminate all the people of Israel. This includes those in hiding and those not in hiding.

THE END TIME SIEGE OF JERUSALEM

The end time siege of Jerusalem will be among the most important events in the end times. The siege will occur approximately at the same time the Psalm 83 campaign takes place. Many places in the Bible describe this end time siege of Jerusalem, including:

- Isaiah 1:25-31, 3:1-26, 5:26-30, 29:1-8, 51:17-23
- Jeremiah 4:5 onward
- Ezekiel 7
- Zechariah 12, 14:1-3

This siege will involve every nation on Earth, including the nations involved in Gog's coalition:[1]

> (2) Behold, I will make Jerusalem a cup of trembling unto all the people round about, **when they shall be in the siege both against Judah and against Jerusalem**. (3) And in that day will I make Jerusalem a burdensome stone for all people: all that burden themselves with it shall be cut in pieces, though **all the people of the earth be gathered together against it**. (Zech 12:2-3)

> **For I will gather all nations against Jerusalem to battle**; and the city shall be taken, and the houses rifled, and the women ravished; and half of the city shall go forth into captivity, and the residue of the people shall not be cut off from the city. (Zech 14:2)

Why the Lord Will Judge Jerusalem

The siege of Jerusalem will not take place without cause. The city's residents will be judged for their wicked conduct (Isa 3:11, Jer 4:18, Ezek 7:3-4). Revelation 11:8 refers to the wicked state of the city at that time by calling it the "great city, which spiritually is called Sodom...". Also, Isaiah 3:9 states that the people of Jerusalem will flaunt their sins like the people of Sodom:[2]

> (8) For Jerusalem is ruined, and Judah is fallen: because their tongue and their doings are against the LORD, to provoke the eyes of his glory.

(9) The shew of their countenance doth witness against them; and they declare their sin as Sodom, they hide it not. Woe unto their soul! for they have rewarded evil unto themselves. (Isa 3:8-9)

The leaders of Jerusalem will oppress their citizens harshly (Isa 3:14-15). The poor quality of leadership in Jerusalem at that time will be a microcosm of the lack of quality leadership that will exist at that time for the people of Israel (Ezek 34:5, 8, Jer 23:1-2, 50:6, Zech 10:2, 11:15-17).[3]

Unsurprisingly, the main target of Jerusalem's judgment will be the political, military, and religious elite of the city:

(1) For, behold, the Lord, the LORD of hosts, doth take away from Jerusalem and from Judah the stay and the staff, the whole stay of bread, and the whole stay of water, (2) The mighty man, and the man of war, the judge, and the prophet, and the prudent, and the ancient, (3) The captain of fifty, and the honourable man, and the counsellor, and the cunning artificer, and the eloquent orator. (Isa 3:1-3, also see Isa 22:1-3, Jer 4:9, Ezek 7:27, Zech 10:3)

The women of Jerusalem will also anger the Lord with their conduct (Isa 3:16-17). They will also face judgment. Zechariah 14:2 describes their fate:

For I will gather all nations against Jerusalem to battle; and the city shall be taken, and the houses rifled, and the women ravished; and half of the city shall go forth into captivity,... (also see Isa 3:18-24)

Mindset of the People in Jerusalem

The most ironic aspect of the siege of Jerusalem is that the attack will catch the city's leaders off guard, even though the Bible details the attack. The city's leaders will have a huge false sense of security:

(25) Destruction cometh; and **they shall seek peace, and there shall be none.** (26) Mischief shall come upon mischief, and rumour shall be upon rumour; then shall **they seek a vision of the prophet; but the law shall perish from the priest, and counsel from the ancients.** (Ezek 7:25-26, also see Isa 29:9-10, Jer 4:10, Amos 8:11-12)

Why will the city's leaders be so complacent? Perhaps the city's leaders will believe they will be immune from persecution and judgment after they collaborate with the Antichrist (Isa 28:15). However, their deal with him will not protect them when the storm of attackers come (Isa 28:16-19).

The Timing of the Siege

I already mentioned that the end time siege of Jerusalem will take place around the time when the Psalm 83 campaign transpires. More precisely, the end time siege of Jerusalem will begin before the end of the tribulation since the siege of Jerusalem will end after tribulation. How do we know this?:

- The treading of Jerusalem will begin at the midpoint of the tribulation (Matt 24:15-21, Luke 21:23-24).
- Revelation 11:2 tells us the Gentiles will tread Jerusalem down for 42 months.
- The Gentiles will never tread Jerusalem again once the Lord acts after the 42 months (Isa 51:17-23, 52:1-3).

I believe the end time siege of Jerusalem will begin near the end of the tribulation. I will discuss the timing of the end time siege of Jerusalem further in upcoming chapters.

Overview of the Siege

A siege is a military blockade that isolates a place from help and supplies. The goal of a siege is to weaken a place until it surrenders or until it can be defeated.

Ezekiel 7:15-16 tells us that armies will impose a siege on Jerusalem. The passage describes a scene where disease and famine are rampant in the city while troops wait outside the city:[4]

> (15) The sword is without, and the pestilence and the famine within: he that is in the field shall die with the sword; and he that is in the city, famine and pestilence shall devour him. (16) But they that escape of them shall escape, and shall be on the mountains like doves of the valleys, all of them mourning, every one for his iniquity. (Ezek 7:15-16)

After camping outside of Jerusalem, the attackers will enter the city, plunder it, and take half of its residents captive:[5]

(1) Behold, the day of the LORD cometh, **and thy spoil shall be divided in the midst of thee.** (2) **For I will gather all nations against Jerusalem to battle; and the city shall be taken, and the houses rifled,** and the women ravished; and half of the city shall go forth into captivity, and the residue of the people shall not be cut off from the city. (Zech 14:1-2, also see Ezek 7:7, 23-24, Joel 2:1, 7-9, Zep 1:13)

They will also enter the temple in Jerusalem to plunder it, defile it, and damage it (Ps 79:1, Isa 63:17-18, Ezek 7:20-22, Joel 3:4-5).

THE DEATH OF THE TWO WITNESSES

During this time of chaos, the Antichrist and his forces will summon enough strength to kill the Two Witnesses while they are in Jerusalem (Rev 11:8). Their corpses will lie in the streets for 3.5 days. The wicked will celebrate their deaths because they punished the people of Earth for their conduct:

And they that dwell upon the earth shall rejoice over them, and make merry, and shall send gifts one to another; because these two prophets tormented them that dwelt on the earth. (Rev 11:10)

However, this is not the end of the Two Witnesses. See chapter seventeen for the rest of the story about the Two Witnesses.

GATHERED TO FIGHT

Troops from all nations will eventually gather in the Valley of Jehoshaphat, which tradition links to the Kidron Valley. The valley begins at the eastern part of Jerusalem and extends towards the Dead Sea:

(12) Let the heathen be wakened, and come up to the valley of Jehoshaphat: for there will I sit to judge all the heathen round about. (13) Put ye in the sickle, for the harvest is ripe: come, get you down; for the press is full, the fats overflow; for their wickedness is great. (14) Multitudes, multitudes in the valley of decision: for the day of the LORD is near in the valley of decision. (Joel 3:12-14)

Jehoshaphat means "Jehovah judges", so the Valley of Jehoshaphat is an appropriate title for the place where the nations will gather since the Lord will severely judge the nations there.

LET'S PAUSE FOR A MOMENT

We learned that the nations will seek to destroy the people of Israel. They will attack those who sought refuge in the wilderness and lay siege on the people of Jerusalem. Here is a look at where the key events described in this chapter fit in our timeline:

Probable Sequence of Events: Ch.15

Midpoint of the Tribulation: Dan 9:27 (Ch.7)

· Abomination of Desolation: Dan 9:27, Matt 24:15 (Ch.7)

· Antichrist's True Identity Revealed: 2Thess 2:3-4 (Ch.8)

· The False Prophet's Ministry Begins: Rev 13:11-16 (Ch.9)

· Great Tribulation Begins: Matt 24:21 (Ch.11)

5th Seal: Rev 6:9-11 (Ch.11)

Trumpets 1-5: Rev 8:7-13, 9:1-12 (Ch.11)

6th Trumpet: Rev 9:13-21 (Ch.12)

Three Angel Announcements: Rev 14:6-13 (Ch.14)

· Gospel of the Kingdom Preached: Rev 14:6-7, Matt 24:14 (Ch.14)

Bowls 1-6: Rev 16:1-16 (Ch.14)

Psalm 83 Attack & Siege of Jerusalem: *Ps 83, Zech 12:1-3, (Ch.15)*

· *Death of the Two Witnesses: Rev 11:7-10 (Ch.15)*

The coming chapters will cover some of the most important events of the end times. It is crucial for you to have a good understanding of the topics discussed thus far. Therefore, I strongly encourage you to take the time to reread any parts that might have been difficult to understand before continuing to the next chapter.

Notes

1. See the appendix section titled "Psalm 83, the Siege, and Gog" for more about Gog's involvement in the siege of Jerusalem.

2. Similarly, Jer 4:16-22 condemns the residents of Jerusalem as wicked, rebellious, and foolish

3. Ezek 34:7-9, Isa 56:10-12, 65:6-7, Zep 3:1-4 may also relate to the conduct of Israel's leaders from a long-term, historical perspective.

4. Remember that food supplies and water supplies may be scarce across the world at that time. As a result, Jerusalem may be short on supplies. If this is indeed the case, the residents of Jerusalem may suffer from the siege quickly.

5. Isa 42:22-25 may relate to the verses about the plundering of Jerusalem. The passage describes how people are prisoners in their homes and how they are robbed. A counterview is that Isa 42:22-25 speaks of Israel instead of the residents of Jerusalem.

CHAPTER 16.

THE COMING OF CHRIST & THE RAPTURE: PART 1

The coming of Jesus Christ will be among the most important events in the future. The Bible has much to say about the time when Christ will return to this world.

We will focus on the events relating to Christ's coming in the next three chapters. We will also discuss whether the Rapture, the gathering of the righteous to meet Christ, relates to the coming of Christ.

THE EVOLUTION OF MY RAPTURE POSITION

I want to discuss my original thinking on the Rapture first. I originally adopted a classic Pre-Wrath Rapture position that places the Rapture after the breaking of the sixth seal. This position argues:

- The great tribulation, which begins after the Antichrist sets up the abomination of desolation (Matt 24:15, Dan 9:27), is the wrath of Satan/Antichrist instead of the wrath of God.

- The wrath of God believers in Christ will not experience spans the seven trumpets and the seven bowl judgments.

My views later shifted towards a classic Post-Trib Rapture position as I studied more. This position posits:

- The Rapture will take place around the time the seventh trumpet sounds.

- The wrath of God believers in Christ will not experience will come after the seventh trumpet sounds.

The Post-Trib Rapture position differs from the Pre-Wrath position in the amount of time that the elect (those chosen by God to be saved) will endure persecution:

- The Pre-Wrath position posits that the persecution of the elect will last less than the forty-two month war against the saints.

- The Post-Trib position asserts that the persecution of the elect will encompass the forty-two month war against the saints.

My position on the Rapture evolved even further as time went on. My current view combines the Pre-Wrath Rapture and the Post-Trib Rapture positions. I believe each position has elements of truth with regard to the Rapture's timing. More specifically,:

- I agree with Pre-Wrath Rapture proponents that the Rapture will take place after the heavenly signs related to the sixth seal appear.

- However, I also agree with the Post-Trib Rapture proponents that these heavenly signs will not appear until near the time of the seventh trumpet's sounding.

My position is nuanced, so you may need to spend some time rereading what I present before you grasp it. However, you may find it compelling once you gain a good understanding of it.

Next, I will discuss four biblical facts that underpin my Rapture position. Then I will start to unveil a detailed sequence of events relating to Christ's coming.

FACTS UNDERPINNING MY RAPTURE POSITION

1. Christians Can Be Persecuted

The notion that believers in Christ will not go through persecution is unbiblical. In fact, 2 Timothy 3, a chapter with end time implications, states that all who live in Christ will face persecution:

(1) This know also, that in the last days perilous times shall come. (2) For men shall be lovers of their own selves, covetous, boasters, proud, blasphemers, disobedient to parents, unthankful, unholy,... (12) Yea, and all that will live godly in Christ Jesus shall suffer persecution. (2Tim 3:1-2, 12)

Believers in Christ should expect to face persecution leading up to the Rapture.[1]

2. Not Appointed to *Orge* Wrath

Even though believers in Christ are subject to persecution, the Bible indicates that they will be delivered from wrath:

> For God **hath not appointed us to wrath, but to obtain salvation by our Lord Jesus Christ**, (1 Thess 5:9)

> Much more then, being now justified by his blood, **we shall be saved from wrath through him**. (Rom 5:9)

> And to wait for his Son from heaven, whom he raised from the dead, even Jesus, which **delivered us from the wrath to come.** (1 Thess 1:10)

Many people interpret these verses to mean that believers in Christ are not subject to any wrath. However, few know that the Greek text distinguishes between different types of wrath through the words *orge* and *thumos*. Thayer defines:

- *Thumos* as "passion, angry heat, … anger forthwith boiling up and soon subsiding again".[2]
- *Orge* as "indignation which has arisen gradually and become more settled…"[3]

The difference between the two terms is the nature of the wrath.

- *Thumos* represents a temporary surge of anger that will rise and quickly subside.
- *Orge* represents anger that lasts for a prolonged period.

Regarding God's wrath in an end time context:

- You can think of *thumos* as the wrath that God will exhibit against the wicked as they refuse to respond to efforts encouraging them to repent.
- You can think of *orge* as God's longstanding wrath against the wicked, who He will punish with lasting consequences (i.e. eternity in the lake of fire).

The word *orge* appears in 1 Thessalonians 1:10, 5:9, and Romans 5:9. This means that *orge* is the type of wrath that believers in Christ are not subject to. Therefore, believers in Christ are not subject to God's deliberate, long-standing wrath against the wicked.

The Tribulation

The tribulation is not the *orge* wrath of God. We do not see the word *orge* used to depict tribulation. Instead, we see the Greek word *thlipsis* used to depict tribulation or afflictions:

> For in those days shall be affliction [*thlipsis*], such as was not from the beginning of the creation which God created unto this time, neither shall be. (Mark 13:19)

> But in those days, after that tribulation [*thlipsis*], the sun shall be darkened, and the moon shall not give her light, (Mark 13:24)

Those who equate the tribulation to the wrath of God that believers in Christ will avoid do not recognize this.

Wrath of Satan: The Great Tribulation

Satan will be full of wrath when he and his angels are cast from Heaven. He will wage war against his enemies, and this war represents the great tribulation:

> (12) …Woe to the inhabiters of the earth and of the sea! for **the devil is come down unto you, having great wrath**, because he knoweth that he hath but a short time…. (17) And **the dragon was wroth with the woman, and went to make war** with the remnant of her seed, which keep the commandments of God, and have the testimony of Jesus Christ. (Rev 12:12, 17)

Revelation 12:12-17 does not speak about the wrath of God. The passage speaks about the wrath of Satan. How does Revelation 12 depict the wrath of Satan?:

- Verse 12 uses the word *thumos*. Satan will lash out against his foes.

- Verse 17 uses the word *orge*. But this is not the *orge* wrath of God. It is Satan's *orge* wrath. Satan has a long-term grudge against his enemies, including those who have the testimony of Jesus.

The great tribulation is not part of the *orge* wrath of God that the Bible promises believers in Christ will not see. The great tribulation is the wrath of Satan, who will lash out against his long-term enemies.[4][5]

Revelation 15:1 states that the bowl judgments, the seven last plagues, will finish or complete the wrath of God:

And I saw another sign in heaven, great and marvellous, seven angels having the seven last plagues; for in them is filled up the wrath of God. (Rev 15:1)

This verse causes many to think the bowl judgments and the events that take place before them are part of the wrath of God that believers in Christ will not see. However, *orge* does not appear in Revelation 15:1. The verse uses *thumos* to depict the wrath of the bowl judgments.

The fact that the bowl judgments will complete or finish the *thumos* wrath means that every event before the bowl judgments is *thumos* wrath and is not *orge* wrath. In other words, God's *orge* wrath has not yet begun at the onset of the bowl judgments.

Revelation 16:2, 10-11 mention that the wicked will refuse to repent as they deal with the plagues of the bowl judgments. This is consistent with our definition of *thumos* when it comes to God's wrath in an end time context. God will exhibit wrath against the wicked as they refuse to repent.

Thumos Orge and the Day of the Lord

The wicked will be punished with very intense *orge*. Recall that the third angel of the three angels mentioned in Revelation 14 will warn people that anyone who worships the beast or receives the Mark of the Beast will drink the wine of the wrath of God that will be poured unmixed into the cup of the Lord's anger:

The same shall drink of the wine of the wrath of God, which is poured out without mixture into the cup of his indignation; and he shall be tormented with fire and brimstone in the presence of the holy angels, and in the presence of the Lamb: (Rev 14:10)

The "wrath" initially associated with the "wine of the wrath of God" is *thumos*. This wine will be poured without mixture or at full strength into the cup of the Lord's anger/*orge*.

Wine traditionally was mixed with water to weaken its effects. However, Revelation 14:10 describes the adding of the wine of the wrath to a cup of *orge* to enhance its potency. The Bible describes the powerful drink that the wicked will partake as *thumos orge*, and their suffering will be for eternity (Rev 14:11).[6]

The wicked will partake in this combination when it is time to unleash *orge* on the people of the earth. The reason for this timing is that *thumos orge* cannot be poured out without *orge* involved, while *thumos* in isolation will be poured out during the bowl judgments.

God will unleash *orge* during the Day of the Lord, a period most people view as synonymous with the wrath of God that believers in Christ will not face. The Apostle Paul wrote that believers in Christ are not appointed to *orge* when he discussed the Day of the Lord (1 Thess 5:2-3, 8-9).

Taking these passages together, we can approximate the beginning of *orge* and thereby *thumos orge* by finding when the Day of the Lord begins.[7] The start of the Day of the Lord will be a topic addressed in the coming chapters in detail.

3. God Can Preserve a Remnant

The Lord is more than capable of preserving His people as plagues harm the wicked. For instance, the Lord inflicted many plagues on the Egyptians and their animals while He protected the Israelites. In addition, Psalm 91 describes how the Lord can protect the righteous as the wicked around them are struck down:

> (7) A thousand shall fall at thy side, and ten thousand at thy right hand; but it shall not come nigh thee. (8) Only with thine eyes shalt thou behold and see the reward of the wicked. (9) Because thou hast made the Lord, which is my refuge, even the most High, thy habitation; (10) There shall no evil befall thee, neither shall any plague come nigh thy dwelling. (11) For he shall give his angels charge over thee, to keep thee in all thy ways. (Ps 91:7-11)

Revelation 15:1 defines the bowl judgments as the final plagues of God's *thumos*.[8] The Lord can preserve His people through these plagues, especially when it is recognized that the main recipients of the bowl judgments are the kingdom of the Antichrist and those who accept the Mark of the Beast.

4. Angels Will Gather the Wicked Before the Righteous

Psalm 91 teaches that God can protect a righteous person from harm as His wrath destroys the wicked around them. A major implication of this teaching is that a righteous person does not need to be removed from the earth to avoid being subjected to God's wrath. This concept is important to grasp because it will help you better understand the harvest of the earth at the end of the age.

Many assume that the harvest of the righteous will occur before the harvest of the wicked during the end times. However, Christ explained that the wicked will be gathered *before* the righteous and separated from the righteous at the end of the age. He illustrated these truths in the Parable of the Wheat and Tares and the Parable of the Dragnet.

The Parable of the Wheat and Tares

Matthew 13 records Christ teaching the Parable of the Wheat and Tares. Christ describes a man who plants wheat in his field. However, his enemy plants tares (a weed that resembles wheat when it is young) in the same field while he sleeps. This created a problem for the man.

The servants of the field ask the man if they should remove the tares from the field. The man tells the servants to not remove the tares because there is a risk that the wheat could get removed:

> (29) But he said, Nay; lest while ye gather up the tares, ye root up also the wheat with them. (30) **Let both grow together until the harvest: and in the time of harvest I will say to the reapers, Gather ye together first the tares, and bind them in bundles to burn them**: but gather the wheat into my barn. (Matt 13:29-30)

Christ said that the wheat and the tares will remain together *until* the time of harvest. The wheat will not be taken away from the field, nor will the tares be removed from the field before the harvest.

Christ revealed the meaning of the Parable of the Wheat and Tares to His disciples. The parable depicts the harvest of the wheat (the righteous) and tares (the wicked) at the end of the age. At that time, Christ will send His angels to harvest the earth:

> (37) He answered and said unto them, He that soweth the good seed is the Son of man; (38) The field is the world; the good seed are the children of the kingdom; but the tares are the children of the wicked one; (39) The enemy that sowed them is the devil; the harvest is the end of the world; and the reapers are the angels. (40) As therefore the tares are gathered and burned in the fire; so shall it be in the end of this world. (41) The Son of man shall send forth his angels, and they shall gather out of his kingdom all things that offend, and them which do iniquity; (42) And shall cast them into a furnace of fire: there shall be wailing and gnashing of teeth. (43) Then shall the righteous shine forth as the sun in the kingdom of their Father. Who hath ears to hear, let him hear. (Matt 13:37-43)

We can draw some meaningful conclusions from the Parable of the Wheat and Tares:

- The righteous and the wicked will be present on Earth until the end of the age as Christ stated that the wheat and tares will grow together until the end of the age.[9]

- The gathering of the wicked will take place before the gathering of the righteous given that the reapers (angels) will have instructions to gather the tares before they gather the wheat.

The Parable of the Dragnet

The Parable of the Dragnet reinforces the idea that the righteous will be present on Earth during the harvest of the earth at the end of the age. Christ explained that the wicked and the righteous will be present on Earth at the end of the age when the angels come to remove the wicked from the righteous and punish the wicked:

> (49) So shall it be at the end of the world: the angels shall come forth, **and sever the wicked from among the just**, (50) And shall cast them into the furnace of fire: there shall be wailing and gnashing of teeth. (Matt 13:49-50)

Like the Parable of the Wheat and Tares, the Parable of the Dragnet does not indicate that the righteous will disappear from the earth before or during the harvesting of the earth. The parable only mentions that the angels will sever the wicked from the righteous.

One Taken, One Left

Luke 17 also indicates that the harvest of the wicked will take place before the harvest of the righteous. Christ told His disciples that some people will be taken at the time of His coming while others will be left behind (Luke 17:34-36). Christ's disciples asked Him where people will be taken. Luke 17:37 records Christ's answer to their question:

> And they answered and said unto him, Where, Lord? And he said unto them, Wheresoever the body is, thither will the eagles be gathered together. (Luke 17:37)[10]

Christ's statement alludes to the gathering of birds that will transpire shortly before the final battle of the war of Armageddon (Rev 19:17-18), the subject of chapter twenty-one. The wicked will die during this battle, and their corpses will serve as subsistence for the birds that gather. I will discuss the gathering of the wicked further in coming chapters. Next, we will begin to look at events leading to Christ's coming.

JERUSALEM UNDER SIEGE

Ezekiel 7 and Isaiah 51 portray the end time siege of Jerusalem as the pouring of the Lord's fury:

- Ezekiel 7 warns the people in the land of Israel and the city of Jerusalem that the Lord will shortly pour out His wrath on them.

- Isaiah 51 describes Jerusalem after drinking from the cup of the Lord's fury or wrath.[11]

> (3) Now is the end come upon thee, and I will send mine anger upon thee, and will judge thee according to thy ways, and will recompense upon thee all thine abominations.... (5) Thus saith the Lord GOD; An evil, an only evil, behold, is come.... (8) Now will I shortly pour out my fury upon thee, and accomplish mine anger upon thee: and I will judge thee according to thy ways, and will recompense thee for all thine abominations. (Ezek 7:3, 5, 8)

Awake, awake, stand up, O Jerusalem, which hast drunk at the hand of the LORD the cup of his fury; thou hast drunken the dregs of the cup of trembling, and wrung them out. (Isa 51:17)

The siege of Jerusalem will leave the city in ruins. Isaiah describes the scene:

(18) There is none to guide her among all the sons whom she hath brought forth; neither is there any that taketh her by the hand of all the sons that she hath brought up. (19) These two things are come unto thee; who shall be sorry for thee? desolation, and destruction, and the famine, and the sword: by whom shall I comfort thee? (20) Thy sons have fainted, they lie at the head of all the streets, as a wild bull in a net: they are full of the fury of the Lord, the rebuke of thy God. (Isa 51:18-20, also see Ps 79)

The Cries for Help

At this desperate time, the survivors will cry out to the Lord for help. Joel 2 states that the surviving priests of Jerusalem will organize a solemn assembly. The priests and others will cry out to the Lord and call on Him for help:

(15) Blow the trumpet in Zion, sanctify a fast, call a solemn assembly: (16) Gather the people, sanctify the congregation, assemble the elders, gather the children, and those that suck the breasts: let the bridegroom go forth of his chamber, and the bride out of her closet. (17) Let the priests, the ministers of the Lord, weep between the porch and the altar, and let them say, Spare thy people, O Lord, and give not thine heritage to reproach, that the heathen should rule over them: wherefore should they say among the people, Where is their God? (Joel 2:15-17, also see Ps 79:1-3, Joel 1:13-15)

The solemn assembly and the cries for help at that time suggest that the gathering during the siege of Jerusalem may coincide with the Jewish holiday, Yom Kippur. The solemn assembly and the cries for help are consistent with the observance of Yom Kippur (Lev 23:27-28).

The Lord Responds to the Cries

The Lord will have mercy on His people (Isa 54:5-8, 57:15-18). He will respond decisively to the cries for help:

(18) **Then will the LORD be jealous for his land, and pity his people.** (19) **Yea, the LORD will answer** and say unto his people, Behold, I will send you corn, and wine, and oil, and ye shall be satisfied therewith: and I will no more make you a reproach among the heathen: (Joel 2:18-19, also see Isa 30:19, 42:14-16, Ps 102:17-21, 107:13-14, 17-19, Mic 7:7-10)

Isaiah 51:22-23 tells us that the Lord will respond by giving the cup that Jerusalem drank to those who attacked Jerusalem. These attackers will meet their demise:

(22) Thus saith thy Lord the LORD, and thy God that pleadeth the cause of his people, Behold, I have taken out of thine hand the cup of trembling, even the dregs of the cup of my fury; thou shalt no more drink it again: (23) But I will put it into the hand of them that afflict thee; which have said to thy soul, Bow down, that we may go over: and thou hast laid thy body as the ground, and as the street, to them that went over. (Isa 51:22-23)

LET'S PAUSE FOR A MOMENT

In this chapter, I introduced my Rapture position and described how the people of Israel will become so desperate that they will cry out to the Lord for help. We pause here, knowing that the Lord will respond to the calls of His people. Here is a look at where the events described in this chapter fit in our timeline:

Midpoint of the Tribulation: Dan 9:27 (Ch.7)

- Abomination of Desolation: Dan 9:27, Matt 24:15 (Ch.7)
- Antichrist's True Identity Revealed: 2Thess 2:3-4 (Ch.8)
- The False Prophet's Ministry Begins: Rev 13:11-16 (Ch.9)
- Great Tribulation Begins: Matt 24:21 (Ch.11)

5th Seal: Rev 6:9-11 (Ch.11)

Trumpets 1-5: Rev 8:7-13, 9:1-12 (Ch.11)

6th Trumpet: Rev 9:13-21 (Ch.12)

Three Angel Announcements: Rev 14:6-13 (Ch.14)

- Gospel of the Kingdom Preached: Rev 14:6-7, Matt 24:14 (Ch.14)

Bowls 1-6: Rev 16:1-16 (Ch.14)

Psalm 83 Attack & Siege of Jerusalem: Ps 83, Zech 12:1-3 (Ch.15)

- Death of the Two Witnesses: Rev 11:7-10 (Ch.15)
- *The People of Israel Cry for Help: Joel 2:15-17 (Ch.16)*

There's been much to absorb in this chapter, so I encourage you to reflect on what you have read and to reread any parts that might have been difficult to understand before continuing to the next chapter. I will continue to discuss the coming of Christ and the Rapture in the next chapter.

Notes

1. Rev 3:7-12 covers Christ's message to the church of Philadelphia. Christ

praised this church for their faithfulness. He promised to keep them from the time of trial that will affect the entire world:

Because thou hast kept the word of my patience, I also will keep thee from **the hour of temptation, which shall come upon all the world**, to try them that dwell upon the earth. (Rev 3:10)

Many view this as a promise that Christ will remove the whole Church before the tribulation. However, the Greek text does not support this view.

The Greek word for "keep" (*tēreō*) means "to guard (from loss or injury, prop. [properly], by keeping the eye upon...)" (Strong, James. "tēreō". *Strong's Exhaustive Concordance of the Bible*. New York, Cincinnati, Eaton & Mains; Jennings & Graham, 1890. G5083.). You can think of this as keeping or guarding your heart as Proverbs 4:23 encourages us to do. You don't remove your heart from your body. You watch over it.

The Greek word for "keep" in Rev 3:7-12:

○ Implies that the faithful believers of the church of Philadelphia will receive protection during a time of difficulty.

○ Conveys nothing about Christians being physically removed from the time of difficulty.

Furthermore, the word "temptation" in Greek (peirasmós) does not mean "wrath", specially the "wrath of God". Instead, the word means, "a putting to proof". (Ibid. "peirasmós". G3986) The great tribulation will be the ultimate test of where people's loyalties lie.

Overall, the Lord promises faithful believers of the church of Philadelphia a degree of protection from the testing that others will endure. The Lord will protect them while they remain on the earth. They have already proven themselves.

2. Thayer, Joseph Henry. "thumos" *Greek-English Lexicon of the New Testament*. 1889. New York, Cincinnati, Chicago: American Book Company, 1889.

3. Ibid. "orge".

4. Why does Satan have *orge* wrath against his enemies? Rev 12:1-6 traces the origins of Satan's grudge against them.

5. Some argue that the absence of the word "church" spanning from Rev 4 until Rev 22:15 is evidence that the Rapture of the Church will take place before the breaking of the seals. This is a weak argument because believers in Christ will face persecution on Earth in the events described from Rev 4 to Rev 22:15. For instance, Rev 6:9-11 and Rev 20:4 together suggest that people will be beheaded for their belief in Christ while Rev 12:17 tells us that people who "keep the commandments of God, and have the testimony of Jesus Christ." will be the target of Satan's wrath.

   The word "church" may not be in Rev 4 to Rev 22:15, but that does not mean that believers in Christ are absent from the situation on Earth.

6. *Thumos orge* and *orge* can both represent God's long-standing wrath against His enemies as the word *orge* is present. *Orge* denotes God's long-standing anger against the wicked. *Thumos orge* is a term that adds that God's long-standing anger against the wicked is very intense.

7. The term *thumos orge* appears in Rev 16:19 and Rev 19:15 and relates to the destruction of Babylon the Great and the defeat of the wicked gathered for battle, respectively. I show that these events will indeed take place during the Day of the Lord later in this book.

8. Many argue that the events related to the seven trumpets are a part of God's wrath. If the trumpets are a part of God's wrath, they are a part of His *thumos* since the succeeding bowl judgments will complete His *thumos*.

9. The finding that the righteous will remain on Earth until the end of the age is consistent with what Christ promised: "I am with you always, even unto the end of the world." (Matt 28:20) Christ made this promise to His followers, knowing they'll be present on Earth at the end of the age.

10. Matt 24:28 corresponds to Luke 17:37, and the word "carcase" appears instead of the word "body" in Matt 24:28.

11. Although Jerusalem will partake in the Lord's fury, it is not the wrath that the third angel of Revelation 14 warns that the wicked will partake in.

CHAPTER 17.

THE COMING OF CHRIST & THE RAPTURE: PART 2

We saw in the previous chapter that the people of Israel will become so desperate that they will cry out to the Lord for help. The Lord will respond to His people's cries for help, and His response is where we begin in this chapter.

THE SIXTH SEAL

Revelation 6:12-17 describes the breaking of the sixth seal and the many events that will follow:

(12) And I beheld when he had opened the sixth seal, and, lo, there was a great earthquake; and the sun became black as sackcloth of hair, and the moon became as blood; (13) And the stars of heaven fell unto the earth, even as a fig tree casteth her untimely figs, when she is shaken of a mighty wind. (14) And the heaven departed as a scroll when it is rolled together; and every mountain and island were moved out of their places. (15) And the kings of the earth, and the great men, and the rich men, and the chief captains, and the mighty men, and every bondman, and every free man, hid themselves in the dens and in the rocks of the mountains; (16) And said to the mountains and rocks, Fall on us, and hide us from the face of him that sitteth on the throne, and from the wrath of the Lamb: (17) For the great day of his wrath is come; and who shall be able to stand? (Rev 6:12-17)[1]

The End of the Great Tribulation

The *orge*/wrath of the Lamb in verse 17 alludes to the Day of the Lord, a period whose beginning relates to the coming of Christ, as we will later see. The Day of the Lord will arrive after startling signs appear in the heavens (the sky) and on the earth. Figure 17.1 describes the signs that will appear just before the Day of the Lord:[2]

Figure 17.1: The Signs Leading up to the Day of the Lord

- **The Darkening of the Sun**

- *Changing of the Moon's Appearance*

- <u>Signs in the Heavens</u>

- *<u>Massive Seismic Activity</u>*

Rev 6:12-14: (12) And I beheld when he had opened the sixth seal, and, lo, there was a great earthquake; and **the sun became black as sackcloth of hair**, *and the moon became as blood*; (13) <u>**And the stars of heaven fell unto the earth, even as a fig tree casteth her untimely figs, when she is shaken of a mighty wind**</u>. (14) <u>**And the heaven departed as a scroll when it is rolled together**</u>; *<u>and every mountain and island were moved out of their places.</u>*

Joel 2:30-31 (also see Acts 2:19-20): (30) <u>**And I will shew wonders in the heavens**</u> *<u>and in the earth</u>*, blood, and fire, and pillars of smoke. (31) **The sun shall be turned into darkness**, *and the moon into blood*, before the great and the terrible day of the LORD come.

Matt 24:29 (also see Mark 13:24-26): Immediately after the tribulation of those days shall **the sun be darkened**, *and the moon shall not give her light*, <u>**and the stars shall fall from heaven, and the powers of the heavens shall be shaken**</u>:

Luke 21:25-26: (25) **And there shall be signs in the sun**, *and in the moon*, **and in the stars**; *<u>and upon the earth distress of nations, with perplexity; the sea and the waves roaring</u>*; (26) Men's hearts failing them for fear, <u>**and for looking after those things which are coming on the earth**</u>: <u>**for the powers of heaven shall be shaken**</u>.

We can glean more insight about this period from these passages:[3]

- We saw that the breaking of the sixth seal will lead to the appearance of the signs in the heavens and on the earth. This means the great tribulation will end before the breaking of the sixth seal (Matt 24:29), and it will end before the Day of the Lord begins.

- People will be terrified of the signs that will appear.

The world will be full of darkness at this time (Isa 60:1-2). Psalm 102:25-27 and Hebrews 1:10-12 compare the heavens at this time to an old garment that is about to be replaced. Hebrews 1:12 alludes to the heavens rolling up like a scroll when it talks about the Lord folding the garment or vesture up:

> And as a vesture shalt thou fold them up, and they shall be changed: but thou art the same, and thy years shall not fail. (Heb 1:12)

Isaiah states that it will look like the heavens vanished:

> Lift up your eyes to the heavens, and look upon the earth beneath: for the heavens shall vanish away like smoke, and the earth shall wax old like a garment, and they that dwell therein shall die in like manner: but my salvation shall be for ever, and my righteousness shall not be abolished. (Isa 51:6)

Job adds that the heavens will be no more at this time:

> So man lieth down, and riseth not: **till the heavens be no more**, they shall not awake, nor be raised out of their sleep. (Job 14:12)

The reason I shared Job 14:12 is that it indicates the dead will not rise until these conditions arise. We will look at the resurrection of the righteous dead soon.

The darkness that will cover the world will make it very easy for people to notice the signs taking place. Some will be so afraid of the signs that will appear that they will seek refuge from them. Revelation 6 captures the panic that the people of Earth will have when they see the startling signs preceding the Day of the Lord:

> (15) And the kings of the earth, and the great men, and the rich men, and the chief captains, and the mighty men, and every bondman, and every free man, hid themselves in the dens and in the rocks of the mountains; (16) And said to the mountains and rocks, Fall on us, and hide us from the face of him that sitteth on the throne, and from the wrath of the Lamb: (17) For the great day of his wrath is come; and who shall be able to stand? (Rev 6:15-17, also see Isa 2:10, 19, Luke 21:25-26)

The people seeking refuge from the face of Him that sits on the throne indicates that they may see a heavenly dimension when the heavens roll up like a scroll. People at that time may even see a manifestation of God and His Son.

The Kingdom of God Is Near

The appearance of the heavenly signs not only signifies that the Day of the Lord (and the coming of Christ) is near. The appearance of the heavenly signs also means that the kingdom of God's arrival is near, according to Luke 21:25-31:

> (25) And there shall be signs in the sun, and in the moon, and in the stars; and upon the earth distress of nations, with perplexity; the sea and the waves roaring; (26) Men's hearts failing them for fear, and for looking after those things which are coming on the earth: for the powers of heaven shall be shaken... (29) And he spake to them a parable; Behold the fig tree, and all the trees; (30) When they now shoot forth, ye see and know of your own selves that summer is now nigh at hand. (31) So likewise ye, when ye see these things come to pass, know ye that **the kingdom of God is nigh at hand.** (Luke 21:25-26, 29-31)

Revelation 11 informs us that the kingdom of God will arrive on the earth after the seventh trumpet sounds. Therefore, the heavenly signs related to the sixth seal will likely appear shortly before the seventh trumpet sounds:

> (15) And the seventh angel sounded; and there were great voices in heaven, saying, **The kingdoms of this world are become the kingdoms of our Lord, and of his Christ; and he shall reign for ever and ever.** (16) And the four and twenty elders, which sat before God on their seats, fell upon their faces, and worshipped God, (17) Saying, We give thee thanks, O Lord God Almighty, which art, and wast, and art to come; because thou hast taken to thee thy great power, and hast reigned. (Rev 11:15-17)

The Raising of the Two Witnesses

Revelation 11:11-13 tells us that the Two Witnesses will rise from the dead and ascend to Heaven to the chagrin of all those who celebrated these men's death.[4] A great earthquake will take place in the same hour that the Two Witnesses ascend to Heaven:[5]

> (11) And after three days and an half the Spirit of life from God entered into them, and they stood upon their feet; and great fear fell upon them

which saw them. (12) And they heard a great voice from heaven saying unto them, Come up hither. And they ascended up to heaven in
a cloud; and their enemies beheld them. (13) And the same hour was
there a great earthquake, and the tenth part of the city fell, and in the
earthquake were slain of men seven thousand: and the remnant were
affrighted, and gave glory to the God of heaven. (Rev 11:11-13)

THE SEVENTH SEAL

Recall that the scroll with seven seals likely represents the title
deed of this planet. The breaking of the seventh seal will allow the
title deed of this world to be redeemed by our kinsman redeemer,
Christ, since all the requirements will be finally met. We will soon
see that the kingdoms of the world will indeed be officially declared
the property of God and Christ.

Heaven will be silent for a half hour after the breaking of the seventh seal (Rev 8:1). It is not fully clear why there will be a period
of silence in Heaven. However, Zephaniah indicates that this silence
could be from those in Heaven awed by the Lord as He readies to
unleash his full fury on the wicked:[6]

> Hold thy peace at the presence of the Lord GOD: for the day of the
> LORD is at hand: for the LORD hath prepared a sacrifice, he hath bid
> his guests. (Zep 1:7)

THE SEVENTH TRUMPET

Revelation 11:15-19 covers the period spanning from the sounding of the seventh trumpet to the destruction of the wicked. The
sounding of the seventh trumpet will usher in several events which
I believe are part of the "restitution of all things" mentioned in Acts
3:21 and by many prophets:[7]

- The ownership of the world will transfer from Satan to God and
  Christ, and they will reign for eternity (Rev 11:15-17, Dan 2:44).[8][9]

- Also, the *orge*/wrath of God will be underway (Rev 11:18-19)

- It will be time to judge the dead and reward the righteous (Rev
  11:18).[10]

The sounding of the seventh trumpet will also coincide with the completion of several events that I will discuss in the next several sections.

The Mystery of God Complete

The mystery of God will reach its completion at the time of the seventh trumpet:

> But in the days of the voice of the seventh angel, when he shall begin to sound, the mystery of God should be finished, as he hath declared to his servants the prophets. (Rev 10:7)

No consensus exists about what the mystery of God entails. But, I believe the coming of God and Christ's eternal reign at the sounding of the seventh trumpet most likely relates to its completion.

The upcoming reign of God and Christ is a development that many who know the Bible understand. However, many do not know this is a future reality since they do not believe in the Bible or take the time to study the Bible.

It is a development that even fewer people will know about during the end times. Most of the world will recognize the Antichrist as the world's ruler at that time.

This development is a mystery in a biblical sense. A biblical mystery is a hidden truth revealed to those receptive to God's words.[11]

Therefore, the completion of the mystery of God may come when the prophecies about the coming eternal reign of God and Christ come to fruition. However, it is not wise to dogmatic about what the mystery of God entails. Only God truly knows what the mystery is.

The End of the 70th Week of Daniel

Recall that several developments will begin to be brought about at the completion of the seventieth week of Daniel, including the bringing in of everlasting righteousness:

> Seventy weeks are determined upon thy people and upon thy holy city, to finish the transgression, and to make an end of sins, and to make reconciliation for iniquity, **and to bring in everlasting righteousness**, and to seal up the vision and prophecy, and to anoint the most Holy. (Dan 9:24)

The seventh trumpet relates to the end of the seventieth week of Daniel. The process to bring in everlasting righteousness will begin with the onset of God and Christ's eternal reign.

The End of the 42 Month-War with the Saints

Recall that the Antichrist will wage war with the saints for the forty-two months that cover the second half of the tribulation (Rev 13:5-7, Dan 7:21, 25-26). Revelation 12:17, 13:10, and 14:12 define who "the saints" represent in this context:

> And the dragon was wroth with the woman, and went to make war with the remnant of her seed, **which keep the commandments of God, and have the testimony of Jesus Christ**. So the dragon was enraged with the woman, and went off to make war with the rest of her children, (Rev 12:17)

> He that leadeth into captivity shall go into captivity: he that killeth with the sword must be killed with the sword. **Here is the patience and the faith of the saints**. (Rev 13:10)

> (12) **Here is the patience of the saints:** here are *they that keep the commandments of God, and the faith of Jesus*. (13) And I heard a voice from heaven saying unto me, Write, Blessed are the dead which die in the Lord from henceforth: Yea, saith the Spirit, that they may rest from their labours; and their works do follow them. (Rev 14:12-13)

This group must refer to Christians and can be no other group besides Christians since Christians believe in Jesus Christ:

- The reference to the patience of the saints in Revelation 13:10 and Revelation 14:12 affirms that Christians will be on the planet enduring hardship during the reign of the Antichrist.

- The recognition of those who die for Christ from now on in Revelation 14:13 suggests the Rapture has not yet taken place at that point of Revelation 14's chronology since the dead in Christ shall rise when the Rapture finally transpires (1 Thess 4:16).

Why the Judgment of the Righteous Did Not Occur Earlier

The judgment of the righteous will not take place until after the seventh trumpet sounds and after ownership of the earth transfers to Christ and God when Antichrist's forty-two month reign ends:

(17) Saying, We give thee thanks, O Lord God Almighty, which art, and wast, and art to come; because thou hast taken to thee thy great power, and hast reigned. (18) And the nations were angry, and thy wrath is come, and **the time of the dead, that they should be judged, and that thou shouldest give reward unto thy servants the prophets, and to the saints, and them that fear thy name, small and great**; and shouldest destroy them which destroy the earth. (Rev 11:17-18)

The judgment of the righteous could not take place beforehand because the dead rested and the living saints had to remain patient as they endure hardship (Rev 13:10, 14:12-13). Each of these groups will become available to be judged with the impending Rapture.

The Fullness of the Gentiles Arrives & Hardening Ends

Recall that the Apostle Paul noted that a hardening of a portion of Israel began after Israel rejected Christ (Rom 11:1-8). He added that their rejection of Christ led to an effort to bring salvation to the Gentiles. The purpose of this effort is to make Israel jealous:

(11) I say then, Have they stumbled that they should fall? God forbid: but rather through their fall salvation is come unto the Gentiles, for to provoke them to jealousy. (12) Now if the fall of them be the riches of the world, and the diminishing of them the riches of the Gentiles; how much more their fulness? (Rom 11:11-12)

Meanwhile, the hardening impacting a portion of Israel will continue until the fullness of the Gentiles arrives:

For I would not, brethren, that ye should be ignorant of this mystery, lest ye should be wise in your own conceits; that blindness [hardening] in part is happened to Israel, until the fulness of the Gentiles be come in. (Rom 11:25)

The word "fulness" in verse 25 is rendered *pleroma* in Greek, which can mean "completion".[12] This means that something related to the Gentiles will reach its end as Israel's hardening ends.

Given that Paul wrote about the effort to save the Gentiles, *the arrival of the fullness of the Gentiles will likely signify that the present effort to save the Gentiles will reach its end.* In its place, an effort to save Israel will start as their hardening ends.

Paul noted that this endeavor will coincide with the coming of the Deliverer-Christ:

> And so all Israel shall be saved: as it is written, There shall come out of Sion the Deliverer, and shall turn away ungodliness from Jacob: (Rom 11:26)

The fullness of the Gentiles will likely come at this point during the end times because it will be time for Christ to come to save His people and to gather His elect.

THE LORD GOES INTO ACTION

The Lord will go to punish the wicked worldwide quickly after the seventh trumpet sounds. Many end time passages describe the Lord arising to punish the earth, including:

- Isaiah 2:20-21, 42:13-15, 59:16-18
- Zephaniah 3:8
- Psalm 102:13, 15-16[13]

Here is Isaiah 42:13-15:

> (13) The Lord shall go forth as a mighty man, he shall stir up jealousy like a man of war: he shall cry, yea, roar; he shall prevail against his enemies. (14) I have long time holden my peace; I have been still, and refrained myself: now will I cry like a travailing woman; I will destroy and devour at once. (15) I will make waste mountains and hills, and dry up all their herbs; and I will make the rivers islands, and I will dry up the pools. (Isa 42:13-15)

THE SEVENTH BOWL JUDGMENT

The seventh bowl judgment will be the most eventful of the bowl judgments (Rev 16:17-21). Many events will transpire after its pouring, but we focus solely on the destruction of Babylon the Great (Rev 16:19) now because it is likely an event that will take place just before Christ's coming.

Recall that Daniel told Nebuchadnezzar that a stone (the kingdom of God) will destroy the kingdoms of the statue in his dream (including the kingdom of the Antichrist) before it grows to fill the whole world (Dan 2:34-35, 44-45). The arrival of the kingdom of God after the seventh trumpet sounds means the time to destroy the kingdom of the Antichrist approaches.

Why Babylon Will Be Judged Severely

God will punish Babylon the Great for her arrogance (Rev 18:7, Isa 47:7-8, 10) and her many sins (Jer 51:9, Rev 18:4-5). He will accomplish this through the ten kings after He puts it into their hearts to destroy Babylon the Great:

> (16) And the ten horns which thou sawest upon the beast, these shall hate the whore, and shall make her desolate and naked, and shall eat her flesh, and burn her with fire. (17) For God hath put in their hearts to fulfil his will, and to agree, and give their kingdom unto the beast, until the words of God shall be fulfilled. (Rev 17:16-17)

The ten kings may also want to destroy Babylon the Great to pay back the Antichrist for his brutal treatment of the world. Habakkuk suggests the Antichrist will be plundered because he has plundered many nations and has caused much violence:

> (6) Shall not all these take up a parable against him, and a taunting proverb against him, and say, Woe to him that increaseth that which is not his! how long? and to him that ladeth himself with thick clay! (7) Shall they not rise up suddenly that shall bite thee, and awake that shall vex thee, and thou shalt be for booties unto them? (8) Because thou hast spoiled many nations, all the remnant of the people shall spoil thee; because of men's blood, and for the violence of the land, of the city, and of all that dwell therein. (Hab 2:6-8)

Given that Babylon the Great will be key to the world economy under the Antichrist (Rev 17:3, 18:11-17, 22-23), the ten kings may destroy her as an act of revenge against his exploitation of the world. They will desolate her with fire (Rev 17:16-17, 18:6, 8).

Heaven's Reaction

The fall of Babylon the Great is significant because it means that the alliance between the ten kings and the Antichrist is over. Their alliance will only remain until the fall of Babylon the Great (Rev 17:16-17). The end of the alliance signifies that the reign of the Antichrist is over because he no longer has control of the ten kings.

Heaven will rejoice after the fall of Babylon the Great. Revelation 19:1-6 records the celebration:

> (1) And after these things I heard a great voice of much people in heaven, saying, Alleluia; Salvation, and glory, and honour, and power, unto the Lord our God:... (6) And I heard as it were the voice of a great multitude, and as the voice of many waters, and as the voice of mighty thunderings, saying, Alleluia: for the Lord God omnipotent reigneth

Verse 6 refers to a "great multitude", a huge group of people who will die during the great tribulation (Rev 7:9-17). The participation of these dead people in this celebration in Heaven means that the resurrection of the righteous has still not occurred yet. However, they will not have to wait much longer for their resurrection since Christ's coming is imminent.

LET'S PAUSE FOR A MOMENT

We learned that the Lord's response to His people's calls for help will come at a critical point in history:

- The sixth and seventh seals will be broken, and the seventh trumpet will sound as the Lord prepares to intervene for His people.

- The persecution of Christians will end while the kingdoms of the world will revert to Christ and God.

Here is a look at where the key events described in this chapter fit in our timeline:

Probable Sequence of Events: Ch.17

Psalm 83 Attack & Siege of Jerusalem: Ps 83, Zech 12:1-3, (Ch.15)

- Death of the Two Witnesses: Rev 11:7-10 (Ch.15)
- The People of Israel Cry for Help: Joel 2:15-17; (Ch.16)

End of the Great Tribulation: Matt 24:29 (Ch.17)

6th Seal: Rev 6:12-17 (Ch.17)

- *The Raising of the Two Witnesses: Rev 11:11-13 (Ch.17)*

7th Seal: Rev 8:1 (Ch.17)

7th Trumpet: Rev 11:15-19 (Ch.17)

- *Kingdom of God & Christ Established on Earth: Rev 11:15 (Ch.17)*
- *End of the Tribulation: Dan 9:24-27 (Ch.17)*
- *Mystery of God Complete: Rev 10:7 (Ch.17)*
- *Fullness of the Gentiles Reached: Rom 11:25 (Ch.17)*

7th Bowl Poured: Rev 16:17-21 (Ch.17)

- *Babylon the Great Destroyed: Rev 16:19, Rev 18 (Ch.17)*

Once again, I encourage you to reflect on what you have read and to reread any parts that might have been difficult to understand before continuing to the next chapter.

Notes

1. The wicked on Earth will ask, "Who shall be able to stand?" in the coming Day of the Lord (Rev 6:17). Jesus answered the question in Luke 21:25-28, 34-36. Believers in Christ will be able to stand!

2. Isa 34:1-4, Joel 3:14-15, Heb 12:24, 26, and Hag 2:6 also refer to the signs that will appear before the start of the Day of the Lord.

3. I believe the great tribulation will last for 1,260 days. Some will argue that the great tribulation cannot last for 1,260 days. They cite Mark 13:20, which states:

   And except that the Lord had shortened those days, no flesh should be saved: but for the elect's sake, whom he hath chosen, he hath shortened the days. (Mark 13:20, also see Matt 24:22)

   The problem with the argument that the great tribulation will be less than 1,260 days is that the Antichrist's persecution of the saints will span 1,260 days or 3.5 years (Dan 7:25, Rev 12:6, 14).

   Christ's statement about the shortening of the days is part of a description about how bad the great tribulation will be. The great tribulation will be an unprecedented time of persecution (Matt 24:21, Mark 13:19).

   I believe Matt 24:22 and Mark 13:20 are statements about how bad the great tribulation will be rather than statements about how it will last for less than 1,260 days. These verses indicate that the persecution will be so severe that there would be no flesh left to save if God allowed it to continue indefinitely.

   Recall that one of the Antichrist's goals will be to destroy those who do not follow him. He would eventually wipe out all his enemies if he were allowed to continue indefinitely.

4. The raising of the Two Witnesses may be a prelude to the upcoming resurrection of the righteous dead that will take place when Christ comes.

5. The term "great earthquake" appears only three times in the Book of Revelation. The term appears with the breaking of the sixth seal, the raising of the Two Witnesses, and the pouring of the seventh bowl judgment.

   The great earthquake of the seventh bowl judgment will exceed all other earthquakes since it will be the biggest in history (Rev 16:18). I believe that the great earthquake linked to the raising of the Two Witnesses may relate to the great earthquake of the sixth seal given that these similar disasters will occur late in the end time timeline.

6. Dan 7:9-11 records the convening of a court in Heaven. This event may take place at this time given that the demise of the Antichrist and his empire will begin after the court renders judgment.

7. Acts 3:21 declares that Christ must remain in Heaven until the "restitution of all things". Therefore, Christ's coming cannot take place until after the seventh trumpet sounds since He will not gain ownership of the world until it sounds.

8. Ps 2:6-8 touches on Christ being given the kingdoms of the earth to reign over.

9. Debate exists about the timing of Dan 7:13-14. Some believe the ascension of Christ fulfilled Dan 7:13-14, while others believe the passage remains unfulfilled. If the passage remains unfulfilled, it may describe the handover of Earth's ownership to Christ as the world watches.

10. The judgment of the dead and rewarding of the righteous refers to the "Bema Seat Judgment". Each person will receive a reward according to what they did on Earth in this judgment (Rom 14:10-12, 1Cor 3:13-15, and 2Cor 5:9-10). I discuss the Bema Seat Judgment further in chapter twenty-three.

11. See the appendix section titled "Babylon the Great's Identity" for a full explanation of what a biblical mystery is.

12. Strong, James. "Pleroma". Strong's Exhaustive Concordance of the Bible. New York, Cincinnati, Eaton & Mains; Jennings & Graham, 1890. G4138.

13. Isa 26:20-21, Isa 30:27-28, and Nah 1:2, 5-8 may also describe the Lord arising to punish the earth. Isa 33:9-12 may also relate to passages that describe the Lord arising to punish the earth.

CHAPTER 18

THE COMING OF CHRIST & THE RAPTURE: PART 3

We just learned that the Lord's response to His people's calls for help will come at a critical point in history. He will come to save His people, and His arrival is what we will focus on next.

THE COMING OF CHRIST

The majesty of Christ's coming is something that the human mind cannot fully grasp until it occurs. The best we can do is to look at the details the Bible provides us to get a sense of the scene's majesty.[1]

He Will Come in the Clouds

A cloud received Christ when He ascended to Heaven after His first coming (Acts 1:9). The disciples who watched His ascension were told that He will return in like manner (Acts 1:11).

Indeed, Christ will come in the clouds of Heaven when He returns. Many passages speak of Him coming in the clouds, including Matthew 24:30, 26:63-64, Mark 13:26, 14:60-62, and Revelation 1:7, 14:14-16). Here is Matthew 24:30:

> And then shall appear the sign of the Son of man in heaven: and then shall all the tribes of the earth mourn, and **they shall see the Son of man coming in the clouds of heaven** with power and great glory.

Revelation 19:11-21 is also about the coming of Christ. However, the passage depicts Christ riding on a white horse:

> And I saw heaven opened, and behold a white horse; and he that sat

upon him was called Faithful and True, and in righteousness he doth judge and make war. (Rev 19:11)

We can reconcile verse 11 with the passages about Christ coming in the clouds by recognizing that Revelation 19:11-21 is full of figurative language. For instance, the passage also depicts a sword coming out of Christ's mouth that will slay the wicked (Rev 19:15, 21).

The Bible is clear that Christ will come in the clouds of Heaven. Therefore, it's likely that the white horse imagery is figurative, like the sword coming out of Christ's mouth is figurative. The depiction of Christ riding on a white horse is a figurative way to say He will come ready for battle. He will come to destroy the wicked.

Angels Will Accompany Him

Revelation 19 also tells us that the armies of Heaven will accompany Christ at the time of His coming:

And the armies which were in heaven followed him upon white horses, clothed in fine linen, white and clean. (Rev 19:14, also see Isa 66:15)

The idea that heavenly armies will accompany the Lord is consistent with passages that state that angels will accompany Christ when He comes. Many angels will accompany Christ when He comes:

And to you who are troubled rest with us, when the Lord **Jesus shall be revealed from heaven with his mighty angels,** (2Thess 1:7, also see Mark 8:38, Jude 1:14-15, Matt 16:27, 25:31)

The Lord Will Come with Fire

2 Thessalonians 1:7-9 provides us with an intriguing detail about the coming of Christ. Christ will appear with flaming fire around Him intending to take vengeance on those who do not know God and fail to obey the gospel of Christ:

(7) And to you who are troubled rest with us, when the Lord Jesus shall be revealed from heaven with his mighty angels, (8) In flaming fire taking vengeance on them that know not God, and that obey not the gospel of our Lord Jesus Christ: (9) Who shall be punished with everlasting destruction from the presence of the Lord, and from the glory of his power; (2Thess 1:7-9)

Many other Bible prophecy passages also depict the Lord coming with fire, including:

- Isaiah 29:6-7, 30:27-28, 66:15-16
- Psalm 50:1-3, 97:1-4

Here are two key details we can glean from these passages:

- Isaiah 29:6-7 (and Isaiah 30:27 onward) concern the Lord's coming to defeat the nations who seek to destroy Jerusalem. This detail reinforces the idea that the Lord will come after the siege of Jerusalem is underway:

> (6) Thou shalt be visited of the LORD of hosts **with thunder, and with earthquake, and great noise, with storm and tempest, and the flame of devouring fire**. (7) And the multitude of all the nations that fight against Ariel [Jerusalem], even all that fight against her and her munition, and that distress her, shall be as a dream of a night vision. (Isa 29:6-7)

- Psalm 97:1 indicates that the context of the Lord's coming with fire is after He begins His reign over the earth. This detail reaffirms that the Lord's coming will take place after the seventh trumpet sounds:

> (1) The LORD reigneth; let the earth rejoice; let the multitude of isles be glad thereof. (2) Clouds and darkness are round about him: righteousness and judgment are the habitation of his throne. (3) **A fire goeth before him, and burneth up his enemies round about**. (4) His lightnings enlightened the world: the earth saw, and trembled. (Ps 97:1-4)

All Will See & Mourn

The awesome coming of the Lord will capture the attention of everyone.[2] Christ stated that everyone will see Him appear with great power and glory when He arrives:[3]

> And then shall appear the sign of the Son of man in heaven: and then shall all the tribes of the earth mourn, and they shall see the Son of man coming in the clouds of heaven **with power and great glory**. (Matt 24:30, also see Mark 13:26, Ps 97:3-6, 102:15-16)

All nations will mourn when He comes (Rev 1:7).

The Gathering of the Wicked

Recall that the harvest of the wicked will take place before the harvest of the righteous. If the kings of the earth and their armies have already assembled for battle before Christ's coming, whom will the angels gather at Christ's coming? Christ stated that His angels will gather all things that offend and practice lawlessness:

> The Son of man shall send forth his angels, and they shall gather out of his kingdom all things that offend, and them which do iniquity; (Matt 13:41)

This refers to those who will accept the Mark of the Beast. Recall that the third of three angels mentioned in Revelation 14 will warn that those who worship the beast and have the Mark of the Beast will be tormented with fire and brimstone in the presence of angels and Christ (Rev 14:9-11).

Therefore, Christ's angels will gather those with the Mark of the Beast before they gather the righteous. Where will the angels take those with the Mark of the Beast?

We learned that the angels will take the wicked to the battlefield of the final battle where birds will be ready to feast on the dead bodies that will come from the battle (Luke 17:34-37). Thus, anyone with the Mark of the Beast who did not travel to take part in the war of Armageddon will ultimately find themselves on the battlefield for the final battle of this war.

The Gathering of the Righteous

The Last Trump

1 Thessalonians 4:16 and Matthew 24:31 indicate that a great trumpet of God will sound at the time when the Rapture takes place:

> And he shall send his angels **with a great sound of a trumpet**, and they shall gather together his elect from the four winds, from one end of heaven to the other. (Matt 24:31)

> For the Lord himself shall descend from heaven with a shout, with the voice of the archangel, **and with the trump of God**: and the dead in Christ shall rise first: (1 Thess 4:16)

The Apostle Paul added that the trumpet which will sound before the Rapture is the "last trump":

(51) Behold, I shew you a mystery; We shall not all sleep, but we shall all be changed, (52) In a moment, in the twinkling of an eye, at the last trump: for the trumpet shall sound, and the dead shall be raised incorruptible, and we shall be changed. (1Cor 15:51-52)

Controversy exists about the significance of the term "last trump". Some argue that the last trump does not relate to the seven trumpets of Revelation. For instance, some posit that a special trumpet will sound multiple times during the Rapture. In this scenario:

- The resurrection of the righteous dead would occur after the first sounding.

- The transformation of the righteous living would occur after the second sounding.

Meanwhile, others argue that the last trump absolutely relates to the time when the seventh trumpet sounds.[4] The detail provided in Matthew 24:31 about who will sound the trumpet (Christ) is important. It may help us identify which event(s) constitutes the sounding of the last trump.

The key to finding which event(s) may constitute the sounding of the last trump is to find when the Lord will sound a trump in the latter stages of the end times. Some assume that the seventh trumpet is the last trump as it is the final trumpet mentioned in the Book of Revelation. However, the seventh trumpet may not be the "last trump" discussed by Paul because an angel will sound that trumpet (Rev 11:15).

This implies that the last trump may be a different trumpet that will sound after the seventh trumpet sounds. Zechariah 9:14, part of a passage that describes the Lord defending the residents of Jerusalem, mentions that the Lord will sound the trumpet when He arises to defend His people. Given that the Lord will rise to action after the seventh trumpet sounds, the trumpet in Zechariah 9:14 is likely the trump of God of 1 Thessalonians 4:16 (and the "last trump") as the Lord will be the One who will sound the trump of God:

And the LORD shall be seen over them, and his arrow shall go forth as the lightning: **and the Lord GOD shall blow the trumpet**, and shall go with whirlwinds of the south. (Zech 9:14)

Therefore, Matthew 24:31, Zechariah 9:14, and 1 Thessalonians 4:16 describe the Lord sounding a trumpet, but from different perspectives: Matthew 24:31 and 1 Thessalonians 4:16 relate to the Rapture, while Zechariah 9:14 relates to the Lord arising to help His people.

The Dead and Living Join Christ

The righteous dead and the living righteous will join Christ and be glorified when He comes (1Thess 5:9-10, Col 3:4). Everyone who will join Christ will come to Him with an incorruptible body. The dead will be raised possessing a spiritual body while those alive at Christ's coming will experience a transformation:

(42) So also is the resurrection of the dead. It is sown in corruption; it is raised in incorruption:... (44) It is sown a natural body; it is raised a spiritual body. There is a natural body, and there is a spiritual body.... (52) In a moment, in the twinkling of an eye, at the last trump: for the trumpet shall sound, and **the dead shall be raised incorruptible, and we shall be changed**. (1Cor 15:42, 44, 52)

The dead will rise first when Christ arrives. Then believers alive at that time will be caught up in the air to join Christ:

Then we which are alive and remain shall be caught up together with them in the clouds, to meet the Lord in the air: and so shall we ever be with the Lord. (1Thess 4:17)

The Greek word for "meet" in 1 Thessalonians 4:17 is *apantesis*. According to *Strong's Exhaustive Concordance, apantesis* means "a (friendly) encounter".[5] However, some argue that the word's usage in the Bible indicates that believers will not only meet Christ but also accompany Him as He travels from the air to Earth.

Apantesis is a word that rarely appears in the Bible. Beyond 1 Thessalonians 4:17, the word only appears in Matthew 25 and Acts 28:15. Each of these instances describes people meeting someone and then accompanying them to their destination. We will highlight the Parable of the Ten Virgins in Matthew 25 since it is about the coming of Christ:

(1) Then shall the kingdom of heaven be likened unto ten virgins, which took their lamps, and went forth to meet [*apantesis*] the bridegroom.... (6) And at midnight there was a cry made, Behold, the bridegroom cometh; go ye out to meet [*apantesis*] him. (7) Then all those virgins arose, and trimmed their lamps. (8) And the foolish said unto the wise, Give us of your oil; for our lamps are gone out. (9) But the wise answered, saying, Not so; lest there be not enough for us and you: but go ye rather to them that sell, and buy for yourselves. (10) And while they went to buy, the bridegroom came; and they that were ready went in with him to the marriage: and the door was shut. (Matt 25:1, 6-10)

Apantesis appears twice in Matthew 25. The prepared virgins (the righteous) meet the bridegroom (Christ) when He comes. These virgins do not stay where they are at. They come to the bridegroom as He arrives. They meet the bridegroom, and they accompany Him to His destination.

Given how *apantesis* is used, it is likely that the righteous will accompany Christ to Earth after they meet Him in the air.

LET'S PAUSE FOR A MOMENT

The Rapture position presented in the past three chapters is unlikely one that most people are familiar with, so it may take time for most readers to grasp it. Therefore, do not feel bad if you feel the need to restudy any aspects of the Rapture position I've presented. Here is a look at where the key events described in this chapter fit in our timeline:

Probable Sequence of Events: Ch.18

Psalm 83 Attack & Siege of Jerusalem: Ps 83, Zech 12:1-3, (Ch.15)

- Death of the Two Witnesses: Rev 11:7-10 (Ch.15)
- The People of Israel Cry for Help: Joel 2:15-17 (Ch.16)

End of the Great Tribulation: Matt 24:29 (Ch.17)

6th Seal: Rev 6:12-17 (Ch.17)

- The Raising of the Two Witnesses: Rev 11:11-13 (Ch.17)

7th Seal: Rev 8:1 (Ch.17)

7th Trumpet: Rev 11:15-19 (Ch.17)

- Kingdom of God & Christ Established on Earth: Rev 11:15 (Ch.17)
- End of the Tribulation: Dan 9:24-27 (Ch.17)
- Mystery of God Complete: Rev 10:7 (Ch.17)
- Fullness of the Gentiles Reached: Rom 11:25 (Ch.17)

7th Bowl Poured: Rev 16:17-21 (Ch.17)

- Babylon the Great Destroyed: Rev 16:19, Rev 18 (Ch.17)

The Coming of Christ: Matt 24:30 (Ch.18)

- *Gathering of the Wicked: Matt 13:41 (Ch.18)*
- *Gathering of the Righteous/the Rapture: Matt 24:31 (Ch.18)*

The next two chapters should help you comprehend my Rapture position better. I will discuss the Day of the Lord, including the relationship between the Rapture and the Day of the Lord.

Notes

1. Matt 24:36 indicates that no one knows the exact moment when Christ will return: *"But of that day and hour knoweth no man, no, not the angels of heaven, but my Father only."*

   I want to emphasize that I have not told you the exact date or hour that Christ will come in this book. Also, Christ's statement does not mean that we cannot know the general time frame that He will come. If we cannot know the general time frame, Christ would not have gave us details about what events will transpire just before His coming.

2. One of the Greek words used to describe Christ's coming is *parousia*, which means "coming" or "presence" (Strong, James. "parousia". *Strong's Exhaustive Concordance of the Bible*. New York, Cincinnati, Eaton & Mains; Jennings & Graham, 1890. G3952.). Some argue that *parousia* refers to either Christ's (supposed) coming before the start of the tribulation or Christ's coming after the tribulation. I believe that *parousia*, in an end time context, only refers to Christ's coming after the tribulation.

   The *parousia* of Christ will involve the resurrection of the righteous dead before the righteous living ascends to join Christ in the air:

   (15) For this we say unto you by the word of the Lord, that we which are alive and remain unto the coming [*parousia*] of the Lord shall not prevent them which are asleep. (16) For the Lord himself shall descend from heaven with a shout, with the voice of the archangel, and with the trump of God: and the dead in Christ shall rise first: (17) Then we which are alive and remain shall be caught up together with them in the clouds, to meet the Lord in the air: and so shall we ever be with the Lord. (1 Thess 4:15-17)

   2 Thess 2 gives us key information about the timing of the *parousia*. The *parousia* in 2 Thess 2 is the same *parousia* in 1 Thess 4:15-17. We know this because 2 Thess 2:1 connects Christ's *parousia* with the gathering of the righteous. The Apostle Paul warned that the *parousia* will not come until after the falling away and after the Antichrist proclaims to be God:

   (1) Now we beseech you, brethren, by the coming [*parousia*] of our Lord Jesus Christ, and by our gathering together unto him,... (3) Let no man deceive you by any means: for that day shall not come, except there come a falling away first, and that man of sin be revealed, the son of perdition;

(2Thess 2:1, 3)

Furthermore, Paul suggested that the *parousia* of Christ relates to the downfall of the Antichrist, an event that will come after the tribulation:

And then shall that Wicked be revealed, whom the Lord shall consume with the spirit of his mouth, and shall destroy with the brightness of his coming [*parousia*]: (2Thess 2:8)

2Thess 2:8 also indicates that the *parousia* of Christ will be a visible event as brightness will be part of Christ's *parousia*. Christ confirmed His *parousia* will be a visible event when He compared it to a lightning strike:

For as the lightning cometh out of the east, and shineth even unto the west; so shall also the coming [*parousia*] of the Son of man be. (Matt 24:27)

Thus, the *parousia* of Christ will not be a secret event like some teach.

I've studied many end time verses where the word *"parousia"* appears. I do not see how these verses can describe different comings. *Parousia* describes just one coming: the coming of Christ after the tribulation.

3. Christ said that the gathering of the "elect" will come at His Coming (Matt 24:30-31, Mark 13:26-27). Some argue that the elect are not Christians. However, the elect are linked to Christians in many places, including Col 3:11-12, Titus 1:1, Rom 8:28-33, and Rev 17:14. Luke 17:23-18:8 also indicate that the elect are Christians.

4. I believe the "last trump" relates to the time when the seventh trumpet will sound. Scripture strongly suggests the coming of Christ and the gathering of His elect will take place shortly after the seventh trumpet sounds.

5. Strong, James. "apantesis". *Strong's Exhaustive Concordance of the Bible*. New York, Cincinnati, Eaton & Mains; Jennings & Graham, 1890. G529.

CHAPTER 19.

THE DAY OF THE LORD DEFINED: PART 1

The Day of the Lord is among the most important end time topics. The Day of the Lord is a future period that will encompass many events related to Christ's arrival and reign on Earth, including:

- The pouring of the *orge* and *thumos orge* wrath of God on the wicked.
- The saving of the people of Israel.

The Day of the Lord is also among the most controversial Bible prophecy topics. Many disagree about when the Day of the Lord will begin and how long it will last.

I have suggested that the Day of the Lord will not start until after the tribulation by not discussing the Day of the Lord in detail until now. This placement is a minority position because most believe the Day of the Lord will begin at the start of tribulation.

The purpose of the next two chapters is to clarify when the Day of the Lord will begin and to examine how long it will last.

THE DAY OF THE LORD AND THE RAPTURE

Several places in the Bible indicate that the arrival of the Day of the Lord closely relates to the Rapture. For example, Christ compared His coming, particularly the Rapture, to the coming of a thief when He spoke of His coming and the end of the age:

(42) Watch therefore: for ye know not what hour your Lord doth come.
(43) But know this, that if the goodman of the house had known in

what **watch the thief would come**, he would have watched, and would not have suffered his house to be broken up. (Matt 24:42-43)

Remember therefore how thou hast received and heard, and hold fast, and repent. If therefore thou shalt not watch, **I will come on thee as a thief**, and thou shalt not know what hour I will come upon thee. (Rev 3:3)

Similarly, the Apostle Paul and Peter compared the arrival of the Day of the Lord to the coming of a thief in the night:

(2) For yourselves know perfectly that **the day of the Lord so cometh as a thief in the night**. (3) For when they shall say, Peace and safety; then sudden destruction cometh upon them, as travail upon a woman with child; and they shall not escape. (1Thess 5:2-3)

But the day of the Lord will come as a thief in the night; in the which the heavens shall pass away with a great noise, and the elements shall melt with fervent heat, the earth also and the works that are therein shall be burned up. (2Pet 3:10)

The thief comparisons made by Paul, Peter, and Christ suggest the Day of the Lord's arrival and the Rapture are closely related events. This idea is advanced further when Peter mentioned the coming of Christ and the Day of the Lord in the same passage (2Pet 3:3-10).

The idea that the coming of the Day of the Lord and the Rapture are closely related events is also in 1 Thessalonians 5. Paul spoke of the Rapture at the end of 1 Thessalonians 4. He continued to discuss the same general time frame of the Rapture when he addressed the coming of the Day of the Lord in 1 Thessalonians 5:

(4:16) For the Lord himself shall descend from heaven with a shout, with the voice of the archangel, and with the trump of God: and the dead in Christ shall rise first: (4:17) Then we which are alive and remain shall be caught up together with them in the clouds, to meet the Lord in the air: and so shall we ever be with the Lord.... (5:1) But of the times and the seasons, brethren, ye have no need that I write unto you. (5:2) For yourselves know perfectly that the day of the Lord so cometh as a thief in the night. (1Thess 4:16-5:2)

Therefore, we can conclude that the Rapture and the onset of the Day of the Lord are closely connected events that will occur around the same time.

THEORIES ON THE LENGTH OF THE DAY OF THE LORD

The length of the Day of the Lord is a topic of debate. Some believe that the Day of the Lord will last for the length of a day, while others believe that the Day of the Lord will last precisely one thousand years. Some even believe, as I once believed, that the Day of the Lord will continue for one year.

The Day of the Lord = One Day?

The appearance of the word "day" in the term "Day of the Lord" causes some to conclude that the Day of the Lord is the length of a day. However, the Hebrew word "day" is *yôwm*, which is a word that was not always used to describe a period of one day in length. In fact, the following definition of the word *yôwm* indicates that the word can be used (figuratively) to describe a period longer than an ordinary day:

> "a day (as the warm hours), whether lit. [literally] (from sunrise to sunset, or from one sunset to the next), or fig. [figuratively] (a space of time defined by an associated term)..."[1]

The Day of the Lord Is More Than Seven Months in Length

Ezekiel 39 refutes the idea that the Day of the Lord is the length of a day. The phrase "in that day", which in an end time context almost always refers to the Day of the Lord, appears this chapter:

- Verse 11 speaks of the Lord giving Gog and his troops a place of burial in "that day".
- Verse 12 indicates that the burying Gog and his troops' graves will take seven months.

These details imply that the Day of the Lord will extend at least seven months beyond the defeat of Gog and his forces:

The Day of the Lord = One Thousand Years?

Some believe that Psalm 90 and 2 Peter 3 show that the Day of the Lord will last for precisely one thousand years. Here are key parts of each chapter contributing to this viewpoint:

For a thousand years in thy sight are but as yesterday when it is past, and as a watch in the night. (Ps 90:4)

But, beloved, be not ignorant of this one thing, **that one day is with the Lord as a thousand years, and a thousand years as one day.** (2Pet 3:8)

If you study these verses, you'll notice that each compares a day with the Lord to a thousand years. The recognition that a comparison is being made is critical because it means that a direct statement that "a day for the Lord is a thousand years" *is not* being made.

The writer of Psalm 90 and Peter used the comparison to convey the notion that the Lord's timing is entirely different from our sense of timing. The Lord is eternal while our lives are relatively short, so a long time to us is not a long time to Him.

DEFINING THE DAY OF THE LORD'S LENGTH

No single verse tells us the precise length of the Day of the Lord in terms of time. Therefore, *it may be better to define the length of the Day of the Lord in terms of events.*

The first step is to identify which prominent end time events will precede the start of the Day of the Lord, so we know which events will not be part of its start. Also, through this process, we will gain a greater understanding of when the Day of the Lord will begin.

We have already discussed the following events in this book, but they are worth covering again to give you a better understanding of what needs to transpire before the start of the Day of the Lord.

The Return of Elijah

Malachi tells us that the Lord will send Elijah before the start of the Day of the Lord. Therefore, the Day of the Lord cannot arrive at least until Elijah has returned to prophesy on Earth:

Behold, I will send you Elijah the prophet before the coming of the great and dreadful day of the LORD: (Mal 4:5)

Recall that Elijah will likely be one of the Two Witnesses who will prophesy for 1,260 days (Rev 11:3-6). Also, remember that it is very likely that the bulk of the Two Witnesses' ministry will transpire during the second half of the tribulation. Given this, the Day of the Lord is unlikely to begin in the early portion of the tribulation.

The Unveiling of the Man of Sin

Paul wrote that the Rapture and the Day of Christ (the Day of the Lord) will not come at least until after the apostasy and the Antichrist sits in the temple of God in Jerusalem and proclaims that he is God:[2]

> (3) Let no man deceive you by any means: for that day shall not come, except there come a falling away first, and that man of sin be revealed, the son of perdition; (4) Who opposeth and exalteth himself above all that is called God, or that is worshipped; so that he as God sitteth in the temple of God, shewing himself that he is God. (2Thess 2:3-4)

Recall that the Antichrist will proclaim that he is God when he sets up an abomination of desolation mentioned by Christ and Daniel (Matt 24:15, Dan 9:27) at the midpoint of the tribulation.

Therefore, the Rapture and the Day of the Lord will unlikely begin until after the abomination of desolation is set up at the midpoint of the tribulation.

The Day of the Lord Is Near Events

The Old Testament prophets often wrote that the Day of the Lord is near when they described an event. Their words signify that an event will take place near the start of the Day of the Lord. Here are some events that will take place when the Day of the Lord is near.

The Antichrist Wages War in Egypt

Ezekiel 30 tells us that the Day of the Lord will be near when the Antichrist crushes Egypt, Ethiopia, and other allies:

> (3) For the day is near, even the day of the LORD is near, a cloudy day; it shall be the time of the heathen. (4) And the sword shall come upon Egypt, and great pain shall be in Ethiopia, when the slain shall fall in Egypt, and they shall take away her multitude, and her foundations shall be broken down. (5) Ethiopia, and Libya, and Lydia, and all the mingled people, and Chub, and the men of the land that is in league, shall fall with them by the sword. (Ezek 30:3-5)

Therefore, the Day of the Lord will unlikely begin until at least after the Antichrist devastates Egypt and its allies. The war between Egypt, its allies, and the Antichrist will likely begin after the the sixth trumpet sounds. Thus, the Day of the Lord is unlikely to start until at least after the sixth trumpet sounds.

The Gathering at Armageddon

Recall that Revelation 16:14-16 describes the gathering of the kings of the earth (and their armies) at Armageddon:

(14) For they are the spirits of devils, working miracles, which go forth unto the kings of the earth and of the whole world, to gather them to the battle of that great day of God Almighty. (15) **Behold, I come as a thief. Blessed is he that watcheth, and keepeth his garments, lest he walk naked, and they see his shame.** (16) And he gathered them together into a place called in the Hebrew tongue Armageddon.

Revelation 16:15 is a very intriguing verse as it is attributed to Christ. Christ states that He will come as a thief, which recall is a reference to coming of the Day of the Lord (1Thess 5:1-3, 2Pet 3:10) and the Rapture (Matt 24:42-44, Rev 3:3).

Some believe Christ's statement in verse 15 is parenthetical and is unrelated to the events of Revelation 16. I believe the statement relates to the events of Revelation 16 and is significant. It indicates that the Day of the Lord and the Rapture have not yet arrived as of the pouring of the sixth bowl. Christ is still yet to come as a thief.

The Siege of Jerusalem & the Gathering of the Nations

The end time siege of Jerusalem will transpire shortly before the Day of the Lord begins. Joel 2:1-11 describes a rush of attackers against the city of Jerusalem as the Day of the Lord nears:

(1) Blow ye the trumpet in Zion, and sound an alarm in my holy mountain: let all the inhabitants of the land tremble: for the day of the LORD cometh, for it is nigh at hand;... (9) They shall run to and fro in the city; they shall run upon the wall, they shall climb up upon the houses; they shall enter in at the windows like a thief. (10) The earth shall quake before them; the heavens shall tremble: the sun and the moon shall be dark, and the stars shall withdraw their shining: (Joel 2:1, 9-10, also see Ezek 7:6-9)

Troops from all nations will eventually assemble in the Valley of Jehoshaphat shortly before the start of the Day of the Lord:

> (12) Let the heathen be wakened, and come up to the valley of Jehoshaphat: for there will I sit to judge all the heathen round about.... (14) Multitudes, multitudes in the valley of decision: for the day of the LORD is near in the valley of decision. (15) The sun and the moon shall be darkened, and the stars shall withdraw their shining. (Joel 3:12, 14-15)

The situation in Jerusalem will become so dire that many of the remaining survivors will gather to beg the Lord to rescue them. Joel 1:14-15 tells us that the Day of the Lord is imminent when this solemn gathering takes place:

> (14) Sanctify ye a fast, call a solemn assembly, gather the elders and all the inhabitants of the land into the house of the LORD your God, and cry unto the LORD, (15) **Alas for the day! for the day of the LORD is at hand**, and as a destruction from the Almighty shall it come.

Therefore, the Day of the Lord will unlikely begin until at least after the nations assemble in the Valley of Jehoshaphat and after a solemn assembly in Jerusalem takes place.

The Appearance of Signs in the Heaven & on the Earth

Recall that strange signs in the heavens and on the earth will appear before the Day of the Lord arrives. The following signs will appear in the heavens and on the earth when the sixth seal is broken just before the Day of the Lord starts (Rev 6:12-17):

- The darkening of the sun
- The darkening of the moon (the moon appears as blood)
- The heavens rolling up like a scroll
- The darkening of the stars of heaven
- Massive seismic instability on the earth

Joel 3:14-15 mentions the darkening of the sun and the moon, which further proves that the gathering of the nations to the Valley of Jehoshaphat will come just before the start of the Day of the Lord:

(14) Multitudes, multitudes in the valley of decision: for the day of the LORD is near in the valley of decision. (15) The sun and the moon shall be darkened, and the stars shall withdraw their shining. (Joel 3:14-15)

The Harvest of Earth

As stated in chapter fourteen, Revelation 14:14-20 depicts the harvest of the earth at the end of the age in two different ways:

- The first depiction (Rev 14:14-16) emphasizes the gathering of Christ's elect.

- The second depiction (Rev 14:17-20) emphasizes the reaping and punishment of the wicked.

Joel 3:13 also references the harvest of the earth at that time with an emphasis on the harvest of the wicked. Figure 19.1 shows the similarities between Joel 3:13 and Revelation 14:17-20:

Figure 19.1: The Harvest of the Wicked

- **Reaping of the Wicked**

- *Preparing to Punish the Wicked*

Rev 14:17-20: (17) And another angel came out of the temple which is in heaven, he also having a sharp sickle. (18) And another angel came out from the altar, which had power over fire; and cried with a loud cry to him that had the sharp sickle, saying, **Thrust in thy sharp sickle, and gather the clusters of the vine of the earth; for her grapes are fully ripe.** (19) **And the angel thrust in his sickle into the earth, and gathered the vine of the earth,** *and cast it into the great winepress of the wrath of God.* (20) And the winepress was trodden without the city, and blood came out of the winepress, even unto the horse bridles, by the space of a thousand and six hundred furlongs.

Joel 3:12-15: (12) Let the heathen be wakened, and come up to the valley of Jehoshaphat: for there will I sit to judge all the heathen round about. (13) **Put ye in the sickle, for the harvest is ripe**: *come, get you down; for the press is full, the fats overflow; for their wickedness is great.* (14) Multitudes, multitudes in the valley of decision: for the day of the LORD is near in the valley of decision. (15) The sun and the moon shall be darkened, and the stars shall withdraw their shining.

Recall that Joel 3:13 is part of a passage about the gathering of all nations in the Valley of Jehoshaphat. The Lord will soon arise to judge them and to protect the city of Jerusalem and His people:

> The LORD also shall roar out of Zion, and utter his voice from Jerusalem; and the heavens and the earth shall shake: but the LORD will be the hope of his people, and the strength of the children of Israel. (Joel 3:16)

Therefore, we can see again that the coming of Christ/the Rapture will take place around the time when the Lord rises up to rescue Jerusalem and punish the nations and will relate to the onset of the Day of the Lord.

LET'S PAUSE FOR A MOMENT

In this chapter, we began to look at the Day of the Lord's timing and discussed how it is best to define the Day of the Lord's length in terms of events. We end this chapter knowing what prominent end time events will transpire before the start of the Day of the Lord.

There's been much information to absorb in this chapter. I encourage you to reflect on what you have read and to reread any parts that might have been difficult to understand before you go to the next chapter. I will discuss events relating to the Day of the Lord in the next chapter.

Notes

1. Strong, James. "Yowm". *Strong's Exhaustive Concordance of the Bible*. New York, Cincinnati, Eaton & Mains; Jennings & Graham, 1890. H3117.

2. I believe the Day of Christ and the Day of the Lord represent the same event but from different perspectives. The Day of Christ is associated with the righteous perspective as the righteous will become blameless and will be rewarded at that time (Phil 1:6, 10, Phil 2:14-17, 1Cor 1:7-8, 1Cor 5:5, 2Cor 1:14), while the Day of the Lord is more associated with the punishment of the wicked (1Thess 5:2-3).

CHAPTER 20.

THE DAY OF THE LORD DEFINED: PART 2

This chapter continues the discussion from the previous chapter about the Day of the Lord. The last chapter covered many prominent end time events that will precede the start of the Day of the Lord.

This chapter provides an overview of many events and developments that will take place from the start of the Day of the Lord to its conclusion.

THE DAY OF THE LORD BEGINS

The Destruction of Babylon the Great

Recall that the beginning of *orge* and *thumos orge* will coincide with the start of the Day of the Lord. Babylon the Great's destruction will occur at the onset of the Day of the Lord since she will likely be the first recipient of God's *thumos orge* wrath:

> And the great city was divided into three parts, and the cities of the nations fell: and great Babylon came in remembrance before God, to give unto her the cup of the wine of the fierceness of his wrath. (Rev 16:19)

The city's destruction will send shock waves across the world (Rev 18:9-24), but it is only a preview of what is coming for the wicked of the world.

Recall that the Lord will respond to the cries for help in Jerusalem by arising for battle:

(17) Let the priests, the ministers of the LORD, weep between the porch and the altar, and let them say, Spare thy people, O LORD, and give not thine heritage to reproach, that the heathen should rule over them: wherefore should they say among the people, Where is their God? (18) **Then will the LORD be jealous for his land, and pity his people.** (Joel 2:17-18, also see Zech 14:2-3)

Christ's coming with a vengeance will be an event that no one on the earth will miss:

Behold, he cometh with clouds; **and every eye shall see him, and they also which pierced him: and all kindreds of the earth shall wail because of him.** Even so, Amen. (Rev 1:7, also see Matt 24:30, Ps 97:1-6)

Christ will unleash vengeance against those who do not know God and disobey the gospel of Christ when He comes to judge the world:[1]

(7) And to you who are troubled rest with us, when the Lord Jesus shall be revealed from heaven with his mighty angels, (8) In flaming fire taking vengeance on them that know not God, and that obey not the gospel of our Lord Jesus Christ: (9) Who shall be punished with everlasting destruction from the presence of the Lord, and from the glory of his power; (2Thess 1:7-9)

The following sections will touch on many events and developments that will take place during the Day of the Lord, including events that relate to the Lord taking vengeance against His enemies.

Pride and the Powerful Brought Down

The Lord will punish the arrogant and humble them during the Day of the Lord. He will humble everyone from the ordinary person to the mighty king:[2]

For the day of the LORD of hosts **shall be upon every one that is proud and lofty, and upon every one that is lifted up; and he shall be brought low:** (Isa 2:12, also see Zep 1:8-9, Ps 110:5-6)

Only God Is Exalted

God will be the only One exalted during the Day of the Lord according to Isaiah 2:

> And the loftiness of man shall be bowed down, and the haughtiness of men shall be made low: and the LORD alone shall be exalted in that day. (Isa 2:17, also see Isa 2:11)

This statement is significant because it means that no one else shall be exalted during the Day of the Lord, including the Antichrist. The Antichrist will reign for forty-two months and will be exalted during his reign as people worship him (Rev 13:11-18). Therefore, this statement confirms that the Day of the Lord cannot begin until after the tribulation, which recall coincides with the end of the Antichrist's forty-two month reign.

An Intense Time of Darkness & Judgment

The Day of the Lord will begin with a period of intense darkness and judgment. Amos describes the intense nature of this period:[3]

> (18) Woe unto you that desire the day of the LORD! To what end is it for you? **The day of the LORD is darkness, and not light**. (19) As if a man did flee from a lion, and a bear met him; or went into the house, and leaned his hand on the wall, and a serpent bit him. (20) Shall not the day of the LORD be darkness, and not light? Even very dark, and no brightness in it? (Amos 5:18-20)

The survival rate will be low during this time of intense judgment. The Lord will make people more rare than fine gold (Isa 13:6, 12).

The Wrath of God

As we saw with the fall of Babylon the Great, the wrath of God will scourge the earth at the onset of the Day of the Lord (Isa 13:9, Zep 1:15). Like Babylon the Great, the wicked recipients of the wrath of God will receive the full strength of God's *thumos orge* wrath:

> (9) And the third angel followed them, saying with a loud voice, If any man worship the beast and his image, and receive his mark in his forehead, or in his hand, (10) The same shall drink of the wine of the wrath

of God, which is poured out without mixture into the cup of his indignation; and he shall be tormented with fire and brimstone in the presence of the holy angels, and in the presence of the Lamb: (Rev 14:9-10, also see Obad 1:15-16, Mic 5:10-15, Ezek 39:21)

Jerusalem's Attackers Defeated

The siege of Jerusalem will conclude at the beginning of the Day of the Lord.[4] The Lord promised that He will punish those that besiege Jerusalem on the Day of the Lord:

(2) Behold, I will make Jerusalem **a cup of trembling** unto all the people round about, when they shall be in the siege both against Judah and against Jerusalem. (3) And in that day will I make Jerusalem a burdensome stone for all people: **all that burden themselves with it shall be cut in pieces, though all the people of the earth be gathered together against it.** (4) In that day, saith the Lord, I will smite every horse with astonishment, and his rider with madness: and I will open mine eyes upon the house of Judah, and will smite every horse of the people with blindness. (Zech 12:2-4, also see Isa 51:17-23)

The defeat of Jerusalem's attackers will be part of an overall effort to free the people of Israel from their oppressors:

For it shall come to pass in that day, saith the LORD of hosts, that **I will break his yoke from off thy neck, and will burst thy bonds, and strangers shall no more serve themselves of him**: (Jer 30:8, also see Joel 2:32, Obad 1:17)

The Judgment of the People of Israel

The people of Israel will have gone through much suffering by the time the Day of the Lord starts. Isaiah 6 suggests that desolation will cover the land of Israel by the time the hardening of Israel ends. Verse 13 suggests that only 10% of the population in the land of Israel may survive to see additional purging:

(12) And the LORD have removed men far away, and there be a great forsaking in the midst of the land. (13) But yet in it shall be a tenth, and it shall return, and shall be eaten: as a teil tree, and as an oak, whose substance is in them, when they cast their leaves: so the holy seed shall be the substance thereof. (Isa 6:12-13)

Thus, it is conceivable that 90% of the population of Israel could perish or be displaced in the tribulation before the remaining people endure the refining related to the Day of the Lord.

Malachi 3:2 compares the Lord's coming to a refiner's fire. This comparison makes sense since the Lord will judge with fire (Isa 66:15-16):

> But who may abide the day of his coming? and who shall stand when he appeareth? for he is like a refiner's fire, and like fullers' soap: (Mal 3:2)

The comparison of the Lord to a refiner's fire is also apt because the Lord is the One who will refine the people of Israel. For instance, Malachi 3:3-4 touches on how the Lord will purify the tribe of Levi:

> (3) And he shall sit as a refiner and purifier of silver: and he shall purify the sons of Levi, and purge them as gold and silver, that they may offer unto the LORD an offering in righteousness. (4) Then shall the offering of Judah and Jerusalem be pleasant unto the LORD, as in the days of old, and as in former years. (Mal 3:3-4)

The refiner analogy is also in Zechariah 13. The Lord will refine His people to get a faithful remnant of His people:

> (8) And it shall come to pass, that in all the land, saith the LORD, two parts therein shall be cut off and die; but the third shall be left therein. (9) And I will bring the third part through the fire, and will refine them as silver is refined, and will try them as gold is tried: they shall call on my name, and I will hear them: I will say, It is my people: and they shall say, The LORD is my God. (Zech 13:8-9)[5]

Finally, let's look again at Romans 11. Recall that the Apostle Paul wrote that a hardening will impact a portion of Israel until "the fulness of the Gentiles be come in" (Rom 11:25).

He also alluded to Isaiah 59:20 when he gave an overview of how all Israel will be saved in Romans 11:26. Christ will come to remove the ungodliness from Israel:

> (26) And so all Israel shall be saved: as it is written, **There shall come out of Sion the Deliverer, and shall turn away ungodliness from Jacob**: (27) For this is my covenant unto them, when I shall take away their sins. (Rom 11:26-27)

> **And the Redeemer shall come to Zion, and unto them that turn from transgression in Jacob**, saith the LORD. (Isa 59:20)

The process will unlikely be as simple as all Israel shall be saved the moment Christ arrives. Christ will come and refine His people so that eventually all Israel shall be saved.

Isaiah 59:17-18 gives the context that Christ will begin this process. The passage confirms that the process will start as the Lord comes to seek vengeance against His enemies:

> (17) For he put on righteousness as a breastplate, and an helmet of salvation upon his head; and he put on the garments of vengeance for clothing, and was clad with zeal as a cloak. (18) According to their deeds, accordingly he will repay, fury to his adversaries, recompence to his enemies; to the islands he will repay recompence.... (20) And the Redeemer shall come to Zion, and unto them that turn from transgression in Jacob, saith the LORD. (Isa 59:17-18, 20)

Therefore, Christ will begin the process to refine His people at the start of the Day of the Lord. The Lord will purify His people so that only the godly will remain.

EVENTS TO BE DISCUSSED LATER

Here is a brief overview of a few prominent Day of the Lord events that I will cover in much more detail later in this book.

The Gathering of the Remnant of Israel

The Lord will gather the remnant of His people from the nations "in that day", the Day of the Lord:

> (11) **And it shall come to pass in that day**, that the Lord shall set his hand again the second time to recover **the remnant of his people**, which shall be left, from Assyria, and from Egypt, and from Pathros, and from Cush, and from Elam, and from Shinar, and from Hamath, and from the islands of the sea. (12) And he shall set up an ensign for the nations, and shall assemble the outcasts of Israel, and gather together the dispersed of Judah from the four corners of the earth. (Isa 11:11-12, also see Isa 27:12-13)

The Millennium Phase

Many passages relating to the Millennium refer to the Day of the Lord ("that day"). The following examples support the idea that the Day of the Lord will extend to the Millennium:

- **Example 1:** Zechariah 14:1 establishes that the phrase "in that day", which appears throughout Zechariah 14, refers to the Day of the Lord. Zechariah 14:1-5 concerns the end time siege of Jerusalem and the Lord's counterattack against the besiegers at the onset of the Day of the Lord. Verses 14:8-9 and 14:20-21, which again use the phrase "in that day", each concern the Millennium.

- **Example 2:** Isaiah 30:23 refers to "that day", the Day of the Lord, when there will be great prosperity in Jerusalem and when the sun will shine several times brighter than normal. We will see in chapter twenty-five that these conditions will not exist until the Millennium.

- **Example 3:** Isaiah 19:21-25 indicates that Egypt and Assyria will eventually be friendly to Israel and will serve the Lord "in that day", the Day of the Lord.

- **Example 4:** Ezekiel 38:8-23 talks about a military campaign against the people of Israel at the end of the Millennium (Rev 20:7-9).[6] The passage indicates that the campaign will take place "in that day", the Day of the Lord, twice (Ezek 38:14, 19).

The Heavens & Earth Pass Away

The current heavens and Earth will pass away during the Day of the Lord:

> But the day of the Lord will come as a thief in the night; in the which the heavens shall pass away with a great noise, and the elements shall melt with fervent heat, the earth also and the works that are therein shall be burned up. (2Pet 3:10)

We will look at this massive event in more detail later in this book.

LET'S PAUSE FOR A MOMENT

I summarized many events and developments that will take place during the Day of the Lord in this chapter. We saw that the Day of the Lord will begin with the punishment of the wicked and will continue through the end of the Millennium.

Here is a look at where the start of the Day of the Lord fits in our timeline:

Probable Sequence of Events: Ch.20

Psalm 83 Attack & Siege of Jerusalem: Ps 83, Zech 12:1-3, (Ch.15)

- Death of the Two Witnesses: Rev 11:7-10 (Ch.15)
- The People of Israel Cry for Help: Joel 2:15-17 (Ch.16)

End of the Great Tribulation: Matt 24:29 (Ch.17)

6th Seal: Rev 6:12-17 (Ch.17)

- The Raising of the Two Witnesses: Rev 11:11-13 (Ch.17)

7th Seal: Rev 8:1 (Ch.17)

7th Trumpet: Rev 11:15-19 (Ch.17)

- Kingdom of God & Christ Established on Earth: Rev 11:15 (Ch.17)
- End of the Tribulation: Dan 9:24-27 (Ch.17)
- Mystery of God Complete: Rev 10:7 (Ch.17)
- Fullness of the Gentiles Reached: Rom 11:25 (Ch.17)

7th Bowl Poured: Rev 16:17-21 (Ch.17)

- *Day of the Lord Begins: Zep 1:7-8 (Ch.19-20)*
- Babylon the Great Destroyed: Rev 16:19, Rev 18 (Ch.17)

The Coming of Christ: Matt 24:30 (Ch.18)

- Gathering of the Wicked: Matt 13:41 (Ch.18)
- Gathering of the Righteous/the Rapture: Matt 24:31 (Ch.18)

I know this chapter and the previous chapter had a lot of information to process. Therefore, I once again encourage you to reflect on what you have read and to reread any parts that might have been difficult to understand before continuing to the next chapter. I will discuss the showdown between Christ and Antichrist next.

Notes

1. Nah 1:2-7 may also relate to end time passages about the Lord coming with anger.

2. Isa 13:11, Isa 24:21-23, and Zep 3:11-12 also refer to how the Lord will humble the arrogant.

3. Isa 5:30, 60:1-2, Jer 4:23, Amos 8:9 also refer to the darkness that will impact the heavens at the start of the Day of the Lord.

4. Zech 14:1, Zep 1:10-12, 17-18, and Ezek 7:19 describe the siege of Jerusalem still underway at the start of the Day of the Lord.

5. It's unclear what events the remaining one-third mentioned in Zech 13 survived before they face refinement:

   ◦ Many believe the remaining one-third represents the survivors of Rome's attacks against the land of Israel and Jerusalem in the first century A.D. (given that verse 13:7 appears to refer to Christ).

   ◦ Others believe that the remaining one-third represents the survivors of the Antichrist's persecution.

   Also, the geographic scope of "all the land" is unclear:

   ◦ Some posit "all the land" in verse 8 represents the land of Israel.

   ◦ Others argue it represents the entire world.

   Given the 10% survival rate mentioned in Isa 6:9-13, I believe it is unlikely that this one-third represents the inhabitants of the land of Israel who survive the Antichrist's persecution. Conversely, it is possible for the one-third to represent the world population of the people of Israel.

6. See the appendix section titled "The Fulfillment of Ezekiel 38" to learn why the events of Ezekiel 38 will take place in the Millennium.

CHAPTER 21.

THE FINAL BATTLE OF THE WAR OF ARMAGEDDON

The wicked will seek to wage war against Christ. However, Christ will defeat them so rapidly and so thoroughly that the final battle of the war of Armageddon will not be much of a fight.

This chapter summarizes the slaughter of the wicked, which represents the burning of the tares at the end of the age (Matt 13:30, 40-42).

THE DAYS OF LOT & DAYS OF NOAH

The slaughter of the wicked will begin right after the Rapture. Christ compared the day of His coming to the days of Lot and the days of Noah when the destruction of the wicked came right after the righteous were saved:

> (26) And as it was in the days of Noe [Noah], so shall it be also in the days of the Son of man. (27) They did eat, they drank, they married wives, they were given in marriage, until the day that Noe entered into the ark, and the flood came, and destroyed them all. (28) Likewise also as it was in the days of Lot; they did eat, they drank, they bought, they sold, they planted, they builded; (29) But the same day that Lot went out of Sodom it rained fire and brimstone from heaven, and destroyed them all. (30) Even thus shall it be in the day when the Son of man is revealed. (Luke 17:26-30)

The Winepress

Revelation 14:18-20 depicts the harvest of the wicked as the gathering of grapes and the slaughter of the wicked as the treading of a winepress. Revelation 14:20 suggests that the blood will cover an area of 1,600 furlongs (around 200 miles) at up to five feet deep:

> (18) And another angel came out from the altar, which had power over fire; and cried with a loud cry to him that had the sharp sickle, saying, Thrust in thy sharp sickle, and gather the clusters of the vine of the earth; for her grapes are fully ripe. (19) And the angel thrust in his sickle into the earth, and gathered the vine of the earth, and cast it into the great winepress of the wrath of God. (20) And the winepress was trodden without the city, and blood came out of the winepress, even unto the horse bridles, by the space of a thousand and six hundred furlongs. (Rev 14:18-20)

We can see from this passage that there will be a great slaughter outside of Jerusalem.[1] Although the massacre will be great, it is conceivable since the Lord will slaughter all the nations in His wrath:

> (3) And in that day will I make Jerusalem a burdensome stone for all people: all that burden themselves with it shall be cut in pieces, though all the people of the earth be gathered together against it.... (9) And it shall come to pass in that day, that I will seek to destroy all the nations that come against Jerusalem. (Zech 12:3, 9, also see Zech 14:1-3, Isa 34:1-3, Zep 3:8)

The Lord in Edom

Recall that Revelation 12:6, 14 tells us that the woman (the remnant of Israel) will find refuge in the wilderness for 1,260 days or until the end of the tribulation. The likely reason they will no longer seek refuge is that the Lord will destroy their enemies and make it safe for them to come out of hiding.

Also, recall that a coalition will seek to destroy the remnant of Israel hiding in the wilderness. I believe troops will enter Edom to pursue them. The troops will betray Edom, a member of this coalition, when they enter their land:

> All the men of thy confederacy have brought thee even to the border: the men that were at peace with thee have deceived thee, and prevailed against thee; they that eat thy bread have laid a wound under thee: there is none understanding in him. (Obad 1:7)

The forces in Edom will fail to destroy the people of Israel because the Lord will come to slaughter them in likely the first stop of His return.[2] Isaiah 34:5-6 focuses on what the Lord will do to Edom. The Lord promises a great slaughter in the land of Edom:

> (5) For my sword shall be bathed in heaven: behold, it shall come down upon Idumea, and upon the people of my curse, to judgment. (6) The sword of the LORD is filled with blood, it is made fat with fatness, and with the blood of lambs and goats, with the fat of the kidneys of rams: for the LORD hath a sacrifice in Bozrah, and a great slaughter in the land of Idumea. (Isa 34:5-6)

Isaiah 63:1-6 covers the aftermath of the Lord's slaughter of the forces in Edom. Verses 1-2 depict Christ traveling from Edom with His garments covered with red stains:

> (1) Who is this that cometh from Edom, with dyed garments from Bozrah? this that is glorious in his apparel, travelling in the greatness of his strength? I that speak in righteousness, mighty to save. (2) Wherefore art thou red in thine apparel, and thy garments like him that treadeth in the winefat? (Isa 63:1-2, also see Hab 3:1-19)

Isaiah 63:3-6 explains why Christ's garments are stained with red. They are red because He slaughtered the armies alone.[3] [4] The red on Christ's garments represents the blood of the troops He defeated:[5]

> I have trodden the winepress alone; and of the people there was none with me: for I will tread them in mine anger, and trample them in my fury; and their blood shall be sprinkled upon my garments, and I will stain all my raiment. (Isa 63:3)

It is unclear whether actual blood will cover Christ's garments, but either way, the troops in Edom will have no chance against Him.

The Jubilee Year

The Lord mentions that it will be His year of redemption when He comes:

> For the day of vengeance is in mine heart, and the year of my redeemed is come. (Isa 63:4)

I believe Christ's slaughter of the forces in Edom and elsewhere will likely coincide with the start of a Jubilee Year. A Jubilee Year takes place every fifty years and starts on Yom Kippur, the date when the tribulation is likely to end.

Leviticus 25 describes the Jubilee Year. Two key aspects of the Jubilee Year involve the return of property to their owner and the return of people to their family. People and property are set free:

> (9) Then shalt thou cause the trumpet of the jubile to sound on the tenth day of the seventh month, in the day of atonement shall ye make the trumpet sound throughout all your land. (10) And ye shall hallow the fiftieth year, and proclaim liberty throughout all the land unto all the inhabitants thereof: it shall be a jubile unto you; and ye shall return every man unto his possession, and ye shall return every man unto his family. (Lev 25:9-10, also see Lev 25:23-34)

I believe Christ refers to the Jubilee Year when he mentions "the acceptable year of the Lord":

> (1) The Spirit of the Lord GOD is upon me; because the LORD hath anointed me to preach good tidings unto the meek; he hath sent me to bind up the brokenhearted, to proclaim liberty to the captives, and the opening of the prison to them that are bound; (2) **To proclaim the acceptable year of the LORD,** and the day of vengeance of our God; to comfort all that mourn; (Isa 61:1-2)

Also, the events described in Isaiah and elsewhere are consistent with what takes place at the start of a Jubilee Year. The Lord will free the people of Israel from their captivity (Isa 61:1-2) and cause them to inherit the land of their ancestors and prosper (Deut 30:5).[6]

After Edom

Christ will lead His people out of Edom. Micah describes Him as the one who will remove obstacles for His people:

> (12) I will surely assemble, O Jacob, all of thee; I will surely gather the remnant of Israel; I will put them together as the sheep of Bozrah [capital city of Edom], as the flock in the midst of their fold: they shall make great noise by reason of the multitude of men. (13) The breaker is come up before them: they have broken up, and have passed through the gate, and are gone out by it: and their king shall pass before them, and the LORD on the head of them. (Mic 2:12-13)

The Lord will likely destroy any resistance He finds as He travels to Jerusalem. The Lord will save the "tents of Judah"-those living in small dwellings near Jerusalem-before He reaches the city:

> The LORD also shall save the tents of Judah first, that the glory of the house of David and the glory of the inhabitants of Jerusalem do not magnify themselves against Judah. (Zech 12:7)

Jerusalem Divides Into Three Parts

The largest earthquake in history will take place after the pouring of the seventh bowl judgment. Revelation 16:19 indicates that the great city, Jerusalem (Rev 11:8), will divide into three parts. Around that same time, Christ will split the Mount of Olives so His people can flee for safety (Zech 14:4-5).

THE SHOWDOWN

Revelation 19:19 describes the kings of the earth and the armies of the earth assembled to wage war against Christ and His army:

> And I saw the beast, and the kings of the earth, and their armies, gathered together to make war against him that sat on the horse, and against his army. (Rev 19:19)

This is a big development since it means the focus of the forces gathered to battle will shift from destroying the people of Israel to waging war against Christ and His army. The change in focus likely relates to the presence of Christ and His army on Earth.

However, the wicked will have no chance against Him. In fact, birds and beasts will receive invites to partake in the slaughter:

> (17) And I saw an angel standing in the sun; and he cried with a loud voice, saying to all the fowls that fly in the midst of heaven, **Come and gather yourselves together unto the supper of the great God**; (18) That ye may eat the flesh of kings, and the flesh of captains, and the flesh of mighty men, and the flesh of horses, and of them that sit on them, and the flesh of all men, both free and bond, both small and great. (Rev 19:17-18, also see Ezek 39:17-20)

The Slaughter

The Antichrist and the False Prophet will be seized and placed in the lake of fire:[7]

And the beast was taken, and with him the false prophet that wrought miracles before him, with which he deceived them that had received the mark of the beast, and them that worshipped his image. These both were cast alive into a lake of fire burning with brimstone. (Rev 19:20)

Meanwhile, the remaining people who gather against Christ and His army will die. Christ will crush them by simply speaking:[8]

(15) **And out of his mouth goeth a sharp sword, that with it he should smite the nations: and he shall rule them with a rod of iron**: and he treadeth the winepress of the fierceness and wrath of Almighty God.... (21) **And the remnant were slain with the sword of him that sat upon the horse, which sword proceeded out of his mouth: and all the fowls were filled with their flesh.** (Rev 19:15, 21, also see Ps 2)

Many places detail the slaughter of Christ's opponents, including the following verses:[9]

And there fell upon men a great hail out of heaven, every stone about the weight of a talent: and men blasphemed God because of the plague of the hail; for the plague thereof was exceeding great. (Rev 16:21, also see Rev 11:19)

(12) And this shall be the plague wherewith the Lord will smite all the people that have fought against Jerusalem; Their flesh shall consume away while they stand upon their feet, and their eyes shall consume away in their holes, and their tongue shall consume away in their mouth. (13) And it shall come to pass in that day, that a great tumult from the Lord shall be among them; and they shall lay hold every one on the hand of his neighbour, and his hand shall rise up against the hand of his neighbour.... (15) And so shall be the plague of the horse, of the mule, of the camel, and of the ass, and of all the beasts that shall be in these tents, as this plague. (Zech 14:12-13, 15, also see Zech 12:4, Isa 30:27-30)

Gog and his forces will meet their demise and will be food for the guests that have gathered to partake in the remains of the slaughter:

(3) And I will smite thy bow out of thy left hand, and will cause thine arrows to fall out of thy right hand. (4) Thou shalt fall upon the mountains of Israel, thou, and all thy bands, and the people that is with thee: I will give thee unto the ravenous birds of every sort, and to the beasts of the field to be devoured. (5) Thou shalt fall upon the open field: for I have spoken it, saith the Lord GOD. (6) And I will send a fire on Magog,

and among them that dwell carelessly in the isles: and they shall know that I am the LORD. (Ezek 39:3-6)

Meanwhile, locals will move to liberate Jerusalem. They will fight as the Lord protects them from the chaos:[10]

And they shall be as mighty men, which tread down their enemies in the mire of the streets in the battle: and they shall fight, because the Lord is with them, and the riders on horses shall be confounded. (Zech 10:5, also see Zech 9:15, 14:15)

In that day will I make the governors of Judah like an hearth of fire among the wood, and like a torch of fire in a sheaf; and they shall devour all the people round about, on the right hand and on the left: and Jerusalem shall be inhabited again in her own place, even in Jerusalem. (Zech 12:6)

Finally, the downfall of the wicked will also include the defeat of Satan's angels. They will likely take part in the war of Armageddon and will be punished at the same time as the kings of the earth:

(21) And it shall come to pass in that day, that the LORD shall punish the host of the high ones that are on high, and the kings of the earth upon the earth. (22) And they shall be gathered together, as prisoners are gathered in the pit, and shall be shut up in the prison, and after many days shall they be visited. (Isa 24:21-22)

Thus, the wicked will lose the final battle of the war of Armageddon in a complete rout.

LET'S PAUSE FOR A MOMENT

This chapter detailed Christ's sweeping victory over the wicked that gathered to wage war against Him. Here is a look at where the key events described in this chapter fit in our timeline:

Probable Sequence of Events: Ch.21

7th Bowl Poured: Rev 16:17-21 (Ch.17)

- Day of the Lord Begins: Zep 1:7-8 (Ch.19-20)
- Babylon the Great Destroyed: Rev 16:19, Rev 18 (Ch.17)

The Coming of Christ: Matt 24:30 (Ch.18)

- Gathering of the Wicked: Matt 13:41 (Ch.18)
- Gathering of the Righteous/the Rapture: Matt 24:31 (Ch.18)

Christ Begins to Liberate His People: Isa 61:1-2 (Ch.21)

Greatest Earthquake of All Time: Rev 16:18 (Ch.21)

Antichrist & False Prophet Cast to Lake of Fire: Rev 19:20 (Ch.21)

Slaughter of the Wicked & Jerusalem Liberated: Rev 19:21, Zech 12:6 (Ch.21)

I believe it is important to reflect on how one-sided Christ's victory will be. He will crush: Satan, the Antichrist, the armies of the world, and Satan's spiritual minions. All the power of evil in this world is nothing compared to the power of Christ!

Notes

1. Joel 3:12-14 refers to the slaughter of the wicked alluded to in Rev 14:18-20. The battleground spans a large area outside of Jerusalem.

2. The Lord will likely visit Edom first, as Isa 63:1-6 describes Him traveling from Edom as He begins His work to save His people at the start of the Jubilee Year.

3. The heavenly armies and the righteous will likely join Christ as He routs the wicked. However, they are unlikely to take part in the slaughter.

Christ will defeat the wicked alone.

4. The slaughter in Edom will not include the forces that besiege Jerusalem. Christ will act alone in Edom while the Lord's people will take part in the defeat of Jerusalem's attackers (Zech 10:3-5, 12:6, 14:15).

5. The treading of the winepress does not always refer to one event. For instance, the phrase describes the defeat of the people of Jerusalem in the time of Nebuchadnezzar (Lam 1:15). Therefore, the treading of the winepress in Isa 63 may be unrelated to the treading of the winepress in Rev 14:18-20.

6. Isa 45:8-17 may also be about the Lord freeing captives at the onset of a Jubilee Year. But some link the passage to the time of Cyrus the Great.

7. 2Thess 2:8 and Isa 14:15-16 indicate that the Antichrist may die. Rev 19:20 states that the Antichrist will be seized and cast alive into the lake of fire.

We can harmonize these verses with the idea that the Antichrist may die at the battle, but then immediately raised from the dead. He will then be cast alive into the lake of fire. Interestingly, Isa 14:19-20 suggests that he will not be buried with those already dead:

(19) But thou art cast out of thy grave like an abominable branch, and as the raiment of those that are slain, thrust through with a sword, that go down to the stones of the pit; as a carcase trodden under feet. (20) Thou shalt not be joined with them in burial, because thou hast destroyed thy land, and slain thy people: the seed of evildoers shall never be renowned. (Isa 14:19-20)

The Antichrist will experience the second death reserved for the wicked immediately.

8. 2Thess 2:8, Isa 11:4, and Isa 30:27-30 also suggest that Christ will destroy the nations by speaking.

9. Ezek 38:18-23 may also be about the slaughter of the wicked although its main fulfillment will be in the Millennium.

10. Mic 4:13 and Isa 41:15-16 may also relate to the battle to free Jerusalem.

CHAPTER 22.

POST-ARMAGEDDON: PART 1

The period after the war of Armageddon is not a time frame that many focus on, as so many events lie ahead of us. However, it is an important time to consider since the Bible has much to say about it.

We cannot gain a full understanding of what God has planned without at least considering what will take place after the war of Armageddon.

The purpose of the next two chapters is to provide a detailed overview of what will take place between the end of the war of Armageddon and the start of the Millennium (henceforth known as the Post-Armageddon period).

THE FIRST THIRTY DAYS

Daniel 12 mentions two periods that will start when the daily sacrifice stops. The first period spans 1,290 days from the time the daily sacrifice stops to the end of the abomination of desolation:

> And from the time that the daily sacrifice shall be taken away, and the abomination that maketh desolate set up, there shall be a thousand two hundred and ninety days. (Dan 12:11)

Since the second half of the tribulation is 1,260 days long, we have a thirty day period to account for after the tribulation. Some believe this extra thirty day period implies:

- The Antichrist will live for another thirty days after the tribulation.
- The war of Armageddon will conclude at the end of the thirty days.

However, the thirty days simply could be the time that passes before the abomination of desolation is removed from the temple ruins. The thirty days may also cover the time it takes for all the remnant of Israel to reach Mount Zion (more on this soon).

SEVENTY-FIVE DAYS

The second period spans 1,335 days from the time the daily sacrifice stops to a time when a living person will be blessed:

> Blessed is he that waiteth, and cometh to the thousand three hundred and five and thirty days. (Dan 12:12)

We may be able to deduce why someone who sees the 1,335th day will be blessed by looking at the calendar:[1]

- Recall that the end of the tribulation will fall 1,260 days after the daily sacrifice stops. This will coincide with Yom Kippur.

- The difference between Yom Kippur at the end of the tribulation and the 1,335th day from the time the daily sacrifice stops is seventy-five days.

- Amazingly, the Jewish holiday of Hanukkah falls around seventy-five days after Yom Kippur!

Hanukkah (Hebrew meaning "dedication") commemorates the rededication of the Second Temple. The temple was purified after Antiochus Epiphanes IV defiled it (see chapter seven).

The potential significance of Hanukkah taking place at the end of this seventy-five day period is that it may celebrate the dedication of a temple from where the Lord will reign (see chapter twenty-three).

The dedication of a temple occurs when it is ready for use. Its dedication likely means that the Lord will be ready to rule the nations of the earth from there. We can conclude from this that the Millennium will likely start after the seventy-five day period and that the full Post-Armageddon period is seventy-five days long.

THE GATHERING OF THE REMNANT OF ISRAEL

This section is the first of many sections in this chapter and the next chapter to detail key developments that will take place in the Post-Armageddon period.

Recall that the Lord promised that He will eventually gather the remnant of Israel from the nations to live prosperously in the land of Israel:

(1) And it shall come to pass, when all these things are come upon thee, the blessing and the curse, which I have set before thee, and thou shalt call them to mind among all the nations, whither the LORD thy God hath driven thee, (2) And shalt return unto the LORD thy God, and shalt obey his voice according to all that I command thee this day, thou and thy children, with all thine heart, and with all thy soul; (3) That then the LORD thy God will turn thy captivity, and have compassion upon thee, and will return and gather thee from all the nations, whither the LORD thy God hath scattered thee. (Deut 30:1-3)

He will begin to bring the remnant of Israel from the nations after the defeat of the wicked in the war of Armageddon:

Therefore thus saith the Lord GOD; Now will I bring again the captivity of Jacob, and have mercy upon the whole house of Israel, and will be jealous for my holy name; (Ezek 39:25)

The Signal to Gather the Remnant of Israel

The Bible depicts the Lord as a shepherd who will recover His flock from the nations:

(11) **For thus saith the Lord GOD; Behold, I, even I, will both search my sheep, and seek them out.** (12) **As a shepherd seeketh out his flock in the day that he is among his sheep that are scattered; so will I seek out my sheep, and will deliver them out of all places where they have been scattered in the cloudy and dark day.** (13) And I will bring them out from the people, and gather them from the countries, and will bring them to their own land, and feed them upon the mountains of Israel by the rivers, and in all the inhabited places of the country. (Ezek 34:11-13, also see Isa 40:11, 56:8, Jer 23:3, 31:7-10, Mic 2:12-13)

Isaiah states that the Lord will set up a signal to the nations, and the remnant of Israel scattered across the world shall assemble:[2]

(11) And it shall come to pass in that day, that the Lord shall set his hand again the second time to recover the remnant of his people, which

shall be left, from Assyria, and from Egypt, and from Pathros, and from Cush, and from Elam, and from Shinar, and from Hamath, and from the islands of the sea. (12) And he shall set up an ensign for the nations, and shall assemble the outcasts of Israel, and gather together the dispersed of Judah from the four corners of the earth. (Isa 11:11-12, also see Isa 43:1, 5-7, 66:19-20)

Isaiah 27:13 states that a great trumpet may also sound when the remnant of Israel gather from places like Assyria and Egypt:[3]

And it shall come to pass in that day, that the great trumpet shall be blown, and they shall come which were ready to perish in the land of Assyria, and the outcasts in the land of Egypt, and shall worship the LORD in the holy mount at Jerusalem. (Isa 27:13)

An Emotional Journey

The remnant of Israel will be emotional as they travel to the land of Israel. In fact, they will weep while they travel:

(8) Behold, I will bring them from the north country, and gather them from the coasts of the earth, and with them the blind and the lame, the woman with child and her that travaileth with child together: a great company shall return thither. (9) **They shall come with weeping, and with supplications will I lead them**: I will cause them to walk by the rivers of waters in a straight way, wherein they shall not stumble: for I am a father to Israel, and Ephraim is my firstborn. (Jer 31:8-9)

(4) In those days, and in that time, saith the LORD, **the children of Israel shall come, they and the children of Judah together, going and weeping: they shall go, and seek the LORD their God**. (5) They shall ask the way to Zion with their faces thitherward, saying, Come, and let us join ourselves to the LORD in a perpetual covenant that shall not be forgotten. (Jer 50:4-5)

The Gentiles Will Provide Help

Several Bible prophecy verses, including Isaiah 49:22 and Isaiah 66:20, indicate that the Gentiles will respond to the Lord's signal. They will escort the remnant of Israel to the land of Israel:

Thus saith the Lord GOD, **Behold, I will lift up mine hand to the Gentiles**, and set up my standard to the people: and **they shall bring thy sons in their arms, and thy daughters shall be carried upon their shoulders**. (Isa 49:22, also see Isa 14:1-2, 60:3-4, 9)

And they [the surviving nations] **shall bring all your brethren for an offering** unto the LORD out of all nations upon horses, and in chariots, and in litters, and upon mules, and upon swift beasts, **to my holy mountain Jerusalem, saith the LORD**, as the children of Israel bring an offering in a clean vessel into the house of the LORD. (Isa 66:20, also see Isa 56:6-8)

The Way of Holiness

Several places in the Bible, including Isaiah 11:15-16, tell us the remnant of Israel in Assyria and Egypt will return using a highway:

(15) And the LORD shall utterly destroy the tongue of the Egyptian sea; and with his mighty wind shall he shake his hand over the river, and shall smite it in the seven streams, and make men go over dryshod. (16) **And there shall be an highway for the remnant of his people**, which shall be left, from Assyria; like as it was to Israel in the day that he came up out of the land of Egypt. (Isa 11:15-16, also see Isa 35:8-10, 40:1-3, 62:10-12, Hos 11:10-11)

The highway will form after the pouring of the seventh bowl judgment when all mountains are brought down (Rev 16:17-20). Isaiah 40:1-4, a passage which saw its first fulfillment with the first coming of Christ (Matt 3:1-3), confirms that a highway will form at the time when every mountain and hill is brought low:

(1) Comfort ye, comfort ye my people, saith your God. (2) Speak ye comfortably to Jerusalem, and cry unto her, that her warfare is accomplished, that her iniquity is pardoned: for she hath received of the LORD'S hand double for all her sins. (3) The voice of him that crieth in the wilderness, Prepare ye the way of the LORD, make straight in the desert a highway for our God. (4) **Every valley shall be exalted, and every mountain and hill shall be made low: and the crooked shall be made straight, and the rough places plain**: (Isa 40:1-4)

Travelers on the highway will find plenty of water to drink. Water will even be found along the desert areas of the highway:

(10) They shall not hunger nor thirst; neither shall the heat nor sun smite them: for he that hath mercy on them shall lead them, even by the springs of water shall he guide them. (11) And I will make all my mountains a way, and **my highways shall be exalted**. (12) Behold, these shall come from far: and, lo, these from the north and from the west;

and these from the land of Sinim. (Isa 49:10-12, also see Jer 31:8-9, Isa 35:6-8, 41:14, 17-18, 43:19, Ps 107:3-6, 35)

Arriving on Mount Zion

Revelation 16:17-20 and Isaiah 40:1-4 indicate that mountains will be brought low after the seventh bowl judgment. However, the Lord can and will restore some mountains, including Mount Zion. The Lord may restore Mount Zion in the early part of the Post-Armageddon period. We can deduce that He will restore Mount Zion at this time since it will be the site where the Gentiles will take the remnant of Israel:

> And they shall bring all your brethren for an offering unto the LORD out of all nations upon horses, and in chariots, and in litters, and upon mules, and upon swift beasts, to my holy mountain Jerusalem, saith the LORD, as the children of Israel bring an offering in a clean vessel into the house of the LORD. (Isa 66:20)

The remnant of Israel already there will be in awe as the Gentiles bring their brethren and wealth for an offering to the Lord:

> (3) And the Gentiles shall come to thy light, and kings to the brightness of thy rising. (4) Lift up thine eyes round about, and see: all they gather themselves together, they come to thee: thy sons shall come from far, and thy daughters shall be nursed at thy side. (5) Then thou shalt see, and flow together, and thine heart shall fear, and be enlarged; because the abundance of the sea shall be converted unto thee, the forces [wealth] of the Gentiles shall come unto thee. (Isa 60:3-5)

The returning remnant of Israel will be witnesses for the Lord. They will be living proof that man can only be saved by the Lord (Ezek 20:41-42, Isa 43:10-13). The Gentiles at that time will begin to view the people of Israel in high regard (Zep 3:19-20).

LET'S PAUSE FOR A MOMENT

This chapter began a look at the Post-Armageddon period. We learned that it will last for seventy-five days. We also learned that the gathering of the people of Israel from the nations will be one of the key developments that will take place at that time.

Here is a look at where the Post-Armageddon period fits in our timeline:

Probable Sequence of Events: Ch.22

The Coming of Christ: Matt 24:30 (Ch.18)

• Gathering of the Wicked: Matt 13:41 (Ch.18)

• Gathering of the Righteous/the Rapture: Matt 24:31 (Ch.18)

Christ Begins to Liberate His People: Isa 61:1-2 (Ch.21)

Greatest Earthquake of All Time: Rev 16:18 (Ch.21)

Antichrist & False Prophet Cast to Lake of Fire: Rev 19:20 (Ch.21)

Slaughter of the Wicked & Jerusalem Liberated: Rev 19:21, Zech 12:6 (Ch.21)

75 Day Post-Armageddon Period: Dan 12:11-12 (Ch.22-23)

• *Gathering of the Remnant of Israel: Isa 11:11-12 (Ch.22)*

I encourage you to reflect on what you have read and reread any parts that might have been difficult to understand before you continue. We will look at several more Post-Armageddon events next.

Notes

1. It is likely that those who see the 1,335th day may take part in the Marriage Supper of the Lamb. I discuss this event in chapter twenty-three.

2. Ps 50:1-6 describes the Lord calling the world to gather at Mount Zion. This call includes an order to gather the remnant of Israel for judgment.

3. Isa 27:13 does not say who will sound the trumpet, so it may not be the Lord who will sound it. However, the trumpet could relate to one that will sound at the Lord's coming if the Lord is the one who sounds it.

CHAPTER 23.

POST-ARMAGEDDON: PART 2

We continue our look at the Post-Armageddon period. We will look at several more events that will take place in this period.

THE SHEEP & GOAT JUDGMENT

The Sheep and Goat Judgment will determine which of the surviving Gentiles will enter the Millennium Kingdom. This event will take place after the surviving nations come to Mount Zion after the Lord's call to bring the people of Israel to their land (Isa 49:22, 66:19-20). Christ will separate the Gentiles into two groups:

> (31) When the Son of man shall come in his glory, and all the holy angels with him, then shall he sit upon the throne of his glory: (32) And before him shall be gathered all nations: and he shall separate them one from another, as a shepherd divideth his sheep from the goats: (Matt 25:31-32)

The sheep will be on the right hand of Christ and will enter the Millennium Kingdom (Matt 24:33-34). The goats will be on the left hand of Christ and will face eternal punishment (Matt 25:33, 41, 46).

The basis of judgment will be how each person treated the Lord's people during their time of need:

- The sheep will be those who help the Lord's people in their time of need (Matt 25:35-40).[1]

- The goats will be those who do not help the Lord's people in their time of need (Matt 25:42-46).

THE BEMA SEAT JUDGMENT

Revelation 11:18 states that the "time" (or "season" based on the Greek word *kairos*) to judge the dead and to hand out rewards will come after the seventh trumpet sounds:[2]

(15) And the seventh angel sounded; and there were great voices in heaven, saying, The kingdoms of this world are become the kingdoms of our Lord, and of his Christ; and he shall reign for ever and ever.... (18) And the nations were angry, and thy wrath is come, and the time of the dead, that they should be judged, and that thou shouldest give reward unto thy servants the prophets, and to the saints, and them that fear thy name, small and great; and shouldest destroy them which destroy the earth. (Rev 11:15, 18)

The rewarding of the righteous will take place at an event commonly known as the "Bema Seat Judgment". Each person's reward will be according to what they did during their life (Rom 14:10-12, 1Cor 3:13-15, 2Cor 5:10-11, 2Tim 4:1-2, 6-8, Rev 22:12, Matt 10:40-42).

The Bema Seat Judgment will likely occur around the time Christ judges the surviving Gentiles. This placement stems from the parallel between Matthew 16:27, a verse about the judging at the Bema Seat Judgment, and Matthew 25:31, a verse about the judging at the Sheep and Goat Judgment:

(27) **For the Son of man shall come in the glory of his Father with his angels; and then** he shall reward every man according to his works. (28) Verily I say unto you, There be some standing here, which shall not taste of death, till they see the Son of man coming in his kingdom. (Matt 16:27-28)

When the Son of man shall come in his glory, and all the holy angels with him, then shall he sit upon the throne of his glory: (Matt 25:31)

Matthew 25:31 notes that Christ will sit on His throne at that time. This throne could serve as the judgment seat of Christ referenced in following passages:

(10) But why dost thou judge thy brother? or why dost thou set at nought thy brother? **for we shall all stand before the judgment seat of Christ.** (11) For it is written, As I live, saith the Lord, every knee shall

bow to me, and every tongue shall confess to God. (12) So then every one of us shall give account of himself to God. (Rom 14:10-12)

For we must all appear before the judgment seat of Christ; that every one may receive the things done in his body, according to that he hath done, whether it be good or bad. (2Cor 5:10)

THE 144,000 SAVED

Recall that Revelation depicts the 144,000 on Mount Zion with Christ (Rev 14:1-5). This scene likely records the 144,000 just after they are saved:

(1) And I looked, and, lo, a Lamb stood on the mount Sion, and with him an hundred forty and four thousand, having his Father's name written in their foreheads. (2) And I heard a voice from heaven, as the voice of many waters, and as the voice of a great thunder: and I heard the voice of harpers harping with their harps: (3) And they sung as it were a new song before the throne, and before the four beasts, and the elders: and no man could learn that song but the hundred and forty and four thousand, which were redeemed from the earth. (Rev 14:1-3)

They are the firstfruits to God and to Christ, which means they are the first of the harvest (Rev 14:4-5). The harvest relates to the salvation of Israel, so they are the first of the saved Israel. The rest will follow quickly.

THE SPIRITUAL PURIFICATION OF ISRAEL

The remnant of Israel will be purified spiritually after they arrive in the land of Israel. Psalm 50:7-23 may describe what the Lord will tell them just before He purifies them. He will explain that He cares far more about their attitude when they worship than what they sacrifice to Him in worship (Ps 50:7-15, 23). He will also explain that He does not tolerate sinful behavior (Ps 50:16-22). The Lord also promises to show the righteous the way of salvation (Ps 50:23).

The Bible describes or alludes to the spiritual purification process in Deuteronomy 30:5-7, Ezekiel 11:17-20, 36:24-28, 37:21-23, and Jeremiah 32:37-39. Here is an overview of the process (see Figure 23.1):

Figure 23.1: The Spiritual Purification Process

- **Gathered**

- *Change of Heart & Spirit*

- <u>**Abominations Removed**</u>

- <u>*Obey the Lord*</u>

Ezek 11:17-20: (17) Therefore say, Thus saith the Lord GOD; **I will even gather you from the people, and assemble you out of the countries where ye have been scattered, and I will give you the land of Israel.** (18) And they shall come thither, and they shall take away <u>all the detestable things thereof and all the abominations thereof from thence</u>. (19) *And I will give them one heart, and I will put a new spirit within you; and I will take the stony heart out of their flesh, and will give them an heart of flesh:* (20) That <u>*they may walk in my statutes, and keep mine ordinances*</u>, and do them: and they shall be my people, and I will be their God.

Ezek 36:24-28: (24) **For I will take you from among the heathen, and gather you out of all countries, and will bring you into your own land.** (25) Then will I sprinkle clean water upon you, and ye shall be clean: <u>**from all your filthiness, and from all your idols, will I cleanse you**</u>. (26) *A new heart also will I give you, and a new spirit will I put within you: and I will take away the stony heart out of your flesh, and I will give you an heart of flesh.* (27) *And I will put my spirit within you,* <u>*and cause you to walk in my statutes, and ye shall keep my judgments, and do them*</u>. (28) And ye shall dwell in the land that I gave to your fathers; and ye shall be my people, and I will be your God.

Notice that Ezekiel 36:25 mentions the word "Then", which confirms that the spiritual purification of the people of Israel will begin after they assemble in the land of Israel.

An Outpouring of the Lord's Spirit

An outpouring of the Lord's Spirit will take place at this time:

- Ezekiel 11:19 says the Lord will put a "new spirit" in His people.

- Ezekiel 36:27 says the Lord will put His Spirit (the Holy Spirit) in them.

Given the parallel between Ezekiel 11:17-20 and 36:24-28, the "new" spirit that the Lord will put in the people of Israel is likely His Spirit, and it is "new" compared to the spirit they had before:

(19) And I will give them one heart, and **I will put a new spirit within you**; and I will take the stony heart out of their flesh, and will give them an heart of flesh: (20) That they may walk in my statutes, and keep mine ordinances, and do them: and they shall be my people, and I will be their God. (Ezek 11:19-20)

(26) A new heart also will I give you, and a new spirit will I put within you: and I will take away the stony heart out of your flesh, and I will give you an heart of flesh. (27) **And I will put my spirit within you**, and cause you to walk in my statutes, and ye shall keep my judgments, and do them. (Ezek 36:26-27, also see Ezek 39:28-29)

Many will mourn right after the people of Israel receive the Lord's Spirit. People will fully grasp how Christ was mistreated in His first coming:

And I will pour upon the house of David, and upon the inhabitants of Jerusalem, the spirit of grace and of supplications: and they shall look upon me whom they have pierced, and they shall mourn for him, as one mourneth for his only son, and shall be in bitterness for him, as one that is in bitterness for his firstborn. (Zech 12:10)

The outpouring of the Lord's Spirit may also lead to the moment when Israel's sons and daughters shall prophesy and old men shall dream dreams:[3]

(27) And ye shall know that I am in the midst of Israel, and that I am the LORD your God, and none else: and my people shall never be ashamed. (28) And it shall come to pass afterward, that I will pour out my spirit upon all flesh; and your sons and your daughters shall prophesy, your old men shall dream dreams, your young men shall see visions: (Joel 2:27-28, also see Acts 2:17-18)

Israel Plunders Its Neighbors

The remnant of Israel will also plunder their neighbors during this period. Isaiah 11:14 states that the remnant of Israel will plunder the Philistines, Edom, Moab, and Ammon:

But they shall fly upon the shoulders of the Philistines toward the west;

they shall spoil them of the east together: they shall lay their hand upon Edom and Moab; and the children of Ammon shall obey them. (Isa 11:14, also see Ezek 39:10, Zep 2:5-9)

The Fall of Edom

Scripture has much to say about the fall of Edom. The first prediction of Edom's fall came thousands of years ago. Balaam told Balak that Israel will one day crush Edom:

(17) I shall see him, but not now: I shall behold him, but not nigh: there shall come a Star out of Jacob, and a Sceptre shall rise out of Israel, and shall smite the corners of Moab, and destroy all the children of Sheth. (18) And Edom shall be a possession, Seir also shall be a possession for his enemies; and Israel shall do valiantly. (19) Out of Jacob shall come he that shall have dominion, and shall destroy him that remaineth of the city. (Num 24:17-19)

Recall that a coalition of Gentile nations will attack Edom when they pursue those in hiding and that Christ will intervene to protect His people. The intervention by Christ to protect His people will not bring the full end of Edom. The end of Edom will come through the hand of the remnant of Israel:[4]

And I will lay my vengeance upon Edom by the hand of my people Israel: and they shall do in Edom according to mine anger and according to my fury; and they shall know my vengeance, saith the Lord GOD. (Ezek 25:14)

(18) **And the house of Jacob shall be a fire, and the house of Joseph a flame, and the house of Esau for stubble, and they shall kindle in them, and devour them;** and there shall not be any remaining of the house of Esau; for the LORD hath spoken it.... (21) And saviours shall come up on mount Zion to judge the mount of Esau; and the kingdom shall be the LORD'S. (Obad 1:18, 21)

Edom will be uninhabitable after the Lord destroys it through the remnant of Israel (Isa 34:9-10).

THE DEDICATION OF THE TEMPLE

Recall that the Post-Armageddon period will likely end with the dedication of the temple from where Christ will reign. Zechariah tells us that Christ will build this temple:

(12) And speak unto him, saying, Thus speaketh the LORD of hosts, saying, Behold the man whose name is The BRANCH; and he shall grow up out of his place, and he shall build the temple of the LORD: (13) Even he shall build the temple of the LORD; and he shall bear the glory, and shall sit and rule upon his throne; and he shall be a priest upon his throne: and the counsel of peace shall be between them both. (Zech 6:12-13)

The temple will sit on Mount Zion (a fact I will discuss further in the next chapter), and Ezekiel 40-46 describes the building in great detail.

THE MARRIAGE SUPPER OF THE LAMB

The Marriage Supper of the Lamb (or Wedding Feast of the Lamb) may usher in the start of the Millennium. Revelation 19:9 mentions the coming Marriage Supper of the Lamb and how those invited to this event are blessed:

And he saith unto me, Write, Blessed are they which are called unto the marriage supper of the Lamb. And he saith unto me, These are the true sayings of God. (Rev 19:9)

The Bride of the Lamb

The Marriage Supper of the Lamb will celebrate the union of Christ and His bride. Many teach that the Church is the bride of Christ. However, Revelation 21:9-10 clarifies that New Jerusalem is the bride of the Christ:[5] [6] [7]

(9) And there came unto me one of the seven angels which had the seven vials full of the seven last plagues, and talked with me, saying, Come hither, I will shew thee the bride, the Lamb's wife. (10) And he carried me away in the spirit to a great and high mountain, and shewed me that great city, the holy Jerusalem, descending out of heaven from God, (Rev 21:9-10)

The Timing of the Marriage Supper of the Lamb

Isaiah 25 provides clues about the timing of the Marriage Supper of the Lamb. Verse 6 mentions a celebration where the Lord will invite all people to a grand feast on Mount Zion and that the feast will include meat and wine:[8]

> And in this mountain shall the LORD of hosts make unto all people a feast of fat things, a feast of wines on the lees, of fat things full of marrow, of wines on the lees well refined. (Isa 25:6)

The presence of wine at the feast is noteworthy because Christ told His disciples that He would not drink wine until He is back on Earth in His Father's kingdom:

> But I say unto you, I will not drink henceforth of this fruit of the vine, until that day when I drink it new with you in my Father's kingdom. (Matt 26:29)

We saw that the feast will be for everyone on Mount Zion. The guests of this feast are blessed (Rev 19:9). This means that this feast must only include the righteous. This also means that the feast must take place after:

- The Sheep and Goat Judgment.
- The Spiritual Cleansing of Israel.

Daniel says that those who see the 1,335th day are blessed (Dan 12:11). The attendees of this feast are the ones who Daniel refers to.

This confirms the Marriage Supper of the Lamb will take place on the last day of the seventy-five day Post-Armageddon period.

The timing of the Marriage Supper of the Lamb suggests that New Jerusalem, the bride of Christ, will appear at the inauguration of the Millennium. Indeed, I believe New Jerusalem will appear at the start of the Millennium. I will discuss this event in more detail in the next chapter.

LET'S PAUSE FOR A MOMENT

This chapter summarized several Post-Armageddon events. We looked closely at the judging and the rewarding of different groups. Here is a look at where the key events described in this chapter fit in our timeline:

Probable Sequence of Events: Ch.23

The Coming of Christ: Matt 24:30 (Ch.18)

* Gathering of the Wicked: Matt 13:41 (Ch.18)
* Gathering of the Righteous/the Rapture: Matt 24:31 (Ch.18)

Christ Begins to Liberate His People: Isa 61:1-2 (Ch.21)

Greatest Earthquake of All Time: Rev 16:18 (Ch.21)

Antichrist & False Prophet Cast to Lake of Fire: Rev 19:20 (Ch.21)

Slaughter of the Wicked & Jerusalem Liberated: Rev 19:21, Zech 12:6 (Ch.21)

75 Day Post-Armageddon Period: Dan 12:11-12 (Ch.22-23)

* Gathering of the Remnant of Israel: Isa 11:11-12 (Ch.22)
* *Sheep & Goat Judgment: Matt 25:31-46 (Ch.23)*
* *Bema Seat Judgment: Rev 11:18 (Ch.23)*
* *The Spiritual Purification of Israel: Ezek 36:24-28 (Ch.23)*
* *Millennial Temple Built: Zech 6:12-13 (Ch.23)*

Marriage Supper of the Lamb: Rev 19:9 (Ch.23)

I encourage you to reflect on what you have read and to reread any parts that might have been difficult to understand before continuing to the next chapter.

Notes

1. It is important to clarify that the sheeps' good works will not save them. Their good works will instead gain them entry into the Millennium Kingdom. The sheep will only be saved if they accept Christ as their Savior

(Eph 2:8-9, 1John 5:11-13, Rom 6:23). They will presumably get saved before the Millennium (see endnote 3).

2. Strong, James. "kairos". *Strong's Exhaustive Concordance of the Bible.* New York, Cincinnati, Eaton & Mains; Jennings & Graham, 1890. G2540.

3. The Lord will pour out His Spirit will on all flesh, so the remaining Gentiles after the Sheep and Goat Judgment may also receive His Spirit.

4. Ezek 35:9, 14-15 tells us that Edom will desolate when the whole world rejoices. Isa 14:5-8 and Ps 98:2-8 tell us that this will happen after evil's defeat in the war of Armageddon.

5. I am not disputing those who teach that the bride of Christ is the Church. I am only pointing out the reality of Rev 21:9-10.

6. Rev 19:7-9 states:

(7) Let us be glad and rejoice, and give honour to him: for the marriage of the Lamb is come, and his wife hath made herself ready. (8) And to her was granted that she should be arrayed in fine linen, clean and white: for the fine linen is the righteousness of saints. (9) And he saith unto me, Write, Blessed are they which are called unto the marriage supper of the Lamb.

The passage does not say that the bride of the Lamb is the Church. It describes the bride of the Lamb arrayed in fine linen that represents the righteous acts of the saints. But this does not mean the Church is the bride. The righteous acts of the saints are only an accessory for the bride.

Rev 19:9 mentions that the guests of the Marriage Supper of the Lamb are blessed. This verse harkens to the Parable of the Wedding Feast in Matt 22, which concerns the guests of the feast rather than the bride herself.

7. The Parable of the Wedding Feast (Matt 22:1-14) depicts the effort to find guests to attend a wedding feast. This wedding feast is likely the Marriage Supper of the Lamb at the start of the Millennium. The guests, the saints, are those who are worthy of attending the feast.

8. The Apostle Paul quotes from Isa 25:8 when he talks about the Rapture in 1Cor 15:51-54. By quoting Isa 25:8, he tells us the Rapture relates to the Marriage Supper of the Lamb. The Rapture will come before the Marriage Supper of the Lamb, but the time between the events will be short. This is more evidence that the Rapture will occur after the tribulation.

CHAPTER 24.

THE MILLENNIUM: PART 1

The Millennium will be a time of relative peace on Earth. The nations will serve the people of Israel while military conflict will be mitigated. Christ will rule with an iron rod; keeping the inhabitants of Earth in line with His statutes.

Sin will exist during the Millennium. But it will be less prevalent due to Christ's strict rule and Satan's imprisonment.

The purpose of the next two chapters is to summarize what conditions will be like during the Millennium.

THE EARLY DAYS OF THE MILLENNIUM

The Renovation of the Heavens & the Earth

Recall that the Lord will come with fire. Peter tells us that the heavens and the earth will burn up on the Day of the Lord.

(10) But the day of the Lord will come as a thief in the night; in the which the heavens shall pass away with a great noise, and the elements shall melt with fervent heat, the earth also and the works that are therein shall be burned up.... (12) Looking for and hasting unto the coming of the day of God, wherein the heavens being on fire shall be dissolved, and the elements shall melt with fervent heat? (13) Nevertheless we, according to his promise, look for new heavens and a new earth, wherein dwelleth righteousness. (2Pet 3:10, 12-13)

Verse 13 mentions the coming of new heavens and a new earth. We can deduce that the burning up of the heavens and the earth (and the impacts from the seals, trumpets, and bowls) could lead to the need for new heavens and a new earth:

- There will be a lack of drinking water because of the water being turned into blood and dead corpses lying in the water.
- The air will be very unhealthy to breathe due to all the smoke in the air.
- It will be very difficult to grow food because of the lack of adequate water and all the smoke blocking out the sun.

Recall that Job 14:12 stated that the resurrection of the dead will take place when the heavens are no more or passed away. The passing away of the heavens and the earth does not mean that they will cease to exist. Psalm 102 tells us that the heavens and the earth will wear out like old clothing, and the Lord will change them:

(25) Of old hast thou laid the foundation of the earth: and the heavens are the work of thy hands. (26) They shall perish, but thou shalt endure: yea, all of them shall wax old like a garment; as a vesture shalt thou change them, and they shall be changed: (Ps 102:25-26)

You can think of the new heavens and the new earth as a full renovation of what already will exist at the time.[1] We see evidence that new heavens and a new earth will arise at the Millennium in Isaiah. He mentions new heavens and a new earth while describing life in the Millennium:

(17) **For, behold, I create new heavens and a new earth:** and the former shall not be remembered, nor come into mind. (18) But be ye glad and rejoice for ever in that which I create: for, behold, I create Jerusalem a rejoicing, and her people a joy. (Isa 65:17-18)

(22) **For as the new heavens and the new earth**, which I will make, shall remain before me, saith the Lord, so shall your seed and your name remain. (23) And it shall come to pass, that from one new moon to another, and from one sabbath to another, shall all flesh come to worship before me, saith the Lord. (Isa 66:22-23)

The Lord will change the heavens and the earth so that life can thrive in the Millennium and beyond. Christ refers to the time when these changes come about as the regeneration (Matt 19:28).[2]

Satan Bound

The world may be much less sinful during the Millennium with Satan not present to deceive the nations. He will spend the Millennium in the abyss:

(1) And I saw an angel come down from heaven, having the key of the bottomless pit and a great chain in his hand. (2) And he laid hold on the dragon, that old serpent, which is the Devil, and Satan, and bound him a thousand years, (3) And cast him into the bottomless pit, and shut him up, and set a seal upon him, that he should deceive the nations no more, till the thousand years should be fulfilled: and after that he must be loosed a little season. (Rev 20:1-3)

WHO WILL ENTER THE MILLENNIUM?

The population that will enter the Millennium is likely to consist of the following groups:

- **The Saints:** They will serve in various administrative and priestly roles, as we will later see. They will have glorified bodies and will not take part in the repopulating of the earth since they will have glorified bodies (1Cor 15:42-53) and will not marry (Matt 22:30).

- **The Saved Remnant of Israel:** These survivors will have mortal bodies and will take part in the repopulating of the earth.

- **The Surviving Gentiles:** These are the sheep from the Sheep and Goat Judgment. They will have mortal bodies and will take part in the repopulating of the earth.

- **Young Children:** Some young children may survive the tribulation. I don't rule out the possibility that these survivors may enter the Millennium. Only God truly knows the answer and knows the best ways to deal with children who will be too young to understand what took place around them.

Rebuilding the Ruins

The remnant of Israel will rebuild the waste places of their land in the early part of the Millennium:[3]

(14) **And I will bring again the captivity of my people of Israel, and**

they shall build the waste cities, and inhabit them; and they shall plant vineyards, and drink the wine thereof; they shall also make gardens, and eat the fruit of them. (15) And I will plant them upon their land, and they shall no more be pulled up out of their land which I have given them, saith the LORD thy God. (Amos 9:14-15, also see Isa 58:12, 61:4-5, Jer 30:18)

The nations may also help rebuild the waste places (Isa 60:10).[4]

The results of the restoration will be impressive. The transformation of the land will be so dramatic that the land will resemble the Garden of Eden (Isa 51:3, Ezek 36:33-35).

Cleansing of the Land

The remnant of Israel will also bury those who perished in the war of Armageddon. The work will extend into the early months of the Millennium since it will take seven months to clear the land:

(11) And it shall come to pass in that day, that I will give unto Gog a place there of graves in Israel, the valley of the passengers on the east of the sea: and it shall stop the noses of the passengers: and there shall they bury Gog and all his multitude: and they shall call it The valley of Hamongog. (12) And seven months shall the house of Israel be burying of them, that they may cleanse the land. (Ezek 39:11-12)

It will also take seven years to dispose of the weapons used in the war of Armageddon (Ezek 39:9-10).

THE PURPOSE OF THE MILLENNIUM

The Millennium is a phase in God's plan to subdue all His foes, particularly death, and to unite all things in Heaven and on Earth under Christ (Eph 1:10). Death will be the last foe to be defeated, and once it is defeated, Christ will subject all things to the Father, including Himself:

(24) Then cometh the end, when he shall have delivered up the kingdom to God, even the Father; when he shall have put down all rule and all authority and power. (25) For he must reign, till he hath put all enemies under his feet. (26) The last enemy that shall be destroyed is death. (27) For he hath put all things under his feet. But when he saith all things are put under him, it is manifest that he is excepted, which did put all things under him. (28) And when all things shall be subdued

unto him, then shall the Son also himself be subject unto him that put all things under him, that God may be all in all. (1Cor 15:24-28)

The Millennium will also bring the fulfillment of several Old Testament covenants. Here is a brief overview of these covenants:

- **Abrahamic Covenant (Gen 12:1-3, Gen 15)**: God will make a great nation out of Abraham, and his descendants will be blessed in a Promised Land.

- **Davidic Covenant (2Sam 7:8-17)**: The line of David (through Christ) will someday rule forever and reaffirms that the people of Israel will live in their appointed land.

- **Land (Palestinian) Covenant (Deut 29:1-30:20)**: This covenant reaffirms that the people of Israel will possess the Promised Land. The Lord will gather His people from the nations from where they are scattered. Also, the people of Israel will have unprecedented prosperity in their land and live safely. They will also be reconciled to the Lord and have a close relationship with Him.

- **New Covenant (Jer 31:31-35, Rom 11:25-27)**: The Lord will change Israel's heart, forgive their iniquity, and no longer remember their sins. Also, Israel and the Lord will be in an eternal relationship (Jer 32:39-40).

THE MILLENNIAL GOVERNMENT

Theocracy will be the main form of government in the Millennium. It will have a clear hierarchy of power:

- Christ will serve as ruler, chief judge, and chief priest of the entire earth.
- Underneath Christ will be kings and judges who will govern over nations, cities, and smaller localities.
- Priests will also play a prominent role as ministers of the Lord.

Christ as King

Christ will be the undisputed ruler of the world during the Millennium (Ps 22:28-29). He will rule the nations with an iron rod, which suggests that He will rule so strictly that there will be severe consequences for those who disobey (Ps 2:8-9, Rev 12:5, 19:5). For instance, nations who do not observe the Feast of Tabernacles will face drought (Zech 14:16-19).

Christ's words will be the basis of the laws of that time:

> And many people shall go and say, Come ye, and let us go up to the mountain of the LORD, to the house of the God of Jacob; and **he will teach us of his ways, and we will walk in his paths: for out of Zion shall go forth the law,** and the word of the LORD from Jerusalem. (Isa 2:3, also see Mic 4:2)

Besides serving as lawmaker, Christ will serve as a righteous judge (Isa 11:1-4). Christ will even judge and settle disputes that arise between nations (Mic 4:3, Isa 9:7).

Christ as High Priest

Christ will serve as High Priest as He rules on His throne:

> (12) And speak unto him, saying, Thus speaketh the LORD of hosts, saying, Behold the man whose name is The BRANCH; and he shall grow up out of his place, and he shall build the temple of the LORD: (13) Even he shall build the temple of the LORD; and he shall bear the glory, and shall sit and rule upon his throne; **and he shall be a priest upon his throne**: and the counsel of peace shall be between them both. (Zech 6:12-13)

Christ's role as king and priest in the Millennium is modeled after Melchizedek, a king who also served as a priest in the time of Abraham (Gen 14:18-20, Heb 6:20, Ps 110:1-4).

Jerusalem: Capital City of the World

Jerusalem will be an elevated plain-exalted above all other places on Earth:

> All the land shall be turned as a plain from Geba to Rimmon south of Jerusalem: and it shall be lifted up, and inhabited in her place, from Benjamin's gate unto the place of the first gate, unto the corner gate, and from the tower of Hananeel unto the king's winepresses. (Zech 14:10)

Fittingly, Jerusalem will serve as the capital city of the entire world as it will be the home of Mount Zion and the temple of the Lord:

(1) Great is the LORD, and greatly to be praised in **the city of our God, in the mountain of his holiness.** (2) **Beautiful for situation, the joy of the whole earth, is mount Zion, on the sides of the north, the city of the great King.** (3) God is known in her palaces for a refuge.... (8) **As we have heard, so have we seen in the city of the LORD of hosts, in the city of our God: God will establish it for ever. Selah.** (Ps 48:1-3, 8, also see Isa 60:14, 62:1-3, Jer 3:16-17, Ps 68:28-30)

Mount Zion will be the highest point on Earth (Ezek 40:1-2). The Lord's temple will be on Mount Zion, and He will dwell with His people:[5]

And he said unto me, Son of man, the place of my throne, and the place of the soles of my feet, where I will dwell in the midst of the children of Israel for ever, and my holy name, shall the house of Israel no more defile, neither they, nor their kings, by their whoredom, nor by the carcases of their kings in their high places. (Ezek 43:7)

(2) And it shall come to pass in the last days, that the **mountain of the LORD'S house shall be established in the top of the mountains**, and shall be exalted above the hills; and all nations shall flow unto it. (3) And many people shall go and say, Come ye, and let us go up to the mountain of the LORD, to the house of the God of Jacob; and he will teach us of his ways, and we will walk in his paths: for out of Zion shall go forth the law, **and the word of the LORD from Jerusalem.** (Isa 2:2-3)

Jerusalem will be a splendid city at that time. A strong case can be made that this Jerusalem described in the Old Testament will be New Jerusalem, which Revelation 21 and 22 cover in great detail.

New Jerusalem shares many key details with Jerusalem in the Millennium. Here are some of the key details they share:

- **The Lord is Jerusalem's Husband:** Isa 54:1-8 (also see Gal 4:26-27), Isa 62:5, Rev 21:2-3, 9-10

- **The Place of the Lord's Throne:** Ps 46:4-5, 48:1-3, Isa 24:23, Jer 3:17, Ezek 37:27, 43:5-7, Zech 2:10-11, Rev 21:3-4, 22, 22:3

- **The City of God:** Ps 46:4, 48:1-2, 8, 87:1-3, 132:13-14, Isa 60:14, Joel 3:17, Heb 12:22, Rev 3:12

- **The Lord Provides Light:** Isa 60:19-20, Rev 21:23-24, 22:5

- **Water of Life & Healing Fruits:** Ps 46:4, Zech 14:8, Ezek 47:1-12, Rev 22:1-2

- **Built with Precious Stones:** Isa 54:11-12, Rev 21:18-21

- **Twelve Gates Named After the Tribes of Israel:** Rev 21:12-13, Ezek 48:31-34

- **The City Gates Do Not Close:** Isa 60:11, Rev 21:25

- **In a Very High Place:** Isa 2:3, Mic 4:1, Ezek 40:2, Rev 21:10

- **The Nations Will Bring Their Honor:** Isa 60:11, Rev 21:24, 26

I do not believe these parallels are a coincidence. It is likely that New Jerusalem is the Jerusalem of the Millennium. They are the same place.[6][7]

New Jerusalem will serve as the eternal home of the saints (John 14:2-4, Rev 22:3-5). Only those whose names are in the Book of Life can enter the city (Rev 21:27). The wicked will not be allowed to enter the city (Rev 21:27, 22:14-15).

THE KINGS OF THE EARTH

The kings of the earth at that time will be subservient to Christ (Ps 72:8-11, 138:4-5), including King David.

King David

The Lord promised David that his seed will reign forever. Christ's reign will fulfill this promise, and David will also receive a high position of power (Ps 89:3-5, 27-29, 34-37). He will serve as ruler of Israel during the Millennium:

But they shall serve the LORD their God, **and David their king, whom I will raise up unto them.** (Jer 30:9)

(24) **And David my servant shall be king over them**; and they all shall have one shepherd: they shall also walk in my judgments, and observe my statutes, and do them. (25) And they shall dwell in the land that I have given unto Jacob my servant, wherein your fathers have dwelt; and they shall dwell therein, even they, and their children, and their children's children for ever: **and my servant David shall be their prince for ever.** (Ezek 37:24-25, also see Ezek 34:23-24)

However, David will be under the authority of Christ, who will be king of the entire world, including Israel. Nevertheless, David will be above the other kings of the earth (Ps 89:27).

Many Judges Under Christ

A group of judges will work under Christ during the Millennium (Jer 3:15, 23:4-5, Isa 1:26-27, 32:1-2). The saints will fill the role as judges as the Apostle Paul revealed that the saints will judge the world and even angels:

(2) Do ye not know that the saints shall judge the world? and if the world shall be judged by you, are ye unworthy to judge the smallest matters? (3) Know ye not that we shall judge angels? how much more things that pertain to this life? (1Cor 6:2-3)

Revelation 20:4 confirms this when it states that the fifth seal martyrs will have the power to judge:[8]

And I saw thrones, and they sat upon them, and judgment was given unto them: and I saw the souls of them that were beheaded for the witness of Jesus, and for the word of God, and which had not worshipped the beast, neither his image, neither had received his mark upon their foreheads, or in their hands; and they lived and reigned with Christ a thousand years. (Rev 20:4)

This fulfills the promise Christ gives to those who remain steadfast in their faith. He promises to grant them authority:[9]

To him that overcometh will I grant to sit with me in my throne, even as I also overcame, and am set down with my Father in his throne. (Rev 3:21)

Christ promised He will give believers power over the nations. This means that they will judge the nations:

> (26) And he that overcometh, and keepeth my works unto the end, **to him will I give power over the nations**: (27) **And he shall rule them with a rod of iron**; as the vessels of a potter shall they be broken to shivers: even as I received of my Father. (Rev 2:26-27)

Christ also promised that twelve apostles will have a special role. They will serve as judges over the restored nation of Israel:

> And Jesus said unto them, Verily I say unto you, That ye which have followed me, in the regeneration when the Son of man shall sit in the throne of his glory, ye also shall sit upon twelve thrones, judging the twelve tribes of Israel. (Matt 19:28)

We can also conclude that what people do on Earth in this life may impact what they will oversee in the Millennium when we consider the Parable of the Pounds (Luke 19:11-27) and the Parable of the Talents (Matt 25:14-30).

Each parable depicts good, faithful servants receiving a reward according to what they had done. Notably, the good servants got the ability to rule over cities in the Parable of the Pounds:

> (16) Then came the first, saying, Lord, thy pound hath gained ten pounds. (17) And he said unto him, Well, thou good servant: because thou hast been faithful in a very little, have thou authority over ten cities. (18) And the second came, saying, Lord, thy pound hath gained five pounds. (19) And he said likewise to him, Be thou also over five cities. (Luke 19:16-19)

Priests of God and Christ

As we have seen, Christ will serve as High Priest. Others will serve in priestly roles as well. Here are those who will serve as priests:

- Some of the Gentiles (Isa 66:20-21)
- The Saints (Rev 20:5-6)
- The Remnant of Israel (Isa 61:6)

Notably, the Levites will serve as priests for the temple of the

Lord. The following passage refers to the role they will play in temple worship:

(15) **But the priests the Levites, the sons of Zadok**, that kept the charge of my sanctuary when the children of Israel went astray from me, they shall come **near to me to minister unto me, and they shall stand before me to offer unto me the fat and the blood,** saith the Lord GOD: (16) **They shall enter into my sanctuary, and they shall come near to my table, to minister unto me, and they shall keep my charge.** (Ezek 44:15-16, also see Mal 3:3, Ezek 43:18-21)

LET'S PAUSE FOR A MOMENT

We looked at Christ's millennial reign in this chapter. Christ will rule the world and serve as its High Priest, chief judge, and chief lawmaker, but He will have kings, judges, and priests assisting Him. Here is a look at where the Millennium fits in our timeline:

Probable Sequence of Events: Ch.24

75 Day Post-Armageddon Period: Dan 12:11-12 (Ch.22-23)

- Gathering of the Remnant of Israel: Isa 11:11-12 (Ch.22)
- Sheep & Goat Judgment: Matt 25:31-46 (Ch.23)
- Bema Seat Judgment: Rev 11:18 (Ch.23)
- The Spiritual Purification of Israel: Ezek 36:24-28 (Ch.23)
- Millennial Temple Built: Zech 6:12-13 (Ch.23)

Marriage Supper of the Lamb: Rev 19:9 (Ch.23)

Millennial Kingdom: Rev 20:4-6 (Ch.24-25)

- *New Heavens & a New Earth: Rev 21:1 (Ch.24)*
- *Satan Bound for 1,000 Years: Rev 20:2 (Ch.24)*
- *New Jerusalem Arrives: Rev 21:2, 10 (Ch.24)*

I encourage you to reflect on what you have read and reread any parts that might have been difficult to understand before continuing to the next chapter. I will discuss what life in the Millennium will be like in the next chapter.

Notes

1. Jer 31:35-37 reinforces the idea that the heavens will not cease to exist before they become new. The passage links the lifespan of the sun, the moon, and the stars to the nation of Israel's lifespan. If they cease to exist, Israel will cease to exist. We know Israel will always exist, so the heavens will continue to exist as well.

2. Some point out:

   - Rev 21:1 indicates that there will be "no more sea" in the new earth.

   - Rev 20:13 mentions the sea at the end of the Millennium.

   They argue that the contrast between the earth of Rev 20 and Rev 21 suggests that the earth of Rev 20, the earth of the Millennium, is not the new earth.

   It is important to realize that Rev 21:1 does not state that no seas will exist. It refers to one sea.

   Some posit that this is the Red Sea, which the Lord will dry up to make a way for the remnant of Israel when they travel from Egypt (Isa 11:15).

   Others posit that "no more sea" means that there will no longer be a continuous body of water spanning across the world like there is now. Instead, there will be many seas in the new earth.

3. We see that the rebuilding of the waste places will occur in the Millennium when we consider Isa 32 and Ezek 36. Isa 32:13-15 and Ezek 36:33 show that the rebuilding of the waste places will only start after the remnant of Israel are purified and after the Lord pours out His Spirit. We saw that these events do not take place until the late in the Post-Armageddon period.

4. Ezek 38:11 depicts the land of Israel lacking walls during the Millennium

yet Isa 60:10 indicates the nations will help to build up the walls.

It is possible that walls may exist in the land of Israel during the early part of the Millennium but later taken down as the inhabitants grow more secure or need room to accommodate their growing livestock population.

5. Mic 4:1-2, Zech 8:3, Joel 3:17-18, Ps 68:15-16, 29, Ps 132:13-14, Isa 24:23, and Ezek 20:40 also indicate that the Lord will reign from Mount Zion.

6. Some skeptics of the view that New Jerusalem is Jerusalem of the Millennium point out:

   ◦ New Jerusalem will not have a temple (Rev 21:22).

   ◦ Jerusalem will have a temple in the Millennium (Ezek 43).

   The Greek word for "temple" in Rev 21:22 does not refer to the whole temple structure. It only refers to the Holy of Holies. No Holy of Holies will exist in New Jerusalem because God and Christ will reign from there. Therefore, saying that New Jerusalem will have a temple does not contradict Rev 21:22.

7. The size of New Jerusalem is disputed. Some believe New Jerusalem is a city that will be too big to fit on the earth in the Millennium. However, others believe New Jerusalem will not be nearly as large as some argue, and it will fit the boundaries of Israel in the Millennium. Regardless of who is right, I believe there is overwhelming evidence for New Jerusalem to be present in the Millennium.

8. John recognized the martyrs he saw after the breaking of the fifth seal (Rev 6:9-11). They are people who lost their lives during the great tribulation for supporting the Word of God and refusing to bow down to the Antichrist. They were resurrected at the Rapture and will reign with Christ during the Millennium.

9. Similarly, Job 36:5-7 says that the righteous will sit on the throne with kings; forever exalted.

CHAPTER 25.

THE MILLENNIUM: PART 2

In this chapter, we will look at what life will be like in the Millennium and look at what will happen at the end of the Millennium.

THE LAND OF ISRAEL IN THE MILLENNIUM

Israel will be a much different place than it is today. We will look at how it will be different in this section.

A Kingdom United

Political divisions will no longer exist between the Kingdom of Israel and the Kingdom of Judah during the Millennium:

> And I will make them one nation in the land upon the mountains of Israel; and one king shall be king to them all: **and they shall be no more two nations, neither shall they be divided into two kingdoms any more at all:** (Ezek 37:22, also see Hos 1:10-11, Isa 11:12-13, Jer 3:17-18, 50:4)

Expanded Borders

The boundaries of Israel will be much larger than they are today. Ezekiel 47:13-20 describes the boundaries of Israel at that time. Their borders will extend into Lebanon and Syria.

Unprecedented Security

The Bible tells us how the people of Israel will dwell safely during the Millennium. They will be afraid of no one:

And they shall no more be a prey to the heathen, neither shall the beast of the land devour them; **but they shall dwell safely, and none shall make them afraid**. (Ezek 34:28, also see Jer 23:5-7, 32:37-38, 33:16, Isa 32:17-20, 60:17, Mic 4:4)

The residents of the land will have great confidence in the Lord to keep them safe. They will have good reason to feel secure. The Lord will have executed judgment against those who despised them:

And they shall dwell safely therein, and shall build houses, and plant vineyards; yea, they shall dwell with confidence, when I have executed judgments upon all those that despise them round about them; and they shall know that I am the LORD their God. (Ezek 28:26)

The Lord will extend peace to Jerusalem and no weapon will succeed against it (Isa 66:10-14, Isa 54:17). The streets of the city will be safe for children to play and for the elderly to rest at (Zech 8:4-6). It's easy to imagine why the people of Israel will dwell safely with confidence. They will know that they have a Protector who can annihilate anyone who may pose a threat to them. The Lord proved His strength through the rout of their enemies during the time of His coming. The Lord will protect them and Jerusalem (Zech 2:5).

Prosperity

The people of Israel will enjoy great prosperity (Zech 8:11-13). For example, they will never see famine. The land will produce great crop yields each year and no one will plunder their food:

(29) I will also save you from all your uncleannesses: **and I will call for the corn, and will increase it, and lay no famine upon you**. (30) And I will multiply the fruit of the tree, and the increase of the field, that **ye shall receive no more reproach of famine among the heathen**. (Ezek 36:29-30, also see Isa 30:23-24, Joel 2:19, Isa 62:6-9)

Also, the people of Israel will have many cattle in their land (Zech 2:4, Ezek 36:10-11).

THE NATIONS IN THE MILLENNIUM

The nations will not resist the Lord and His people in the Millennium like they will during the end times. Instead, they will serve Christ and His people.

Servants of Christ

The nations of the earth will serve Christ and seek to live according to His ways during the Millennium. The nations will serve the Lord while the kings of the earth submit to the Lord's authority (Ps 72:11, Isa 56:6).

The Nations Will Worship the Lord

The worship of the Lord will be a global practice. People across the world will worship the Lord from their respective locations:

> The LORD will be terrible unto them: for he will famish all the gods of the earth; **and men shall worship him, every one from his place, even all the isles of the heathen.** (Zep 2:11)

> For from the rising of the sun even unto the going down of the same **my name shall be great among the Gentiles; and in every place incense shall be offered unto my name, and a pure offering: for my name shall be great among the heathen,** saith the LORD of hosts. (Mal 1:11)

People from around the world will also take part in temple worship and sacrifice in Jerusalem. The temple will be a place of prayer for everyone:

> (6) Also the sons of the stranger, that join themselves to the LORD, to serve him, and to love the name of the LORD, to be his servants, every one that keepeth the sabbath from polluting it, and taketh hold of my covenant; (7) **Even them will I bring to my holy mountain, and make them joyful in my house of prayer: their burnt offerings and their sacrifices shall be accepted upon mine altar; for mine house shall be called an house of prayer for all people.** (8) The Lord GOD which gathereth the outcasts of Israel saith, Yet will I gather others to him, beside those that are gathered unto him. (Isa 56:6-8, also see Ps 22:27, 86:9)

People will offer gifts to the Lord when they visit His temple:

> (28) Thy God hath commanded thy strength: strengthen, O God, that which thou hast wrought for us. (29) **Because of thy temple at**

Jerusalem shall kings bring presents unto thee. (Ps 68:28-29, also see Ps 45:12, 72:8-10, Isa 60:13)

Also, as previously stated, the nations will be expected to attend major events like the Feast of Tabernacles (Zech 14:16-19).

Followers of the Lord's Word

Many people living in the nations will seek to live according to the Lord's Word:

And many people shall go and say, Come ye, and let us go up to the mountain of the LORD, to the house of the God of Jacob; and he will teach us of his ways, and we will walk in his paths: for out of Zion shall go forth the law, and the word of the LORD from Jerusalem. (Isa 2:3, also see Mic 4:2, Zech 8:20-23)

The nations will not be ignorant of the Lord's ways. His teachings will be readily available (Isa 11:9).

Peaceful Relations

The nations will ask Christ to settle disputes instead of waging war with one another. Christ will resolve their disputes and serve as the judge of the nations. As a result, war will not exist, and the weapons of war will be repurposed:

And he shall judge among the nations, and shall rebuke many people: **and they shall beat their swords into plowshares, and their spears into pruninghooks: nation shall not lift up sword against nation, neither shall they learn war any more.** (Isa 2:4, also see Mic 4:3, Hos 2:18)

Therefore, Christ's title as "The Prince of Peace" will be fitting with the absence of war (Isa 9:6-7).

The Servants of Israel & Jerusalem

Beyond serving Christ, the nations will serve Israel and Jerusalem lest they receive severe punishment:

(12) **For the nation and kingdom that will not serve thee shall perish; yea, those nations shall be utterly wasted.**... (14) **The sons also of them that afflicted thee shall come bending unto thee; and all**

they that despised thee shall bow themselves down at the soles of thy feet; and they shall call thee, The city of the LORD, The Zion of the Holy One of Israel. (Isa 60:12, 14, also see Isa 49:23)

CONDITIONS IN THE MILLENNIUM

Life during the Millennium will have some similarities to life today, but will have some significant differences as well.

Life Expectancy and Sin

The lifespan of humans will be much greater during the Millennium than it is today and may be comparable to pre-flood days. In fact, those who die at one hundred years of age at that time will be deemed to have died young:

> There shall be no more thence an infant of days, nor an old man that hath not filled his days: for the child shall die an hundred years old; but the sinner being an hundred years old shall be accursed. (Isa 65:20)

The fact that people will die during the Millennium is proof that sin will still exist since the wages of sin is death (Rom 6:23).[1]

Peaceful Animal & Human Interaction

The Lord will make a covenant with all creatures (Hos 2:18). This will bring peace between animals and animals and humans that we do not see today:

> (6) **The wolf also shall dwell with the lamb**, and the leopard shall lie down with the kid; and the calf and the young lion and the fatling together; and a little child shall lead them. (7) And the cow and the bear shall feed; their young ones shall lie down together: and the lion shall eat straw like the ox. (8) And the sucking child shall play on the hole of the asp, and the weaned child shall put his hand on the cockatrice' den. (9) **They shall not hurt nor destroy** in all my holy mountain: for the earth shall be full of the knowledge of the LORD, as the waters cover the sea. (Isa 11:6-9, also see Isa 65:25, Ezek 34:25)

Brighter Sun & Moon

The light given by the sun and by the moon will be many times brighter in the Millennium than before the Millennium:

Moreover the light of the moon shall be as the light of the sun, and the light of the sun shall be sevenfold, as the light of seven days, in the day that the LORD bindeth up the breach of his people, and healeth the stroke of their wound. (Isa 30:26)

THE END OF THE MILLENNIUM

The end of the Millennium will bring the end of Satan after he makes one last attempt to thwart God's plan to subdue all His foes. The judgment of the remaining dead and the end of death will also take place.

Satan's Release & Gog's Attacks

Satan will be set free at the end of the Millennium to deceive the nations one last time. The result will be a new invasion featuring Gog and Magog:[2]

(7) And when the thousand years are expired, Satan shall be loosed out of his prison, (8) And shall go out to deceive the nations which are in the four quarters of the earth, Gog and Magog, to gather them together to battle: the number of whom is as the sand of the sea. (Rev 20:7-8)

Ezekiel 38, particularly verses 8-23, records Gog's invasion at the end of the Millennium as it describes the people of Israel gathered from all the nations and living prosperously in complete safety:[3]

(8) After many days thou shalt be visited: in the latter years thou shalt come into the land that is brought back from the sword, and is gathered out of many people, against the mountains of Israel, which have been always waste: but it is brought forth out of the nations, and they shall dwell safely all of them.... (11) And thou shalt say, I will go up to the land of unwalled villages; I will go to them that are at rest, that dwell safely, all of them dwelling without walls, and having neither bars nor gates, (12) To take a spoil, and to take a prey; to turn thine hand upon the desolate places that are now inhabited, and upon the people that are gathered out of the nations, which have gotten cattle and goods, that dwell in the midst of the land. (Ezek 38:8, 11-12)

The Lord will again intervene to defeat Gog.[4] Revelation 20:9 tells us that the Lord will send fire to destroy Gog and his forces:

And they went up on the breadth of the earth, and compassed the camp of the saints about, and the beloved city: **and fire came down from God out of heaven, and devoured them**. (Rev 20:9, also see Ezek 38:18-23)

Satan will be sent to the lake of fire for eternity after the defeat of Gog and his forces:

> And the devil that deceived them was cast into the lake of fire and brimstone, where the beast and the false prophet are, and shall be tormented day and night for ever and ever. (Rev 20:10)

The Great White Throne Judgment

The judgment of the remaining dead will follow. This judgment is known as the "Great White Throne Judgment" since it will take place at God's great white throne.[5] Those involved will be judged with the Book of Life and judged according to their works:

> (11) And I saw a great white throne, and him that sat on it, from whose face the earth and the heaven fled away; and there was found no place for them. (12) And I saw the dead, small and great, stand before God; and the books were opened: and another book was opened, which is the book of life: and the dead were judged out of those things which were written in the books, according to their works. (13) And the sea gave up the dead which were in it; and death and hell delivered up the dead which were in them: and they were judged every man according to their works.… (15) And whosoever was not found written in the book of life was cast into the lake of fire. (Rev 20:11-13, 15)

The judgment of wicked angels that rebelled against the Lord is also likely to take place at this time. Many angels have been locked up in hell (or *Tartarus* in Greek) and await the time when the wicked will receive their final judgment (2Pet 2:4, 9, Jude 1:6). Hell will give up its captives for the Great White Throne Judgment (Rev 20:13).

The End of Death

Death and hell will be eliminated at this time by being cast into the lake of fire (Rev 20:14). Given that the wages of sin is death (Rom 6:23), the end of death implies that sin will finally be eliminated.

With death and sin defeated, the remaining people will have the pleasure to be with God and Christ forever in a perfect world. *No more suffering. No more pain. No more tears. No more problems.*[6]

This is something that all who believe in Christ as their Lord and Savior can look forward to. Christians should not forget that the Lord is not slack concerning His promises (2Pet 3:9). This includes His promises for a better future, as we wait patiently or impatiently for end time events to take place.

LET'S PAUSE FOR A MOMENT

This chapter covered life in the Millennium and the events that will take place when it is over. Israel will enjoy great prosperity while the nations of the earth serve them and Christ.

Satan will have a last opportunity to thwart God's plans at the end of the Millennium. He will fail and will be cast into the lake of fire to suffer for eternity alongside the wicked. Here is where these events fit in our timeline:

Probable Sequence of Events: Ch.25

75 Day Post-Armageddon Period: Dan 12:11-12 (Ch.22-23)

• Gathering of the Remnant of Israel: Isa 11:11-12 (Ch.22)

• Sheep & Goat Judgment: Matt 25:31-46 (Ch.23)

• Bema Seat Judgment: Rev 11:18 (Ch.23)

• The Spiritual Purification of Israel: Ezek 36:24-28 (Ch.23)

• Millennial Temple Built: Zech 6:12-13 (Ch.23)

Marriage Supper of the Lamb: Rev 19:9 (Ch.23)

Millennium Kingdom: Rev 20:4-6 (Ch.24-25)

• New Heavens & a New Earth: Rev 21:1 (Ch.24)

• Satan Bound for 1,000 Years: Rev 20:2 (Ch.24)

• New Jerusalem Arrives: Rev 21:2, 10 (Ch.24)

Satan Released & Defeated: Rev 20:7-10 (Ch.25)

Great White Throne Judgment: Rev 20:11-13, 15 (Ch.25)

THANK YOU FOR YOUR TIME

Thank you for your patience and for your effort to seek out Bible prophecy truth. You've done a great job and accomplished a lot! I also want to thank you for considering the information presented in this book, whether or not you agreed with my conclusions. This book is certainly not perfect, but God and His Word are perfect. Keep studying God's Word, and you will learn even more!

You have reached the end of the main part of this book. Next, you will encounter several appendix sections where I expand on topics that I could not cover earlier in this book.

Notes

1. Isa 65 tells us that death will exist in the Millennium. However, Rev 21:4 tells us that there will be no more death and pain.

    No more death and no more pain in Rev 21:4 refers to what will take place in the confines of New Jerusalem. Death and sin will exist outside of New Jerusalem. We can see that sin will exist outside the city in the Millennium from the fact that some will not be allowed to enter the city (Rev 21:27, 22:14-15).

2. I do not know for sure why Gog appears in Rev 20:7-9. One possibility is that there could be another leader who adopts the name or title "Gog" at the end of the Millennium to lead the forces described in Rev 20.

3. A complete explanation of why Ezek 38's primary fulfillment will come at the end of the Millennium is found in the appendix section titled "The Fulfillment of Ezekiel 38".

4. Ezek 38 mentions that God will show the nations that He is the Lord and mentions how God will be sanctified in the destruction of Gog. The question arises: "Why would the Lord need to show the nations who He is and need to be sanctified again if the fulfillment of Ezekiel 38 is post-millennial? The nations will have served Him and His people for an entire Millennium and lived according to His ways."

The likely answer to why the Lord will need to show the nations who He is and need to be sanctified again is that Satan will deceive the nations upon his release from imprisonment. The nations will again regress to a state where they will be opponents of God with Satan's corrupting influence.

5. Some believe that Rev 20:11 records the passing away of heaven and earth. However, we have seen evidence that the heavens and the earth will pass away when Christ comes. How should we view Rev 20:11?

   Some argue that Rev 20:11 is a verse that describes God (or gives a title to God) based on what He's already accomplished in the past:

   - To help you understand this, think of another title for God. He is often referred to as the God who rescued His people from Egypt. The people of Israel glorified God for rescuing them from Egypt many generations after the event. A Jew living in the fifth century B.C. may refer to God as the "One who rescued us from the hand of Egypt". God did not rescue the people of Israel at that time from Egypt, but He has the title because He did that in the past.

   - Similarly, people may glorify God for causing the first heavens and the first earth to pass away and for creating new heavens and a new earth. John expands on what the Lord accomplished at the start of the Millennium in Rev 21 and 22.

   Others argue that Rev 20:11 conveys the notion that heaven and earth will have nowhere to escape from God.

   I lean towards the first position. Replacing the heavens and the earth will be a huge accomplishment that will be worth praise.

6. Christians will get to experience this perfect existence when the new heavens and new earth arise. But, here I am making a general statement about how nice the whole world will be when death and sin are gone.

IS "GOG" THE ANTICHRIST?

I believed for many years that Gog and the Antichrist were the same individuals. I thought that "Gog" simply was a nickname for the Antichrist.

However, after much study, I believe Gog is a different person than the Antichrist. Gog will lead a different set of nations than the Antichrist will lead. His demise will also be different from the Antichrist.

GOG'S ALLIES VS. ANTICHRIST'S ALLIES

I once believed that Gog's allies aligned with the kings that the Antichrist will work with, as Ezekiel 38 lists many nations. But after much study, I no longer link the allies of Gog, the king of the north, with the kings that align with the Antichrist. Here is why:

The Duration of the Alliance

The king of the north revolts against the Antichrist after the sixth trumpet sounds. Thus, the ten kings would have to rebel against the Antichrist soon after the sixth trumpet sounds if Gog's allies align with the kings that will work with the Antichrist.

However, the ten kings will remain loyal to the Antichrist until they betray him by destroying Babylon the Great (Rev 17:16-17). The ten kings will destroy her after the pouring of the seventh bowl judgment, so the alliance between the ten kings and the Antichrist will be intact until that time (see chapter seventeen).

Ezekiel Does Not List Ten Nations

Ezekiel 38:1-6 lists eight nations that will join Gog when he attacks. The fact that Ezekiel 38 does not list ten nations is more proof that Gog's allies may not align with the kings that Antichrist will work with. You'd think that Ezekiel would mention ten nations instead of the eight nations listed if he meant to reveal the nations that the ten kings will rule.

THE DEMISE OF GOG VS. DEMISE OF ANTICHRIST

The demise of the Antichrist and the demise of Gog appear to be different events. Revelation 19 indicates that the Antichrist will not receive a burial. He will be cast alive into the lake of fire:

> And the beast was taken, and with him the false prophet that wrought miracles before him, with which he deceived them that had received the mark of the beast, and them that worshipped his image. These both were cast alive into a lake of fire burning with brimstone. (Rev 19:20)

In contrast, Ezekiel 39 states that Gog will have his corpse buried after his defeat:

> And it shall come to pass in that day, that I will give unto Gog a place there of graves in Israel, the valley of the passengers on the east of the sea: and it shall stop the noses of the passengers: and there shall they bury Gog and all his multitude: and they shall call it The valley of Hamongog. (Ezek 39:11)

The Assyrian vs. King of Babylon

The prophets often wrote their prophecies so that their audience could grasp what they saw, even though they described times and events well into the future. Isaiah did this when he wrote about the Assyrian and the king of Babylon. For instance, Isaiah described the king of Babylon as a very arrogant king:

> (12) How art thou fallen from heaven, O Lucifer, son of the morning! how art thou cut down to the ground, which didst weaken the nations! (13) For thou hast said in thine heart, I will ascend into heaven, I will exalt my throne above the stars of God: I will sit also upon the mount of the congregation, in the sides of the north: (14) I will ascend above the heights of the clouds; I will be like the most High. (Isa 14:12-14)

This passage has led many to link the king of Babylon to the Antichrist. I agree that the king of Babylon represents the Antichrist in end time passages since the Antichrist will be a very arrogant man, as described in prior chapters of this book.

Isaiah also refers to the Assyrian (the king of Assyria) in end time passages. He will meet his demise after he attacks Jerusalem.

I believe the distinction between the king of Assyria and the king of Babylon suggests that the terms represent different individuals:

- The end time king of Babylon represents the Antichrist.
- The king of Assyria represents Gog in end time passages.

I don't think it is a coincidence that Gog and the Assyrian will meet their fate upon the mountains of Israel.[1]

> That I will break the Assyrian in my land and upon my mountains tread him under foot: then shall his yoke depart from off them, and his burden depart from off their shoulders. (Isa 14:25)

> Thou shalt fall upon the mountains of Israel, thou, and all thy bands, and the people that is with thee: I will give thee unto the ravenous birds of every sort, and to the beasts of the field to be devoured. (Ezek 39:4)

A SUMMARY ON GOG

Gog is not the Antichrist. He represents the "Assyrian" (the king of Assyria) and Daniel 11:40's "king of the north" who will come against the Antichrist during the end times.

Notes

1. Ezek 38:8, 21 show that the mountains of Israel are the Lord's mountains so we can equate "my mountains" in Isa 14:25 to the mountains of Israel:

IDENTIFYING GOG'S COALITION

Many people, including myself at one time, linked the ten kingdoms that the Antichrist will control with the allies of Gog. However, I no longer link the ten kingdoms of the Antichrist's empire with the allies of Gog because:

1. The Antichrist and Gog are not the same individuals. Gog and the Antichrist are powerful leaders who will oppose each other during the latter portion of the end times. I expanded upon this in chapter twelve and in the appendix section titled "Is 'Gog' the Antichrist?".

2. The Antichrist's empire will consist of ten kingdoms during the end times. Ezekiel 38 lists only eight nations who will join Gog.

Gog will attack the Antichrist when the Antichrist faces challenges to his power in the latter part of his reign (see chapter twelve). The Book of Daniel describes the Antichrist facing challenges from the king of the south and the king of the north:

> And at the time of the end shall the king of the south push at him: and the king of the north shall come against him like a whirlwind, with chariots, and with horsemen, and with many ships; and he shall enter into the countries, and shall overflow and pass over. (Dan 11:40)

The king of the north is Gog, from the land of Magog, mentioned in Ezekiel 38:1-7 and Ezekiel 39. Many allies will join Gog, including the nations referred to in Ezekiel 38:2-6:

- Magog, Meshech, Tubal
- Gomer, Togarmah, Persia, Ethiopia, Libya

The nations that join Gog will unlikely be a part of the Antichrist's ten kingdom empire, since they will revolt against the Antichrist when the ten kings (and their kingdoms) will still be loyal to him.

The ten kings who will cooperate with the Antichrist will keep their support for him until the destruction of Babylon the Great at the pouring of the seventh bowl judgment (see chapter seventeen):

(12) And the ten horns which thou sawest are ten kings, which have received no kingdom as yet; but receive power as kings one hour with the beast. (13) These have one mind, and shall give their power and strength unto the beast.... (16) And the ten horns which thou sawest upon the beast, these shall hate the whore, and shall make her desolate and naked, and shall eat her flesh, and burn her with fire. (17) For God hath put in their hearts to fulfil his will, and to agree, and give their kingdom unto the beast, until the words of God shall be fulfilled. (Rev 17:12-13, 16-17)

Consequently, *we may gain a better understanding of which geographic areas will comprise the Antichrist's empire by eliminating the allies of Gog from consideration.*

LOCATING THE ALLIES OF GOG

We have seen that Gog's coalition will comprise many nations (or people groups). We will look at where the allies of Gog will come from. The identification of Gog's allies will help us eliminate them from being part of the Antichrist's empire.

Most try to locate where these nations are today. This method is very unreliable.

The main problem is that it is hard to track where many people groups have migrated to over thousands of years. Some people groups have vanished. Others have integrated into other groups.

The difficulty of tracking people groups over time may be why many disagree about where some nations are at today. For instance:

• Some argue that Gomer is in modern day Germany.
• Others believe Gomer is in other areas of Western Europe.

Another issue is that this method allows for political bias to affect where people locate nations in modern times. For instance, many taught that Meshech and Tubal were in the Soviet Union in the 1980s. Many felt these nations must be in the Soviet Union since it was the chief enemy of the West at that time.

For these reasons, we cannot reliably identify where Gog's allies will come from if we rely on finding where these nations are now.

A more reliable way to identify the locations of Gog's allies is to:

1. View their locations as Ezekiel and his audience at the time did.

2. Identify the modern day places that correspond to these locations.

Ezekiel's audience at the time linked the nations he wrote about to certain locations. Let's consider Ezekiel 27:13. The verse tells us that Meshech and Tubal were nations that traded with Tyre:

> Javan, Tubal, and Meshech, they were thy merchants: they traded the persons of men and vessels of brass in thy market. (Ezek 27:13)

The people of Ezekiel's time knew where these nations lived. This same understanding applied when they saw these nations again in Ezekiel 38:

> (2) Son of man, set thy face against Gog, the land of Magog, the chief prince of Meshech and Tubal, and prophesy against him, (3) And say, Thus saith the Lord GOD; Behold, I am against thee, O Gog, the chief prince of Meshech and Tubal: (Ezek 38:2-3)

The people of Ezekiel's day did not think that "Meshech and Tubal" in Ezekiel 27 resided in different places than "Meshech and Tubal" in Ezekiel 38, since Ezekiel used the same names to identify these nations in both chapters.

This method avoids the major problems of the previous method:

- We do not need to track the movements of many people groups over thousands of years. Instead, we only need to focus on where these people groups resided at Ezekiel's time.

- We also do not need to worry about political bias. We are more than 3,500 years removed from the politics of Ezekiel's time.

- Moreover, the findings from this method have a biblical basis. They are linked to the period when Ezekiel recorded his prophecies.

The issue with using this method is that we lack a map from the sixth century B.C. that shows where Gog's allies lived. However, we can get a good idea where Gog's allies lived by relying on Bible atlases and Bible dictionaries. Figure 1 summarizes where Gog's allies lived in Ezekiel's time:

Figure 1: The Allies of Gog

- **Magog:** Turkey
- **Tubal:** Turkey
- **Meshech:** Turkey
- **Togarmah:** Turkey
- **Gomer:** Turkey
- **Persia:** Iran
- **Ethiopia:** N. Sudan
- **Libya:** Large Parts of N. Africa, including Libya.

Ezekiel 30: Egypt and Its Allies

The king of the south will also challenge the Antichrist's power. In fact, it is likely that the king of the south and the king of the north will be allies given that they share common allies (Ethiopia and Libya) and a common enemy (Antichrist). The king of the south represents the leader of Egypt. Daniel 11:41-43 records the Antichrist coming against Egypt and some of its allies:

> (41) He shall enter also into the glorious land, and many countries shall be overthrown: but these shall escape out of his hand, even Edom, and Moab, and the chief of the children of Ammon. (42) He shall stretch forth his hand also upon the countries: and the land of Egypt shall not escape. (43) But he shall have power over the treasures of gold and of silver, and over all the precious things of Egypt: and the Libyans and the Ethiopians shall be at his steps. (Dan 11:41-43)

Ezekiel 30:1-9 also refers to the king of the south's challenge against the Antichrist. Verse 4-5 mentions the allies who will aid the king of the south's challenge against him:

(4) And the sword shall come upon Egypt, and great pain shall be in Ethiopia, when the slain shall fall in Egypt, and they shall take away her multitude, and her foundations shall be broken down. (5) Ethiopia, and Libya, and Lydia, and all the mingled people, and Chub, and the men of the land that is in league, shall fall with them by the sword. (Ezek 30:4-5)

Figure 2 summarizes the modern day locations of the participants who will challenge the Antichrist from the south:

Figure 2: The Southern Coalition

- **Egypt:** Egypt
- **Ethiopia**): N. Sudan
- **Libya & Put:** Large Parts of N. Africa, including Libya.
- **Chub:**N. Africa
- **Mingled People:** Mercenaries from various countries
- **Lydia:** Turkey

Psalm 83 Participants

Psalm 83 describes a future campaign against the people of Israel involving many nations (see chapter fifteen). Verses 6-8 names the participants of this attack:

(6) The tabernacles of Edom, and the Ishmaelites; of Moab, and the Hagarenes; (7) Gebal, and Ammon, and Amalek; the Philistines with the inhabitants of Tyre; (8) Assur also is joined with them: they have holpen the children of Lot. Selah. (Ps 83:6-8)

Figure 3 lists the modern day locations of the nations involved in the events of Psalm 83:

Figure 3: Psalm 83 Participants

- **Amalek:** Sinai
- **Edom, Ammon, Moab:** Jordan
- **Hagarenes:** Jordan (1Chr 5:10)
- **Gebal & Tyre:** Lebanon
- **Assur:** N. Iraq, parts of Syria & Turkey
- **Philistines:** Gaza Strip
- **Ishmaelites:** Saudi Arabia

We can find whom these nations *will not be loyal* to by looking at the fate of Edom. Daniel indicates that Edom will be relatively safe from the Antichrist's counterattack against his foes:

> He shall enter also into the glorious land, and many countries shall be overthrown: but these shall escape out of his hand, even Edom, and Moab, and the chief of the children of Ammon. (Dan 11:41)

Some may argue that Edom is an ally of the Antichrist, since he will spare them. However, two important details suggest Edom will not be an ally of Antichrist:

- Daniel 11:41 states that Edom shall "escape" from the Antichrist's hand. The use of the word "escape" implies that the Antichrist will pose a threat to Edom, but Edom will avoid the advances of the Antichrist. The threat of an attack on Edom suggests that Edom will not be a protectorate of the Antichrist.

- A group of nations will attack Edom during a time of conflict (see chapter twenty-one). Obadiah 1:1, 7, suggest that Edom's allies will betray them. These allies are most likely the other members of the Psalm 83 coalition. Given Daniel 11:41 tells us that Edom will escape the advances of the Antichrist, we can conclude that Edom's attackers are unaffiliated with the Antichrist as well.

From this, we can conclude that the areas where Edom and the other Psalm 83 coalition members encompass will not be a part of the Antichrist's empire.

Kings of the East

We can infer that the kingdoms belonging to the kings of the east will not be a part of the Antichrist's empire since they are a distinct group in the Book of Revelation:

> And the sixth angel poured out his vial upon the great river Euphrates; and the water thereof was dried up, that the way of the kings of the east might be prepared. (Rev 16:12)

The Remaining Possibilities

You may be reluctant to accept the view that Gog will come from Turkey since many teach that Gog is the Antichrist and will come from Russia. However, this view might be easier for you to accept when you understand that Gog *is not* the Antichrist.

The coming of Gog from Turkey only means that the Antichrist will not come from Turkey and that Turkey will not be one of the Antichrist's ten kingdoms. Therefore, it is still possible under this framework for Russia to be one of the Antichrist's ten kingdoms and for Russia to be a place where the Antichrist arises.

Besides Russia, most, if not all, of Europe may be part of the Antichrist's empire. Europe is likely to be part of the Antichrist's empire, since the last empire of Daniel's statue has metal that represents the Roman Empire (see chapter ten).

SUMMARY

The empire of the Antichrist will comprise ten kingdoms led by leaders who will surrender their power to him. The borders of the Antichrist's empire will not span the whole world:

- Its borders may encompass parts of Europe and Russia.

- Its borders may not include many Mideast countries, including Egypt and Turkey. In fact, some of these countries may revolt against the Antichrist when the sixth trumpet sounds.

BABYLON THE GREAT'S IDENTITY

We will look at Babylon the Great in detail in this section. We will focus on:

• The "mystery" of Babylon the Great.

• The geographic scope of Babylon the Great.

• The significance of Babylon's title "MOTHER OF HARLOTS AND ABOMINATIONS OF THE EARTH".

DETAILING THE HARLOT

The Nature of the Harlot's Mystery

One reason many people do not believe Babylon the Great represents Babylon, Iraq is the word "mystery" in Revelation 17:5:

> ...MYSTERY, BABYLON THE GREAT, THE MOTHER OF HARLOTS AND ABOMINATIONS OF THE EARTH.

This word leads many to think that the answer (the site of Babylon the Great in this case) is not so obvious.

We will see if this is a reasonable conclusion by examining the "mystery" of Babylon the Great.

Defining a "Mystery"

Many think of a mystery as an enigma that is hard to solve (i.e. a crime mystery). However, a New Testament mystery is not the same thing. It is a hidden truth revealed to the godly.

For example, Christ told His disciples that they could understand the mysteries of the kingdom of God/Heaven while others could not understand:

> (9) And his disciples asked him, saying, What might this parable be? (10) And he said, Unto you it is given to know the mysteries of the kingdom of God: but to others in parables; that seeing they might not see, and hearing they might not understand. (Luke 8:9-10, also see Matt 13:10-13, Mark 4:10-12)

The idea that a mystery is a hidden truth revealed to the godly is also seen in 1 Corinthians 2:7-10, Romans 16:25-26, and Colossians 1:25-28.

Also, consider Revelation 1:20. The word "mystery" appears in relation to the seven stars and seven lampstands in the first part of the verse. Christ revealed their meaning for John and his readers in the second part of the verse:

> The mystery of the seven stars which thou sawest in my right hand, and the seven golden candlesticks. The seven stars are the angels of the seven churches: and the seven candlesticks which thou sawest are the seven churches. (Rev 1:20)

Thus, a "mystery" is a hidden truth revealed to the godly.

Also, note that she is not called "MYSTERY, BABYLON THE GREAT" elsewhere in the Book of Revelation. Instead, she is called "Babylon the great", "great city Babylon", and "great Babylon". This fact means that the word "mystery" is not a big part of her name (i.e. a way to signal that her location is symbolic).

The way to signify that a place is symbolic is in Revelation 11:8. The word "spiritually" (Greek: *pneumatikōs*) tells readers that Sodom and Egypt represent a great city where the Lord was crucified. That city is Jerusalem.

The Greek word for "mystery" in Revelation 17:5 is *musterion*, so it is not the word used to signify that a place is symbolic. The word "mystery" is not a reason to dismiss Babylon, Iraq as a candidate to be Babylon the Great.

What Is the "Mystery" of the Woman?

The angel that was with John told him that the mystery of the woman and the beast that carries her would be revealed (Rev 17:7).

Revelation 17:8-14 describe the mystery of the beast. Revelation 17:15-18 describe the mystery of the woman, Babylon the Great:

(15) And he saith unto me, The waters which thou sawest, where the whore sitteth, are peoples, and multitudes, and nations, and tongues. (16) And the ten horns which thou sawest upon the beast, these shall hate the whore, and shall make her desolate and naked, and shall eat her flesh, and burn her with fire. (17) For God hath put in their hearts to fulfil his will, and to agree, and give their kingdom unto the beast, until the words of God shall be fulfilled. (18) And the woman which thou sawest is that great city, which reigneth over the kings of the earth.

The "mystery" is no longer unclear after the angel speaks. The woman represents a great city that rules over the kings of the earth and the people of the earth.

Babylon the *Mega Polis*

The Book of Revelation calls Babylon the Great a "great city" (Rev 14:8, 17:18, 18:10, 18:21). Debate exists about her geographic scope. Although she is known as a "great city", some argue she represents a country or even the entire world.

The Greek term for "great city" is mega polis (mega = great, polis = city). It is not the same term as "megapolis", which we use to describe a large area that contains several major cities. The term we use was popularized by geographer Jean Gottmann in 1961. Therefore, it is wrong to think of Babylon the Great as a large area that covers several major cities (like a country or the world).

The term *mega polis* also appears in the Book of Revelation to describe Jerusalem and New Jerusalem:

- It appears in Revelation 21:10 to describe the breathtaking nature of New Jerusalem.
- It appears in Revelation 11:8 concerning Jerusalem.

Why Jerusalem qualifies as a *mega polis* is unclear. The fact that the term is used for a city is more evidence against the notion that Babylon the Great represents a country or the world.

Interestingly, Jeremiah mentions that Babylon's *cities* (plural) will fall during the attack on Babylon:

(41) How is Sheshach taken! and how is the praise of the whole earth surprised! how is Babylon become an astonishment among the nations! (42) The sea is come up upon Babylon: she is covered with the multitude of the waves thereof. (43) **Her cities are a desolation, a dry land, and a wilderness**, a land wherein no man dwelleth, neither doth any son of man pass thereby. (Jer 51:41-43, also see Jer 50:31-32)

Jeremiah 50:40 compares Babylon's ruin to the ruin of Sodom, Gomorrah, and nearby cities (Deut 29:23). This reinforces the idea that Babylon and her cities will fall at the same time:

As God overthrew Sodom and Gomorrah and the neighbour cities thereof, saith the LORD; so shall no man abide there, neither shall any son of man dwell therein. (Jer 50:40)

I believe that Babylon the Great will be a great city surrounded by several smaller cities:

- The "great" (*mega*) aspect of Babylon the Great refers to the city's stature. Babylon the Great City will be extremely wealthy while it reigns over the kings of the earth (Rev 17:18).

- The smaller neighboring cities will probably depend heavily upon on Babylon the Great economically.

Therefore, I do not believe Babylon the Great represents a country or the central city of a network of cities that spans the world. I believe she will be a very powerful city that will fall along with her smaller neighboring cities.

The Mother of Harlots

Babylon the Great is known as the Mother of Harlots (Rev 17:5). I will provide three potential ways to view the significance of Babylon the Great's title in this section.

The Source of Anti-God, Religious Opposition

One possibility is to view Babylon the Great as the source of anti-God, religious opposition. Some cite the Tower of Babel incident recorded in Genesis 11 as the first post-flood revolt against God:

- Babylon is traditionally viewed as the site of the Tower of Babel, although the tower's exact location is unknown.

- The people of the earth constructed the Tower of Babel at a time when they defied God's instructions to spread across the world and built the tower with the intention of giving themselves glory (Gen 11:4).

Many bring up the controversial book by Alexander Hislop called *The Two Babylons*. They use this book to argue that many false religious practices come from Babylon. Hislop's work claims that many practices of the Roman Catholic Church come from Babylon:

- Some present Hislop's book as an authoritative work on the subject.

- Others, like Ralph Woodrow, a former Hislop defender who later became one of his biggest critics, portray the book as unreliable.

- It is up to each reader to decide whether to believe Hislop's claims or not.

The view that Babylon the Great is the source of anti-God, religious opposition suggests that the city is ancient. Notably, Babylon, Iraq was a city long before Jerusalem and Rome; two cities many think are strong candidates to be Babylon the Great.

Two Other Possibilities

Here are two other ways to explain Babylon the Great's title:

- The title is an idiom. Babylon the Great is a harlot of an unprecedented level. Her influence as a harlot will be felt around the world.

- The title could refer to Ishtar. Ishtar was the Mesopotamian goddess of prostitution. Ancient Mesopotamia covered a vast territory, including the city of Babylon.

WHY BABYLON, IRAQ IS BABYLON THE GREAT CITY

I explain why I believe Babylon, Iraq represents Babylon the Great in these upcoming sections. Here is how I will make my case:

- I begin by showing how Old Testament prophecies about the fall of Babylon, Iraq are unfulfilled.

- Afterward, I present extensive evidence that a part of Israel will be in Babylon, Iraq before she falls during the end times.

- Finally, I present several close parallels between Babylon, Iraq and Babylon the Great.

Unfulfilled Prophecies Remain

Old Testament prophecies about the fall of Babylon, Iraq are not fulfilled yet. I focus on two aspects of her fall that are unfulfilled in this section.

Like Sodom & Gomorrah

Old Testament prophets wrote that the fall of Babylon would be so complete that no human will ever live there again. The Bible compares her fall to the fall of Sodom and Gomorrah:

> (19) And Babylon, the glory of kingdoms, the beauty of the Chaldees' excellency, **shall be as when God overthrew Sodom and Gomorrah.** (20) **It shall never be inhabited, neither shall it be dwelt in from generation to generation: neither shall the Arabian pitch tent there; neither shall the shepherds make their fold there.** (Isa 13:19-20, also see Jer 50:39-40)

Many assume these prophecies were fulfilled when Medo-Persia conquered Babylon. However, the city was not ruined by them. In fact, records from the time suggest they took the city peacefully, although the king was killed (Dan 5:30).[1]

Babylon continued as a city long after the Medo-Persian Empire. For instance:

- Alexander the Great died in Babylon in the 4th century B.C.

- Benjamin of Tudela reported that thousands of Jewish worshippers used a large synagogue near Babylon in the 12th century A.D.[2]

Babylon is currently nowhere near the place that it once was in stature. Much of the location is in ruins and needs restoration work. However, efforts have been made in recent decades by Saddam

Hussein and by the World Monument Fund's "Future of Babylon" project to preserve and to restore key sites at Babylon. These efforts suggest the prophecies about Babylon's fall remain unfulfilled. It is not an eternal wasteland yet.

Sudden Destruction

Jeremiah 51:8 predicted that Babylon would be destroyed "suddenly" at the time of her desolation:

> Babylon is suddenly fallen and destroyed: howl for her; take balm for her pain, if so be she may be healed. (Jer 51:8)

The continuance of the city of Babylon after the fall of the Babylonian Empire suggests that the sudden destruction aspect of Babylon's destruction also remains unfulfilled.

The Fulfillment of Babylon's Prophecies

Isaiah 13 and Jeremiah 50 can help to pinpoint when the prophecies about Babylon's demise will take place. Isaiah 13 is about Babylon's fall during the Day of the Lord (see chapter nineteen):

> (6) Howl ye; for the day of the LORD is at hand; it shall come as a destruction from the Almighty.... (19) And Babylon, the glory of kingdoms, the beauty of the Chaldees' excellency, shall be as when God overthrew Sodom and Gomorrah. (Isa 13:6, 19)

We can see the end time relevance of Jeremiah 50 in the details about the Kingdom of Israel and Judah. Both will return together (Jer 50:4), seek to join with the Lord in an everlasting covenant (Jer 50:5), and will not have sin found in them (Jer 50:20). The unification of the Kingdom of Israel and Judah will take place after their end time return from Babylon. (see chapter twenty-five):

> (4) In those days, and in that time, saith the LORD, **the children of Israel shall come, they and the children of Judah together**, going and weeping: they shall go, and seek the LORD their God. (5) They shall ask the way to Zion with their faces thitherward, saying, Come, and let us join ourselves to the LORD in a perpetual covenant that shall not be forgotten. (Jer 50:4-5)

In those days, and in that time, saith the LORD, **the iniquity of Israel** shall be sought for, and there shall be none; and the sins of Judah, and they shall not be found: for I will pardon them whom I reserve. (Jer 50:20)

From this, we can conclude that the prophecies about the fall of Babylon will take place during the end times. This makes Babylon, Iraq a prime candidate to represent Babylon the Great.

The Presence of Israel in Babylon During the End Times

Many end time prophecies reveal that a part of Israel will be in Babylon, Iraq. This is notable since Revelation 18:4 tells us that the Lord's people will be in Babylon the Great just before the judgment of the city:

> And I heard another voice from heaven, saying, Come out of her, my people, that ye be not partakers of her sins, and that ye receive not of her plagues. (Rev 18:4)

Next, I present examples from the Book of Jeremiah, the Book of Zechariah, and the Book of Isaiah that suggests a portion of Israel will be present in Babylon near the time of the city's destruction.

Jeremiah

Jeremiah 24:5-7 states that the Lord will bring His people from the "land of the Chaldeans", which is in the vicinity of Babylon (Ezek 12:13), to the land of Israel and will not allow them to be removed from the land again. He will also give His people a new heart upon their return, and His people will fully commit to Him:

> (5) Thus saith the LORD, the God of Israel; Like these good figs, so will I acknowledge them that are carried away captive of Judah, whom I have sent out of this place into the land of the Chaldeans for their good. (6) For I will set mine eyes upon them for good, and I will bring them again to this land: and I will build them, and not pull them down; and I will plant them, and not pluck them up. (7) And I will give them an heart to know me, that I am the LORD: and they shall be my people, and I will be their God: for they shall return unto me with their whole heart. (Jer 24:5-7)

These details are in passages about the Post-Armageddon gathering of Israel (see chapter twenty-three and Jer 31:33-34, 32:37-40).

Therefore, a portion of Israel will be near Babylon during the end times and will travel to the land of Israel from Babylon in the Post-Armageddon period.

Recall that Jeremiah 50 is about the end time fall of Babylon. The people of Israel are encouraged to flee from there just before her fall in Jeremiah 50 and in Jeremiah 51:

(8) **Remove out of the midst of Babylon, and go forth out of the land of the Chaldeans,** and be as the he goats before the flocks. (9) For, lo, I will raise and cause to come up against Babylon an assembly of great nations from the north country: and they shall set themselves in array against her; from thence she shall be taken: their arrows shall be as of a mighty expert man; none shall return in vain. (Jer 50:8-9)

(5) For Israel hath not been forsaken, nor Judah of his God, of the LORD of hosts; though their land was filled with sin against the Holy One of Israel. (6) **Flee out of the midst of Babylon, and deliver every man his soul:** be not cut off in her iniquity; for this is the time of the LORD'S vengeance; he will render unto her a recompence. (Jer 51:5-6)

Therefore, a part of Israel will be near Babylon and urged to flee from Babylon when it is about to be destroyed.

Zechariah

Zechariah 2 also has evidence that a part of Israel will be in Babylon during the end times:

- Verse 6 onward encourages the part of the Lord's people situated in the "land of the north" (a phrase that I will soon show often refers to Babylon) to flee with a promise of a better future.

- The detail how the Lord will dwell with His people in verses 10-11 places verse 6 in the future instead of the post-exilic return. He will begin to dwell with His people in the Millennium (Rev 20:6):

(6) **Ho, ho, come forth, and flee from the land of the north,** saith the LORD: for I have spread you abroad as the four winds of the heaven, saith the LORD. (7) Deliver thyself, O Zion, that dwellest with the daughter of Babylon.... (10) Sing and rejoice, O daughter of Zion: for, lo, I come, and I will dwell in the midst of thee, saith the LORD. (11) And many nations shall be joined to the LORD in that day, and shall be

my people: and I will dwell in the midst of thee, and thou shalt know that the LORD of hosts hath sent me unto thee. (Zech 2:6-7, 10-11)

Jeremiah 3:17-18 is another end time passage that tell us the people of Israel will travel from the land of the north to Israel:

(17) At that time they shall call Jerusalem the throne of the LORD; and all the nations shall be gathered unto it, to the name of the LORD, to Jerusalem: neither shall they walk any more after the imagination of their evil heart. (18) **In those days the house of Judah shall walk with the house of Israel, and they shall come together out of the land of the north** to the land that I have given for an inheritance unto your fathers. (Jer 3:17-18, also see Jer 16:14-15)

The land of the north in this context refers to Babylon, Iraq (compare Jer 3:18, 23:6-8, 46:10).[3]

Isaiah

Isaiah 48:20-21, a passage about the end times, describes the people of Israel leaving Babylon as the Lord redeems them.[4] Verse 21 states the Lord will provide His people with water from rocks so they will not thirst as they travel through the desert:[5]

(20) Go ye forth of Babylon, flee ye from the Chaldeans, with a voice of singing declare ye, tell this, utter it even to the end of the earth; say ye, The LORD hath redeemed his servant Jacob. (21) And they thirsted not when he led them through the deserts: he caused the waters to flow out of the rock for them: he clave the rock also, and the waters gushed out. (Isa 48:20-21)

The passage harkens back to Exodus 17:1-6, which describes how the Lord gave His people water from rocks while they were thirsty in the wilderness. However, the Lord giving His people water from rocks as they travel back from Babylon is a development that many believe did not happen in the sixth century B.C.

Thus, several chapters prove that a part of the Lord's people will be in Babylon during the end times. Their presence in Babylon, Iraq just before her end time fall end means that Revelation 18:4 may refer to them in Babylon, Iraq.

The Many Strong Parallels

Many strong parallels between the Book of Revelation, the Book of Jeremiah, and the Book of Isaiah concerning Babylon, Iraq and Babylon the Great exist. The parallels are so strong that it seems they are all speaking about the same event.

This section covers many of these parallels, and they span from Babylon's height of power, her fall, and the aftermath of her fall.

Parallel 1: Global Influence

The Book of Revelation indicates that Babylon the Great will have global influence while the prophecies of the Old Testament suggest that Babylon will have global influence:

- Revelation describes Babylon the Great as a harlot who has made all the nations of the earth intoxicated (Rev 17:1-2, 18:3).

- Jeremiah describes a time when all the earth will be drunk from Babylon's wine (Jer 51:7).

Similarly:

- Revelation describes the harlot sitting upon many waters, which represents all kinds of people, just before her judgment (Rev 17:1, 15).

- Jeremiah also describes Babylon as dwelling upon many waters just before her destruction (Jer 51:13).

- Isaiah describes Babylon as the lady (queen) of kingdoms just before her desolation (Isa 47:5).

Parallel 2: Extreme Arrogance

Babylon the Great will be a very arrogant city:

- Revelation describes Babylon the Great as a queen who brags that she will never see loss (Rev 18:7).

- Isaiah depicts Babylon claiming that she is a queen who will suffer no heartache (Isa 47:7-8).

- Jeremiah refers to Babylon as an arrogant one (Jer 50:31).

The sins that Babylon the Great will commit will so great that it'll reach to the skies:

- Revelation mentions that the sins of Babylon the Great will reach up to heaven when the Lord is about to judge her (Rev 18:5).
- Jeremiah 51 states that the judgment of Babylon will reach up to heaven when her desolation approaches (Jer 51:9). This statement implies that her sin will reach up to heaven. Babylon will receive punishment according to what she has done.

Parallel 4: Flee from Babylon

We saw that the Lord's people will be in Babylon, Iraq and Babylon the Great before her destruction:

- The Lord's people are told to flee from Babylon the Great before her judgment (Rev 18:4).
- Isaiah and Jeremiah suggest that the judgment of Babylon, Iraq will come shortly after the Lord's people flee from there (Isa 48:14, 20, Jer 50:8-9, 51:5-6).

Parallel 5: Sudden Destruction

Babylon the Great will fall quickly when the Lord destroys her:

- Revelation states that Babylon will fall in one day or in one hour (Rev 18:8, 17-19).
- Isaiah says that Babylon will fall suddenly in just one day (Isa 47:9).
- Jeremiah describes Babylon's fall as sudden (Jer 51:8).

Parallel 6: Burned with Fire

Fire will incinerate Babylon the Great when she falls:

- Revelation states that Babylon the Great will be burned with fire (Rev 18:8).
- Jeremiah says that Babylon's high gates will be set on fire (Jer 51:58).

No man will ever live in Babylon the Great again when she falls:

- Revelation states that Babylon will not be found again (Rev 18:21).
- Isaiah compares the fall of Babylon to the fall of Sodom and Gomorrah. No man will live there again (Isa 13:19-20, 14:21-24).
- Jeremiah also compares the fall of Babylon to fall of Sodom and Gomorrah. Man will not live there again (Jer 50:39-40, 51:60-64).

COUNTERARGUMENTS

Some will dispute that Babylon, Iraq is Babylon the Great:

- Some will argue that Babylon the Great must be a specific location.
- Others will claim that it is impossible for Babylon, Iraq to represent Babylon the Great.

This section contains rebuttals to these critics.

Jerusalem is a "Great City"

Some argue Jerusalem is Babylon the Great. The theory rests on the fact that Jerusalem is called a "great city". But the theory has several issues.

The theory implies that "Babylon" should be seen spiritually. The problem with this is that Revelation 11:8 only spoke of Jerusalem as spiritual Sodom and spiritual Egypt. The verse does not speak of the city as *spiritual Babylon*.

Another weakness of the theory is that many end time passages state that the Lord will rescue Jerusalem and its residents while it is under siege. The fact that the Lord will defend the city poses a big problem for those who argue that the city is Babylon the Great City. It does not seem to make much sense for the Lord to intervene to protect Jerusalem if He will later allow the destruction of the city.

Revelation 18:21 is a very challenging verse for Jerusalem proponents to reconcile. The verse states that Babylon the Great City will not be found anymore:

And a mighty angel took up a stone like a great millstone, and cast it into the sea, saying, Thus with violence shall that great city Babylon be thrown down, and shall be found no more at all. (Rev 18:21)

The reason Revelation 18:21 is difficult for Jerusalem proponents to reconcile is that several Bible prophecy verses like Zechariah 12:6 suggest that Jerusalem will be inhabited *again* after the siege:

In that day will I make the governors of Judah like an hearth of fire among the wood, and like a torch of fire in a sheaf; and they shall devour all the people round about, on the right hand and on the left: and **Jerusalem shall be inhabited again** in her own place, even in Jerusalem. (Zech 12:6)

In contrast, several end time verses state that Babylon will not be rescued and will be desolate like Sodom and Gomorrah.

A Non-Babylon Location Other than Jerusalem

The main issue with non-Babylon locations other than Jerusalem is a lack of direct references to them and their fall in the Bible. We would have to spiritualize the term "Babylon" in many end time chapters about her and her fall. This would be hard. Many of these chapters mention areas and terms exclusive to Babylon, Iraq, such as the land of the Chaldeans.

Example: Rome

Rome merits special attention. Many believe that Rome is Babylon the Great City. One verse often cited by these people is Revelation 17:9, which states that the woman sits on seven mountains:

And here is the mind which hath wisdom. The seven heads are seven mountains, on which the woman sitteth. (Rev 17:9)

Many link the seven mountains to the seven hills of Rome. However, the seven mountains are linked to seven kings rather than to seven hills by Revelation 17:10. The emphasis of the seven mountains is on power rather than geography.

Proponents also try to point out that Rome is related to the empire of the Antichrist. However, the Bible lacks any direct reference to Rome's fall. Rome is only mentioned eight times directly by the Bible, and none of the verses pertain to its fall.

In contrast, many chapters in the Old Testament relate to the fall of Babylon, Iraq during the end times, as we saw earlier.

Babylon Lacks Infrastructure

Babylon the Great City will be the economic and political center of the world. Many see Babylon, Iraq's lack of infrastructure, as a huge weakness for the theory that it will be Babylon the Great.

Indeed, even the biggest supporter of the idea that Babylon, Iraq is Babylon the Great must concede that Babylon, Iraq is far from ready to serve as the economic and political center of the world.

However, one of the main goals of studying Bible prophecy is to get an idea of what might take place in the future. Some future events may seem difficult for us to envision because our conception of the future is shaped by what we see now. But we do not know for sure what tomorrow will bring (let alone the next several years). We need to be careful about saying what is and is not possible.

It may not seem that Babylon, Iraq can develop into a major city in the near future at the city's current pace of development. However, we don't know how quickly that will change future. The Antichrist could speed it up a lot.

Interestingly, Habakkuk 2 condemns the Antichrist, the end time king of Babylon, for building a city with bloodshed. This city that he will build is likely Babylon, Iraq. This conclusion is based on the parallels between Habakkuk 2:13 and Jeremiah 51:58:

> (12) Woe to him that buildeth a town with blood, and stablisheth a city by iniquity! (13) Behold, is it not of the LORD of hosts that **the people shall labour in the very fire, and the people shall weary themselves for very vanity**? (Hab 2:12-13)

> Thus saith the LORD of hosts; The broad walls of Babylon shall be utterly broken, and her high gates shall be burned with fire; and **the people shall labour in vain, and the folk in the fire, and they shall be weary**. (Jer 51:58)

Remember that Babylon the Great will draw her power from the Antichrist's power (see chapter ten). This relationship is crucial. It means the city does not need to look like New York City to become the center of global economic activity and political power.

The Antichrist can position Babylon to serve as the center of the global economy and political power with his vast influence. This is the approach that he may follow. Habakkuk 2:12 indicates that he will build a city ruthlessly.

CONCLUSION

The prophecies about the fall of Babylon, Iraq will be fulfilled in the end times. As a result, Babylon, Iraq must at least be a significant city during the end times regardless of whether she serves as Babylon the Great or not.

The many parallels between the Old Testament end time prophecies about Babylon, Iraq's fall and the prophecies about Babylon the Great's fall strongly suggest they describe the same event.

Although Babylon, Iraq lacks the infrastructure that many major cities have, it is not impossible for it quickly to become the center of global economic and political power with the help of the Antichrist.

Notes

1. See the Cyrus Cylinder and the Nabonidus Chronicle for more.

2. Adler, Marcus Nathan, translator. *The Itinerary of Benjamin of Tudela*. By Benjamin (of Tudela), London: Henry Frowde, Oxford University Press, 1907. 42

3. Some may wonder why Babylon is called the "land of the north" in the Bible when it is due east of Israel. The hostile deserts of the region forced the Babylonians to attack Israel from the north. Thus, Babylon is known by the direction their people attacked Israel from.

4. Isa 43:1-6, 14, 44:22-24, 51:11, Jer 31:10-12, 50:33-34, Mic 4:7-13 are end time passages that also refer to the Lord as the redeemer of His people.

5. Isa 41:14-18 and 49:6-12 also refer to the Lord as the redeemer of His people who will provide His people with water as they travel.

PSALM 83, THE SIEGE, & GOG

We can find when the events of Psalm 83 will take place by comparing it with Psalm 79 and Ezekiel 39. Psalm 79 and Psalm 83 share at least three details in common (see Figure 1):

Figure 1: The Similarities Between Psalm 79 & Psalm 83

• **A Call for the Lord to Arise to Help the Distressed People**

• *A Call for the Lord to Punish the Attackers*

• <u>The Heathen Don't Know the Lord, but Will When He Acts</u>

Ps 83:1-2, 17-18: (1) **Keep not thou silence, O God: hold not thy peace, and be not still, O God.** (2) For, lo, thine enemies make a tumult: and they that hate thee have lifted up the head.... (17) *Let them be confounded and troubled for ever; yea, let them be put to shame*, and perish: (18) <u>That men may know that thou, whose name alone is JEHOVAH, art the most high over all the earth.</u>

Ps 79:6-10: (6) *Pour out thy wrath upon the heathen* <u>that have not known thee, and upon the kingdoms that have not called upon thy name</u>. (7) For they have devoured Jacob, and laid waste his dwelling place. (8) O remember not against us former iniquities: let thy tender mercies speedily prevent us: for we are brought very low. (9) **Help us, O God of our salvation, for the glory of thy name: and deliver us, and purge away our sins, for thy name's sake.** (10) Wherefore should the heathen say, Where is their God? <u>let him be known among the heathen in our sight by the revenging of the blood of thy servants which is shed</u>.

The parallels between Psalm 79, a chapter about the end time siege of Jerusalem, and Psalm 83 suggest:

- The events of Psalm 83 may relate to the events of Psalm 79.
- The events of Psalm 83 may take place around the time of the end time siege of Jerusalem.

We may also get an idea of when the events of Psalm 83 will take place by examining the contrast between Psalm 83:17-18 and Ezekiel 39:6-7:

- Psalm 83:17-18 calls for the Lord to make His name known to men.
- Ezekiel 39:6-7 states that the nations will realize who the Lord is when He destroys Gog and his forces.

(17) Let them be confounded and troubled for ever; yea, let them be put to shame, and perish: (18) **That men may know that thou, whose name alone is JEHOVAH, art the most high over all the earth.** (Ps 83:17-18)

(6) And I will send a fire on Magog, and among them that dwell carelessly in the isles: and **they shall know that I am the LORD.** (7) So will I make my holy name known in the midst of my people Israel; and I will not let them pollute my holy name any more: **and the heathen shall know that I am the LORD, the Holy One in Israel.** (Ezek 39:6-7)

The people's realization about the Lord when He destroys Gog and his forces suggests that the Lord will destroy Gog and his forces after the attack of Psalm 83 begins. *Therefore, the events of Psalm 83 may take place around the end time siege of Jerusalem but before the Lord destroys Gog and his forces.*

I believe the events of Psalm 83 relate to the events of the end time siege of Jerusalem, but the chapter does not describe the siege itself:

- Psalm 83 describes a focused attack on a remnant of Israel hiding in the wilderness (Ps 83:3).
- The end time siege of Jerusalem targets those living in the city.
- However, both are part of an overall effort to destroy the people of Israel (Ps 83:4).

The relationship between Psalm 83 and the demise of Gog and his forces is less clear when we only compare Psalm 83 and Ezekiel 39:

- The Psalm 83 attack appears it will come before the demise of Gog and his forces.
- But it is unclear how much time will pass between events or whether the attack by Gog and his forces relate to the attack in Psalm 83.

However, we may get a better idea of how the events of these chapters relate by looking at the link between Ezekiel 39 and passages about the end time siege of Jerusalem.

EZEKIEL 39 & THE SIEGE

Interestingly, some details found in Ezekiel 39 relate to details found in passages about the end time siege of Jerusalem. Notably, the Lord's arrival to defeat the forces that lay siege against the city.

Ezekiel 39:21-22 states that the Lord will set His glory among the nations and that the house of Israel will also know that He is the Lord when He judges Gog and his forces:

(21) And I will set my glory among the heathen, and all the heathen shall see my judgment that I have executed, and my hand that I have laid upon them. (22) So the house of Israel shall know that I am the LORD their God from that day and forward. (Ezek 39:21-22)

Each of these details are in passages about the end time siege of Jerusalem.

The Lord Shall Set Glory Among the Nations

As was just mentioned, the Lord will set His glory among the nations when He destroys Gog and his forces (Ezek 39:21). Psalm 102:13-16 and Isaiah 59:18-20 mention that the Lord will set His glory to the nations when He rescues a besieged Jerusalem. Figure 2 displays the parallels between Ezekiel 39:21, Psalm 102:13-16, and Isaiah 59:18-20:

Figure 2: The Context of the Lord Setting His Glory

- **The Lord Will Set His Glory to the Nations**

- *The Redeeming of Jerusalem*

Ezek 39:21: **And I will set my glory among the heathen**, and all the heathen shall see my judgment that I have executed, and my hand that I have laid upon them.

Ps 102:13-16: (13) *Thou shalt arise, and have mercy upon Zion: for the time to favour her, yea, the set time, is come.* (14) For thy servants take pleasure in her stones, and favour the dust thereof. (15) **So the heathen shall fear the name of the LORD, and all the kings of the earth thy glory.** (16) *When the LORD shall build up Zion,* **he shall appear in his glory.**

Isa 59:18-20: (18) According to their deeds, accordingly he will repay, fury to his adversaries, recompence to his enemies; to the islands he will repay recompence. (19) **So shall they fear the name of the LORD from the west, and his glory from the rising of the sun.** When the enemy shall come in like a flood, the Spirit of the LORD shall lift up a standard against him. (20) *And the Redeemer shall come to Zion,* and unto them that turn from transgression in Jacob, saith the LORD.

House of Israel Shall Know the Lord

The house of Israel shall know the Lord when He destroys Gog and his forces (Ezek 39:22). This detail implies that the house of Israel will not know the Lord before the destruction of Gog and his forces.

Isaiah 35:4-5 states that Israel's spiritual eyes will become open when the Lord comes with a vengeance. Isaiah 59:17-20 tells us He will come with a vengeance when it is time to redeem Jerusalem (see Figure 3):

Figure 3: The House of Israel Shall Know the Lord

- **Spiritual Eyes Will Become Open**

- *The Lord Will Come with Vengeance*

Ezek 39:21-22: (21) And I will set my glory among the heathen, and all the heathen shall see my judgment that I have executed, and my hand that I have laid upon them. (22) **So the house of Israel shall know that I am the LORD their God from that day and forward.**

Isa 35:4-5 (also see Isa 42:13-16): (4) Say to them that are of a fearful heart, Be strong, fear not: behold, your *God will come with vengeance, even God with a recompence; he will come and save you.* (5) **Then the eyes of the blind shall be opened, and the ears of the deaf shall be unstopped.**

Isa 59:17-20: (17) *For he put on righteousness as a breastplate, and an helmet of salvation upon his head; and he put on the garments of vengeance for clothing, and was clad with zeal as a cloak.* (18) *According to their deeds, accordingly he will repay, fury to his adversaries, recompence to his enemies; to the islands he will repay recompence....* (20) And the Redeemer shall come to Zion, and unto them that turn from transgression in Jacob, saith the LORD.

The parallels between Ezekiel 39 and the passages about the end of the siege at the Lord's coming (like Isa 59:17-20) suggest:

- The demise of Gog and his forces relates to the end time siege of Jerusalem.

- The demise of Gog and his forces relates to the Lord's coming.

Here is a summary of the order of events just described:

Mini Timeline of Events

Event 1: A Large-Scale Effort to Destroy the people of Israel:

- The Psalm 83 attack and the end time siege of Jerusalem appear to be parts of this effort.

- The Psalm 83 attack and the end time siege of Jerusalem will occur around the same time.

Event 2: The Destruction of Gog and His Forces:

• The destruction of Gog and his forces will take place at the same time as the demise of the forces that attack Jerusalem. It appears this event will coincide with the Lord's coming.

Given this, it is likely that the invasion of Gog and his forces will also be part of the effort that already connects the attack of Psalm 83 and the end time siege of Jerusalem.

The verses and passages presented do not directly link the attack of Psalm 83 with the invasion by Gog and his forces. But, the relationship between all the passages presented suggest the invasion by Gog and his forces will take place at or near the time of the siege (*and thereby the time of the Psalm 83 attack*).

GOG TAKES PART IN THE SIEGE

Gog's allies will take part in the siege of Jerusalem. We can see why by looking at the parallels between the fate of Gog and the fate of Jerusalem's besiegers.

I showed that the "Assyrian" (the king of Assyria) refers to Gog in an end time context in the appendix section titled: "Is 'Gog' the Antichrist?". We can learn about what Gog will do by looking at the end time exploits of the Assyrian.

Similarity 1: Used to Punish Jerusalem and Then Destroyed

The Assyrian will attack Israel and Jerusalem during the end times. Let's take a look at this passage about the siege from Isaiah 10:

> (5) O Assyrian, the rod of mine anger, and the staff in their hand is mine indignation. (6) **I will send him against an hypocritical nation, and against the people of my wrath** will I give him a charge, to take the spoil, and to take the prey, and to tread them down like the mire of the streets.... (12) Wherefore it shall come to pass, that when the Lord hath performed his whole work upon **mount Zion and on Jerusalem**, I will punish the fruit of the stout heart of the king of Assyria, and the glory of his high looks. (Isa 10:5-6, 12)

Notice that the Assyrian's defeat will come after the Lord uses him to deal with those in Jerusalem (Isa 10:12). He shares the same fate as those who attack Jerusalem (see Figure 4):

Figure 4: The Fate of the Assyrian and Jerusalem's Besiegers

- **Jerusalem Besieged**
- *Attackers Punished*

Isa 10:12: Wherefore it shall come to pass, that **when the Lord hath performed his whole work upon mount Zion and on Jerusalem,** *I will punish the fruit of the stout heart of the king of Assyria, and the glory of his high looks.*

Zech 14:2-3: (2) **For I will gather all nations against Jerusalem to battle; and the city shall be taken, and the houses rifled, and the women ravished; and half of the city shall go forth into captivity,** and the residue of the people shall not be cut off from the city. (3) *Then shall the LORD go forth, and fight against those nations, as when he fought in the day of battle.*

Similarity 2: Jerusalem's Affliction Ends

The demise of the Assyrian will lead to a major change. The yoke will depart from Jerusalem when the Lord defeats him:[1]

That I will break the Assyrian in my land, and upon my mountains **tread him under foot: then shall his yoke depart from off them,** and his burden depart from off their shoulders. (Isa 14:25, also see Isa 10:24-27)

Similarly, Jerusalem's affliction will end after the siege:

(1) Awake, awake; put on thy strength, O Zion; put on thy beautiful garments, O Jerusalem, the holy city: for henceforth there shall no more come into thee the uncircumcised and the unclean. (2) Shake thyself from the dust; arise, and sit down, **O Jerusalem: loose thyself from the bands of thy neck, O captive daughter of Zion.** (Isa 52:1-2)

Similarity 3: The Lord Makes His Name Known

Similarly, again consider the result of Gog's destruction and the result of Jerusalem besiegers' destruction (see Figure 5):

- The Lord will make His name known to the house of Israel and the nations when He defeats Gog and his forces (Ezek 39:5-7, 20-22).

- The Lord's people will know the Lord when He destroys His enemies in battle at Jerusalem (Ps 76:1-3, 6).

Figure 5: The Aftermath of Annihilation

- **The Lord Is Known**

- *The Attackers*

Ps 76:1-3, 6: (1) **In Judah is God known: his name is great in Israel.** (2) In Salem also is his tabernacle, and his dwelling place in Zion. (3) There brake he the arrows of *the bow, the shield, and the sword, and the battle.* Selah.... (6) At thy rebuke, O God of Jacob, *both the chariot and horse are cast into a dead sleep.*

Ezek 39:5-7, 20-22: (5) Thou shalt fall upon the open field: for I have spoken it, saith the Lord GOD. (6) And I will send a fire on Magog, and among them that dwell carelessly in the isles: and **they shall know that I am the LORD.** (7) **So will I make my holy name known in the midst of my people Israel**; and I will not let them pollute my holy name any more: and the heathen shall know that I am the LORD, the Holy One in Israel.... (20) Thus ye shall be filled at my table *with horses and chariots, with mighty men, and with all men of war,* saith the Lord GOD. (21) And I will set my glory among the heathen, and all the heathen shall see my judgment that I have executed, and my hand that I have laid upon them. (22) **So the house of Israel shall know that I am the LORD their God from that day and forward.**

All these similarities suggest that Gog and his forces will take part in the end time siege of Jerusalem.

Notes

1. Nah 1:12-13, 15 and Jer 30:4, 7-9 suggest that the final removal of the yoke from the Lord's people will not take place until the end times.

THE FULFILLMENT OF EZEKIEL 38

Most believe that Ezekiel 38 and Ezekiel 39 relate to events at the start and/or the end of the tribulation. My position on these chapters differs from most people:

- I believe Ezekiel 38:1-7 and Ezekiel 39 relate to the invasion led by Gog during the war of Armageddon.
- In contrast, I believe that Ezekiel 38:8-23 mainly covers an invasion led by Gog at the end of the Millennium (Rev 20:7-9).

We will look at several details from Ezekiel 38:8-12 which prove that Gog's Ezekiel 38 invasion cannot take place until the Millennium.

GATHERED FROM THE NATIONS

We can get a good idea of when Gog's Ezekiel 38 invasion will take place by looking at verse 12. The verse states that the people of Israel have already gathered from the nations before the invasion:

> To take a spoil, and to take a prey; to turn thine hand upon the desolate places that are now inhabited, and upon **the people that are gathered out of the nations**, which have gotten cattle and goods, that dwell in the midst of the land.(Ezek 38:12)

This is not a partial gathering. All of them will dwell safely:

> After many days thou shalt be visited: in the latter years thou shalt come into the land that is brought back from the sword, and is gathered out of many people, against the mountains of Israel, which have been

always waste: but it is brought forth out of the nations, and they shall dwell safely **all of them**. (Ezek 38:8)

In this book, I proved that a full gathering of the people of Israel from the nations will not take place until the Post-Armageddon period. Therefore, the Ezekiel 38 invasion will not take place at the war of Armageddon. Instead, it will take place in the Millennium (Rev 20:7-9).

DWELLING IN THE MOUNTAINS OF ISRAEL

A key to identifying when the Ezekiel 38 invasion will take place is to find when a predominantly Israeli population will live in the mountains of Israel as verse 8 describes:

After many days thou shalt be visited: in the latter years thou shalt come into the land that is brought back from the sword, and is gathered out of many people, against the mountains of Israel, which have been always waste: but it is brought forth out of the nations, and they shall dwell safely all of them. (Ezek 38:8)

Ezekiel 36 is a critical chapter for identifying when the people of Israel will be the main population group on the mountains of Israel. Verses 1-7 pertain to how the nations, including Edom, will control the mountains of Israel until the time when the Lord will punish them. Verses 5-7 focus on the fact that the Lord will punish them:

(5) Therefore thus saith the Lord GOD; Surely in the fire of my jealousy have I spoken against the residue of the heathen, and against all Idumea, which have appointed my land into their possession with the joy of all their heart, with despiteful minds, to cast it out for a prey. ... (7) Therefore thus saith the Lord GOD; I have lifted up mine hand, Surely the heathen that are about you, they shall bear their shame. (Ezek 36:5, 7)

The Lord also spoke against Edom and the nations in several passages that pertain to the Day of the Lord, including Ezekiel 35:9-12, Obadiah 1:8-9, 15, and Isaiah 34:6-8 (see Figure 1):

Figure 1: The Lord Spoke Against the Heathens & Edom

- **Make a Desolation**

- *False Claim of Ownership*

- <u>The Day of the Lord</u>

Ezek 36:5: Therefore thus saith the Lord GOD; Surely in the fire of my jealousy have I spoken against the residue of the heathen, and against all Idumea, *which have appointed my land into their possession with the joy of all their heart*, with despiteful minds, to cast it out for a prey.

Ezek 35:9, 12: (9) **I will make thee perpetual desolations**, and thy cities shall not return: and ye shall know that I am the LORD.... (12) And thou shalt know that I am the LORD, and that I have heard all thy blasphemies which thou *hast spoken against the mountains of Israel, saying, They are laid desolate, they are given us to consume.*

Isa 34:6, 8: (6) The sword of the LORD is filled with blood, it is made fat with fatness, and with the blood of lambs and goats, with the fat of the kidneys of rams: for the LORD **hath a sacrifice in Bozrah, and a great slaughter in the land of Idumea**.... (8) <u>For it is the day of the LORD'S vengeance, and the year of recompences for the controversy of Zion.</u>

Obad 1:8-9, 15: (8) Shall I not in that day, saith the LORD, even destroy the wise men out of Edom, and understanding out of the mount of Esau? (9) And thy mighty men, O Teman, shall be dismayed, to the end that every one of the mount of Esau may be cut off by slaughter.... (15) <u>For the day of the LORD is near upon all the heathen: as thou hast done, it shall be done unto thee: thy reward shall return upon thine own head</u>.

Consequently, we can conclude that the nations and Edom will lose control of the mountains of Israel during the Day of the Lord:

Ezekiel 36:8-12 contains a promise to the mountains of Israel that the people of Israel will arrive from the nations and shall inherit them when the Lord finishes punishing Edom and the nations:

Yea, I will cause men to walk upon you, even my people Israel; and they shall possess thee, and thou shalt be their inheritance, and thou shalt no more henceforth bereave them of men. (Ezek 36:12)

This passage alludes to Ezekiel 34:12-15, which pertains to the Post-Armageddon period and the Millennium. The Lord will gather His people and allow them to live on the mountains of Israel:

> I will feed them [remnant of Israel] in a good pasture, and upon the high mountains of Israel shall their fold be: there shall they lie in a good fold, and in a fat pasture shall they feed upon the mountains of Israel. (Ezek 34:14, also see Isa 65:8-10)

Finally, the Kingdom of Israel and the Kingdom of Judah will be united when the people of Israel dwell on the mountains of Israel. This development will be realized in the Millennium (see chapter twenty-five, Ezek 37:21-22, Isa 11:12-13).

Therefore, Gog's Ezekiel 38 invasion cannot happen until the Millennium since the people of Israel will not possess the mountains of Israel fully until then.

RUINS THAT ARE NOW INHABITED

Ezekiel 38:12 mentions that Gog will attack the places that were once desolate. This verse also suggests that the residents of these places will enjoy great prosperity:

> To take a spoil, and to take a prey; to turn thine hand upon the desolate places that are now inhabited, and upon the people that are gathered out of the nations, which have gotten cattle and goods, that dwell in the midst of the land. (Ezek 38:12)

The land of Israel is likely one of the places spoken of in Ezekiel 38:12 as they will be inhabited and restored after the war of Armageddon (Isa 51:1-3, 62:1-4, Ezek 36:28, 33-36, Amos 9:13-15).

The mountains of Israel are likely also among the places spoken of in Ezekiel 38:12. Ezekiel 36 indicates that they will be desolate when the nations control them:

> (2) Thus saith the Lord GOD; Because the enemy hath said against you, Aha, even the ancient high places are ours in possession: (3) Therefore prophesy and say, Thus saith the Lord GOD; Because they have made you desolate, and swallowed you up on every side, that ye might be a possession unto the residue of the heathen, and ye are taken up in the lips of talkers, and are an infamy of the people: (Ezek 36:2-3)

We saw that the people of Israel will inhabit the mountains of Israel after the war of Armageddon. Ezekiel tells us that they will thrive when they inhabit them:

(8) But ye, O mountains of Israel, ye shall shoot forth your branches, and yield your fruit to my people of Israel; for they are at hand to come. (9) For, behold, I am for you, and I will turn unto you, and ye shall be tilled and sown: (10) And I will multiply men upon you, all the house of Israel, even all of it: and the cities shall be inhabited, and the wastes shall be builded: (Ezek 36:8-10)

Therefore, Gog's Ezekiel 38 invasion will not take place before the Millennium since the conditions described by Ezekiel 38:12 will not be met until the Millennium.

LIVE SECURELY

The people of Israel will live securely when Gog invades. The Hebrew word for "securely" in Ezekiel 38:8 is *betach*. The word appears in verses that refer to the security that Israel will enjoy in the Millennium. Ezekiel 34:25-28 is an example where the word appears in this context:

(25) And I will make with them a covenant of peace, and will cause the evil beasts to cease out of the land: and they shall dwell safely [*betach*] in the wilderness, and sleep in the woods.... (28) And they shall no more be a prey to the heathen, neither shall the beast of the land devour them; but they shall dwell safely [*betach*], and none shall make them afraid. (Ezek 34:25, 28)

Other examples of *betach* applying to the people of Israel dwelling safely in the Millennium include:

- Jeremiah 23:5-7, 32:37-39
- Zechariah 14:10-11

As I stated in chapter twenty-five, it's easy to imagine why the inhabitants of Israel will dwell safely with confidence in the Millennium. They will know that they have a Protector who can annihilate anyone who may pose a threat. The Lord proved His strength through the rout of their enemies.

Ezekiel 38:16, 22-23 tells us that the Lord will be sanctified in the eyes of the nations through the defeat of Gog and his army:

> (16) And thou shalt come up against my people of Israel, as a cloud to cover the land; it shall be in the latter days, and I will bring thee against my land, that the heathen may know me, when I shall be sanctified in thee, O Gog, before their eyes.... (22) And I will plead against him with pestilence and with blood; and I will rain upon him, and upon his bands, and upon the many people that are with him, an overflowing rain, and great hailstones, fire, and brimstone. (23) Thus will I magnify myself, and sanctify myself; and I will be known in the eyes of many nations, and they shall know that I am the LORD. (Ezek 38:16, 22-23)

However, passages like Ezekiel 39:27-28 suggest that the Lord will be sanctified in the eyes of the nations through His people:

> (27) **When I have brought them again from the people, and gathered them out of their enemies' lands, and am sanctified in them in the sight of many nations**; (28) Then shall they know that I am the LORD their God, which caused them to be led into captivity among the heathen: but I have gathered them unto their own land, and have left none of them any more there. (Ezek 39:27-28, also see Ezek 20:41-42, 28:25-26, 36:23-25)

These two facts can be reconciled by recognizing that Ezekiel 38 and Ezekiel 39 describe different events:

- Ezekiel 39 covers the Lord being sanctified through the return of His people from the nations after the war of Armageddon.

- Ezekiel 38 covers the Lord being sanctified through the final defeat of Gog and his forces at the end of the Millennium. Satan will deceive the nations for the last time (Rev 20:8), so the Lord may need to sanctify Himself again in the eyes of the nations.

PROBABLE SEQUENCE OF EVENTS

The Start of the Tribulation: Dan. 9:27 (Ch.5)

1st to 4th Seal: Rev 6:1-8 (Ch.7)

- Start of Temple Sacrifice: Dan 8:13-19 (Ch.7)
- War in Heaven: Rev 12:7-12 (Ch.7)
- 144,000 Sealed: Rev 7:1-8 (Ch.13)
- The Two Witnesses' Ministry Begins: Rev 11:3-6 (Ch.9)

Midpoint of the Tribulation: Dan 9:27 (Ch.7)

- Abomination of Desolation: Dan 9:27, Matt 24:15 (Ch.7)
- Antichrist's True Identity Revealed: 2Thess 2:3-4 (Ch.8)
- The False Prophet's Ministry Begins: Rev 13:11-16 (Ch.9)
- Great Tribulation Begins: Matt 24:21 (Ch.11)

5th Seal: Rev 6:9-11 (Ch.11)

Trumpets 1-5: Rev 8:7-13, 9:1-12 (Ch.11)

6th Trumpet: Rev 9:13-21 (Ch.12)

Three Angel Announcements: Rev 14:6-13 (Ch.14)

- Gospel of the Kingdom Preached: Rev 14:6-7, Matt 24:14 (Ch.14)

Bowls 1-6: Rev 16:1-16 (Ch.14)

Psalm 83 Attack & Siege of Jerusalem: Ps 83, Zech 12:1-3 (Ch.15)

- Death of the Two Witnesses: Rev 11:7-10 (Ch15)
- The People of Israel Cry for Help: Joel 2:15-17 (Ch.16)

End of the Great Tribulation: Matt 24:29 (Ch.17)

6th Seal: Rev 6:12-17 (Ch.17)

- The Raising of the Two Witnesses: Rev 11:11-13 (Ch.17)

7th Seal: Rev 8:1 (Ch.17)

7th Trumpet: Rev 11:15-19 (Ch.17)

- Kingdom of God & Christ Established on Earth: Rev 11:15 (Ch.17)
- End of the Tribulation: Dan 9:24-27 (Ch.17)
- Mystery of God Complete: Rev 10:7 (Ch.17)
- Fullness of the Gentiles Reached: Rom 11:25 (Ch.17)

7th Bowl Poured: Rev 16:17-21 (Ch.17)

- Day of the Lord Begins: Zep 1:7-8 (Ch.19-20)
- Babylon the Great Destroyed: Rev 16:19, Rev 18 (Ch.17)

The Coming of Christ: Matt 24:30 (Ch.18)

- Gathering of the Wicked: Matt 13:41 (Ch.18)
- Gathering of the Righteous/the Rapture: Matt 24:31 (Ch.18)

Christ Begins to Liberate His People: Isa 61:1-2 (Ch.21)

Greatest Earthquake of All Time: Rev 16:18 (Ch.21)

Antichrist & False Prophet Cast to Lake of Fire: Rev 19:20 (Ch.21)

Slaughter of the Wicked & Jerusalem Liberated: Rev 19:21, Zech 12:6 (Ch.21)

75 Day Post-Armageddon Period: Dan 12:11-12 (Ch.22-23)

- Gathering of the Remnant of Israel: Isa 11:11-12 (Ch.22)
- Sheep & Goat Judgment: Matt 25:31-46 (Ch.23)
- Bema Seat Judgment: Rev 11:18 (Ch.23)
- The Spiritual Purification of Israel: Ezek 36:24-28 (Ch.23)
- Millennial Temple Built: Zech 6:12-13 (Ch.23)

Marriage Supper of the Lamb: Rev 19:9 (Ch.23)

Millennial Kingdom: Rev 20:4-6 (Ch.24-25)

- New Heavens & a New Earth: Rev 21:1 (Ch. 24)
- Satan Bound for 1,000 Years: Rev 20:2 (Ch.24)
- New Jerusalem Arrives: Rev 21:2, 10 (Ch.24)

Satan Released & Defeated: Rev 20:7-10 (Ch.25)

Great White Throne Judgment: Rev 20:11-13, 15 (Ch.25)

INDEX

SCRIPTURE INDEX

- 42:13-16: 267
- 42:14-16: 142
- 42:22-25: 131n
- 43:1, 5-7: 200
- 43:1-6, 14: 262n
- 43:10-13: 202
- 43:19: 202
- 44:22-24: 262n
- 47:5: 257
- 47:7-8: 257
- 47:7-8, 10: 155
- 47:9: 258
- 48:14, 20: 258
- 48:20-21: 256
- 49:6-12: 262n
- 49:8, 12-15: 23
- 49:10-12: 201-202
- 49:22: 200, 204
- 49:23: 231
- 51:1-3: 274
- 51:3: 217
- 51:6: 148
- 51:11: 262n
- 51:17: 141
- 51:17-23: 126, 128, 182
- 51:18-20: 141
- 51:22-23: 142
- 52:1-2: 269
- 52:1-3: 128
- 54:1-8: 221
- 54:5-8: 141
- 54:7-11: 25n

- 54:11-12: 221
- 54:17: 228
- 55:8-9: 8
- 56:6: 229
- 56:6-8: 201, 229
- 56:8: 199
- 56:10: 131n
- 57:15-18: 141
- 58:12: 217
- 59:16-18: 154
- 59:17-18, 20: 184
- 59:17-20: 266, 267
- 59:18-20: 265-266
- 59:20: 183
- 60:1-2: 148, 187n
- 60:3-4, 9: 200
- 60:3-5: 202
- 60:10: 217, 226n
- 60:11: 221
- 60:12, 14: 230-231
- 60:13: 230
- 60:14: 220, 221
- 60:17: 228
- 60:19-20: 221
- 61:1-2: 191
- 61:4-5: 217
- 61:6: 223
- 62:1-3: 220
- 62:1-4: 274
- 62:5: 221
- 62:6-9: 228
- 62:10-12: 201

BY THE SAME AUTHOR

Prophecy Proof Insights on the Last Generation

A Study on the Timing of Christ's Return

The world is full of chaos. Many wonder if we are living in the last days. Will we see the end time events described in the Bible come to pass soon? Are we the last generation before the coming of Christ?

Prophecy Proof Insights on the Last Generation tackles the question: "Are we the last generation before the coming of Christ?"

We will look at often-overlooked biblical clues about the timing of key end time events. These clues empower us to identify plausible start dates and end dates for the tribulation and the Second Coming of Christ.

The Bible promises us that Christ will return and gives us clues about the timing of His return. Learn which upcoming dates are possible by getting your copy of this book.

You can get your copy of *Prophecy Proof Insights on the Last Generation* by visiting: https://www.prophecyproof.org/lastgeneration/

ABOUT THE AUTHOR

Wayne Croley is a Bible prophecy researcher, commentator, and author from Sacramento, California.

He has studied and written extensively about Bible prophecy since he was a teenager with the goal of helping people understand current events and the truth about the end times. Wayne is the founder of *Prophecy Proof Insights*, a Bible prophecy website attracting readers from across the globe.[1]

Wayne holds an MBA from the California State University, Sacramento. He also holds a degree in Managerial Economics (graduating with highest honors) and a degree in Political Science (graduating with high honors) from the University of California, Davis.

He is also a winner of the prestigious Clyde Jacobs and Larry Peterman Distinguished Scholar Award.

Notes

1. https://www.prophecyproof.org

Made in the USA
Middletown, DE
18 December 2022

19382115R00189